IMAGES
of America

DODGE CITY

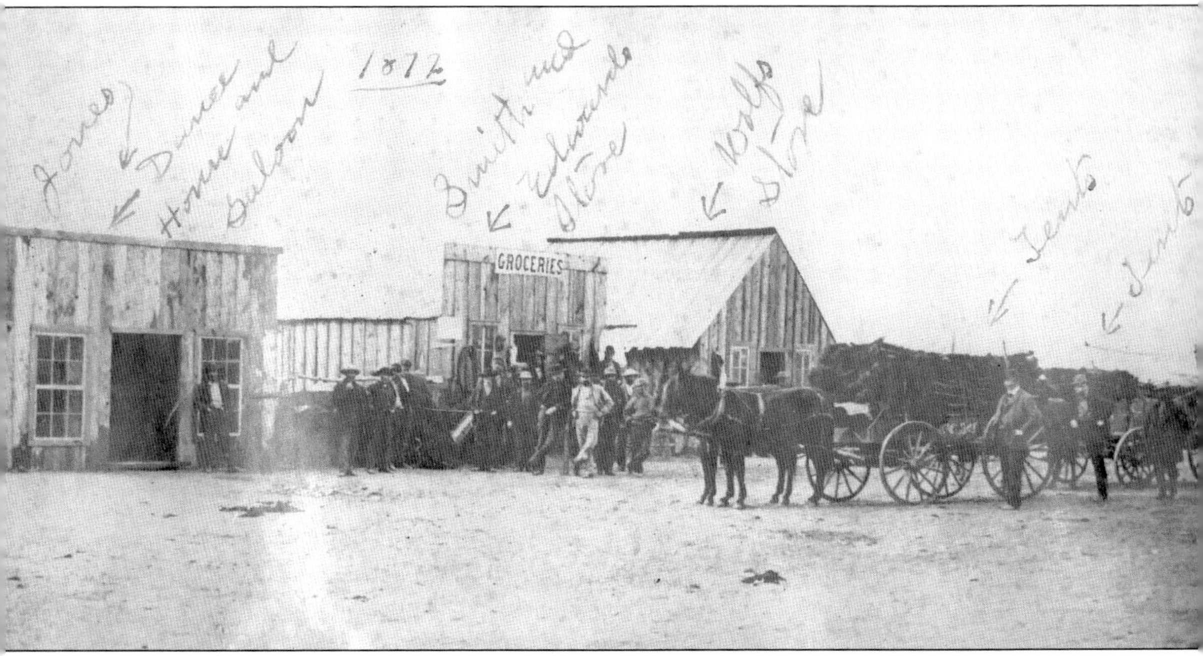

Dodge City was incorporated on August 15, 1872. The first name, Buffalo City, had been taken already, so the town's name was changed to Dodge City after Fort Dodge, although Robert Wright is quoted by Heinie Schmidt as saying it was named after Col. Richard Dodge. Above is the oldest known photograph of Dodge City, dated September 1872. It was taken on the Santa Fe Trail (now Trail Street) and shows the first block south of the Santa Fe Railroad tracks, with tents and wood storefronts. The north side of the tracks was developed very rapidly, and by the fall of 1872, buildings were present on Front Street (Main Street at the time). George M. Hoover's saloon, the first business in town, is behind this row of buildings, immediately south of the tracks. Hoover later moved to Front Street. The Jones Dance Hall and Saloon, Smith and Edwards Store, and Wolfe's Store (Daniel Wolfe later drowns in a river) are the storefront buildings. The wagon holds buffalo hides. (Courtesy of the Ford County Historical Society.)

ON THE COVER: The first Dodge City High School baseball team is pictured in 1898. Louie Schmidt is in the back row, the second from the right. Each uniform was handmade. Note the disparity in style. Baseball became popular during the Civil War, and buffalo hunter H.H. Raymond writes of playing the game with W.B. "Bat" Masterson. All of these players were born after about 1880, the first generation of pioneer children in southwest Kansas. Family names include Trebilcock, Tarbox, Miller, Milton, Jones, Straeter, Baird, Evans, and Rev. William Westwood, the "umpire." (Courtesy of the Ford County Historical Society.)

IMAGES
of America

DODGE CITY

George Laughead Jr.

ARCADIA
PUBLISHING

ISBN 978-0-7385-5225-5

Published by Arcadia Publishing
Charleston, South Carolina

Printed in the United States of America

Library of Congress Control Number: 2007943175

For all general information, please contact Arcadia Publishing:
Telephone 843-853-2070
Fax 843-853-0044
E-mail sales@arcadiapublishing.com
For customer service and orders:
Toll-Free 1-888-313-2665

Visit us on the Internet at www.arcadiapublishing.com

For pioneer Dodge City history, there are people who have read the original documents and collected the photographs, and had families live through it—Dr. C. Robert Haywood, Lola Adams Crum, Fredric R. Young, Betty Braddock, Noel Ary, KU history professor emeritus Dr. Lynn H. Nelson, and my father, George R. Laughead Sr.—my history mentors.

Contents

ACKNOWLEDGMENTS

I would like to thank the late Betty Braddock for the years of volunteer work she completed, including a Kansas Humanities Council (KHC) grant that paid for archive supplies and organizing and archiving photographs that had been collected by Heinrich Schmidt, Henry Mueller, Ida Ellen Rath, Lola Adams Crum, and Betty herself, among others. Betty also helped start (and later became the longtime director of) the Kansas Heritage Center in Dodge City. Current KHC director Barbara Vincent, with Dave Webb and Janice Scott, still provide the first place to go for research on Dodge City and Old West Kansas—much thanks to them. Others in my hometown who were always helpful when I had questions include Louis Sanchez, Troy Robinson, Charles Meade, Ann Warner, Dr. Gus E.A. Liebl, Ken Felts, and Jim Sherer. Chris Cecil helped me find time. I would like to thank the staff at Arcadia Publishing, particularly editors Ted Gerstle (at the start) and Winnie Rodgers (at the finish) for their kindness and patience; they allowed me to work on this project for a lot longer time than they had planned. Historians Karen Holliday Tanner, Glenn Boyer, Jeff Guinn, and Dr. Ann Kirschner helped make this book possible. Ellen Ellis at Legends Printing in Dodge City scanned photographs. All photographs are courtesy of the Ford County Historical Society Archives. Any errors found are my own.

INTRODUCTION

The founding of the American West can be studied in no better place than Dodge City, Ford County, Kansas. Whether it is frontier forts, trails, cow towns, farms, or ranches, Dodge City has original examples of each.

Common among the settlers of Dodge City and Ford County was their journey and struggle to build a civilized society. These pioneer settlers had a multitude of business, civic, and religious interests, including the Masons, Knights of Columbus, and Order of the Eastern Star. Every town on the plains had common elements, from the early merchants wanting schools built, supporting churches and getting libraries organized, business clubs started, and of course, the various orders.

Founder Robert M. Wright describes early Dodge City in his 1913 book, *Dodge City: The Cowboy Capital and the Great Southwest in the Days of the Wild Indian, the Buffalo, the Cowboy, Dance Halls, Gambling Halls and Bad Men* (actual title):

> It has already been said that Dodge City was established in 1872, upon the advent of the Atchison, Topeka & Santa Fe Railroad. Dodge was in the very heart of the buffalo country. Hardly had the railroad reached there, long before a depot could be built (they had an office in a box car), business began; and such a business! Dozens of cars a day were loaded with hides and meat, and dozens of carloads of grain, flour, and provisions arrived each day. The streets of Dodge were lined with wagons, bringing in hides and meat and getting supplies from early morning to late at night.

With trains moving continually, mail went from Dodge City to Chicago in a day or less. The *Sunday Boston Herald* arrived at the Mueller-Schmidt House (now a county museum) on Tuesday. The telegraph and the telephone appeared as early as anywhere outside the northeast.

Dodge City was the buffalo capital until mass slaughter destroyed the huge herds and left the prairie littered with decaying carcasses. An estimated 1.5 million buffalo hides were shipped from Dodge from 1872 to 1878. For years after that, farmers gathered buffalo bones and sold them for $6 to $8 a ton. The bones were used in the manufacture of china and fertilizer. By 1875, the buffalo were gone as a source of revenue, but the longhorn cattle of Texas drove the dollars into town. For 10 more years, over five million head of cattle were driven up the western branch of the Chisholm Trail and the Great Western Trail, to Dodge City.

Law and order came riding into town with such respectable law officers as W.B. "Bat" Masterson, Ed Masterson, Wyatt Earp, Bill Tilghman, H.B. "Ham" Bell, and Charlie Bassett. Out of these personalities evolved the famous fictional characters of *Gunsmoke* and Marshal Matt Dillon. In 1877, the population was 1,200, and 19 businesses were licensed to sell liquor.

During those first years, the population varied according to the season, swelling during the summer with the influx of cowboys, cattle buyers, gamblers, and prostitutes. Business houses, dance halls, and saloons catered to the Texas trade. Saloonkeepers served brandies, liqueurs, and the latest mixed drinks. Ice was available so even beer could be served cold. Some saloons advertised anchovies and Russian caviar on their cold menus.

Gambling ranged from a game of 5¢ "Chuck-aluck" to $1,000 poker pots. Many saloons offered some type of musical entertainment—a piano player, a singer, or as in Chalk Beeson's Long Branch, a five-piece orchestra. Beeson also organized and led the famous Cow Boy Band that entertained all over the west at cattlemen's conventions, concerts, dances, and in Washington, DC, at the inauguration of President Harrison.

Fort Dodge, Kansas, closed in 1882, and due to a January 1886 blizzard, the cattle drives ended. Robert Wright wrote:

> What made Dodge City so famous was that it was the last of the towns of the last big frontier of the United States. When this was settled, the frontier was gone, it was the passing of the frontier with the passing of the buffalo, and the Indian question was settled forever. Here congregated people from the east, people from the south, people from the north, and people from the west. People of all sorts, sizes, conditions, and nationalities; people of all color, good, bad, and indifferent, congregated here, because it was the big door to so vast a frontier. Some came to Dodge City out of curiosity; others strictly for business; the stock man came because it was a great cattle market . . . the cowboy came because it was his duty as well as delight, and here he drew wages and spent them; the hunter came because it was the very heart of the greatest game country on earth; the freighter came because it was one of the greatest overland freight depots in the United States, and he hauled material and supplies for nearly four hundred miles, supplying three military posts, and all the frontier for that far south and west; last but not least, the gambler and the bad man came because of the wealth and excitement, for obscene birds will always gather around a carcass.

Stuart Lakes's *Wyatt Earp: Frontier Marshal*, published in 1931, remains one of the most famous books on that era. In fact, it was only after the 1930s that the fame of the first decade of Dodge City became part of movies, television, and books. The 1900s generation did not value that history, nor want to hear about it. My grandfather George E. Laughead (1880–1953) was one of those persons. George E. Laughead was city treasurer and then Dodge City street commissioner (who put in brick streets) on pioneer George M. Hoover's first city council, formed in 1911, of which old-timer Hamilton B. Bell was mayor.

Dodge City, now 140 years old, remains iconic. Few other towns have had as many travelers pass through it to the West or as many cattle driven to it; millions of both left the main body of the United States on the Santa Fe Trail, west from Dodge City.

One

Pioneer Families of Dodge City

The names of the most famous lawmen, outlaws, and gamblers of the Old West are well known, such as the Earp brothers, the Masterson brothers, and John Henry Holliday. The men, women, and children who settled the frontiers of Kansas have names not as recognizable and are certainly not famous. Whether it is 19-year-old Robert M. Wright—who would become Dodge City's founder—driving wagons on contract in 1859 from Westport, Missouri, to Denver, Colorado; John Mueller coming out from Ohio to make his fortune in boots; Adam Schmidt, the first blacksmith in Dodge City after serving in the Union Army; Elizabeth Berg Schmidt, who was raised in Ohio; Charles Rath, the leading buffalo hunter and an immigrant from Germany; or Canadian immigrant George M. Hoover, the first merchant of Dodge City, these less-famous persons built the West as it is now known.

Of the hardships and joys on the frontier, Robert M. Wright wrote:

> As I look back and endeavor to recall the events of that period, a kaleidoscopic panorama presents itself to my mind—a picture ever changing, ever restless, with no two days alike in experience. In those days, one lived ten years of life in one calendar year. Indians, drought, buffaloes, bad men, the long horn, and, in fact, so many characteristic features of that time present themselves that I am at a loss where to begin. If you wish to feel yourself more comfortable than a king while listening to the sweetest strains of music, come back into a warm, pleasant home with its comforts and listen to the crackle of a cheerful, open wood fire, after being out in cold and storm for a month or two, never, during that time, being near a house or comfortable habitation, while every moment being in terror of Indian attack, or suffering from cold and storm really more terrible than Indian attack, sitting up the greater part of the night to keep from freezing, and riding hard all day on the morrow. In the joy of the change, you will imagine yourself in the heaven of heavens. How many of us have often experienced these feelings on the frontier of Kansas in the early days. Yet this kind of a life gives one a zest for adventure, for it is a sort of adventure to which he not only becomes accustomed but attached. In fact, there is a fascination about it difficult to resist, and having once felt its power, one could not permit himself to give it up.

The children of the early pioneers, who survived very rough conditions, would go on to enjoy the fruits of their parents' labors, including sports, theater, music, books, fine food and clothes, and Victorian houses. Luxury was just as much a part of Dodge City in the 1880s and 1890s as in the cities of the East. Few descendants of the early settlers of Dodge City remain, although some are still present in southwest Kansas.

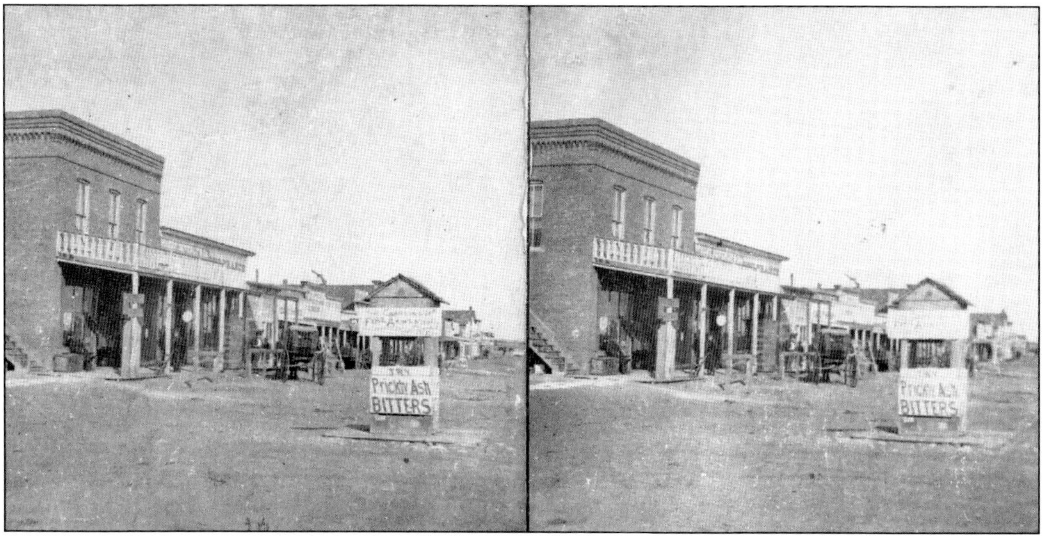

Pictured above is a stereo photograph of Robert Wright's brick general store and Front Street, c. 1875. Early Dodge City depended on buffalo hunting, cattle drives, the Santa Fe Trail, and the railroad for business. Wheat harvesting in southwest Kansas began decades after the 1870s. The bottom photograph shows a wheat threshing rig around 1915 near Dodge City. The end of the cattle drives in 1886 lead to farmers replacing ranching with wheat and other grain crops.

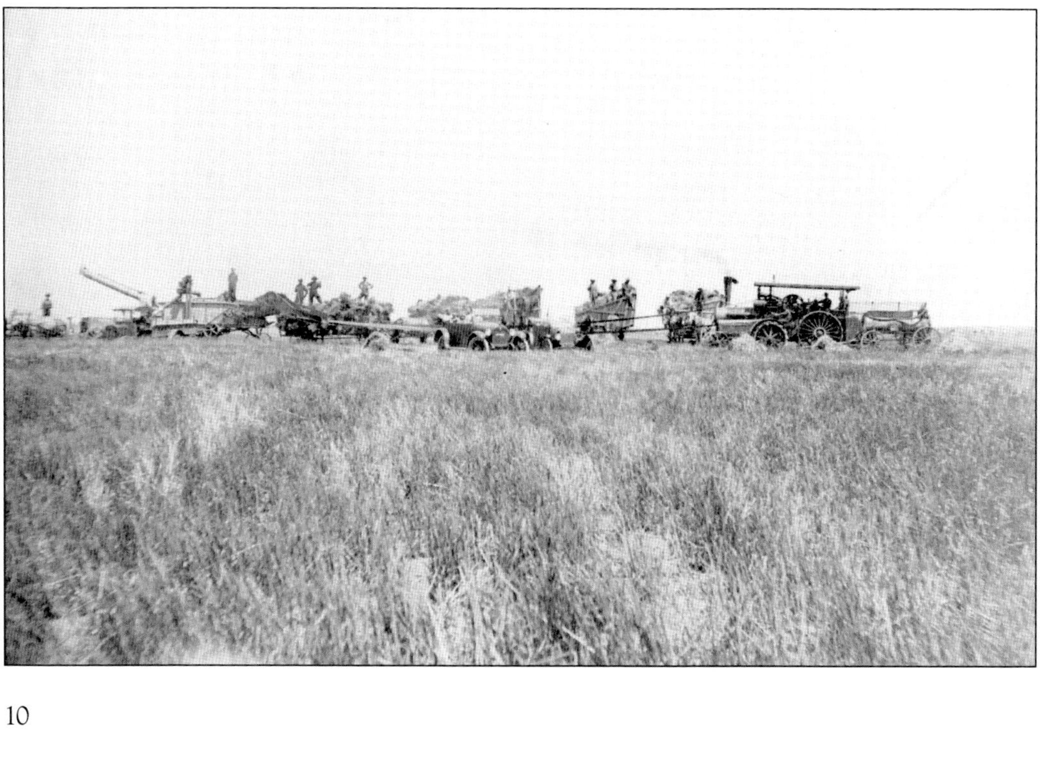

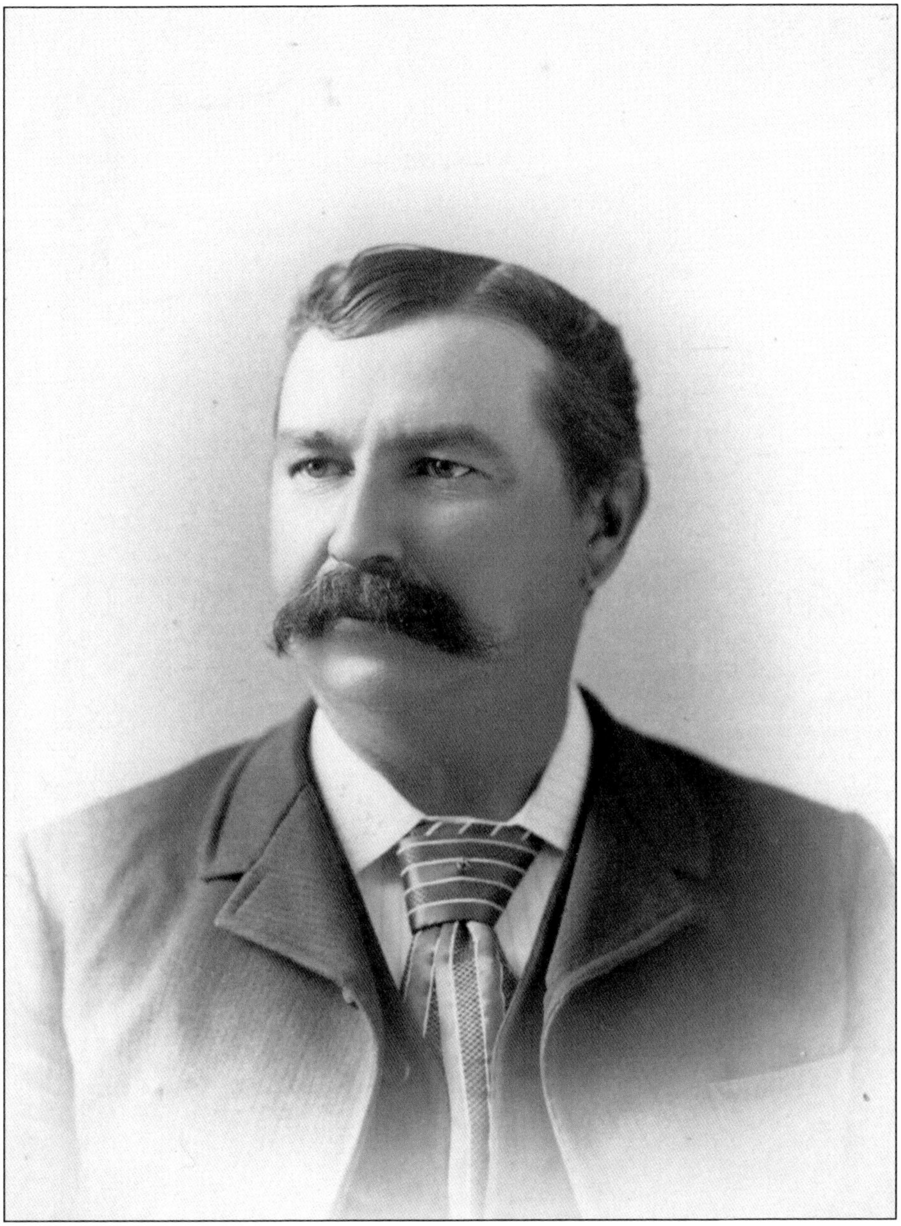

Few cities were founded by a man with the background of Dodge City's own town president, Robert M. Wright. Wright came west at age 16 to make his mark on the world. He married his 13-year-old first cousin, Alice, when he was 19. Wright rose from "bullwhacker," or freight wagon driver, to owner of the largest commercial empire in the area, making and losing a fortune on the cattle trade, starting trails and towns. In 1872, by the time he owned a general store in Dodge City, Wright was making huge amounts of money from the Santa Fe Trail, buffalo hunter, and cattle trade. In *The Merchant Prince of Dodge City: The Life and Times of Robert M. Wright*, Dr. C. Robert Hayward gives evidence that Wright was taking in $200,000 a month during the cattle season of 1880—over $4 million today. In his final years, Wright was asking for help selling the last of his land and cattle in 1906. The letter was written from a drug rehabilitation hospital in Kansas City.

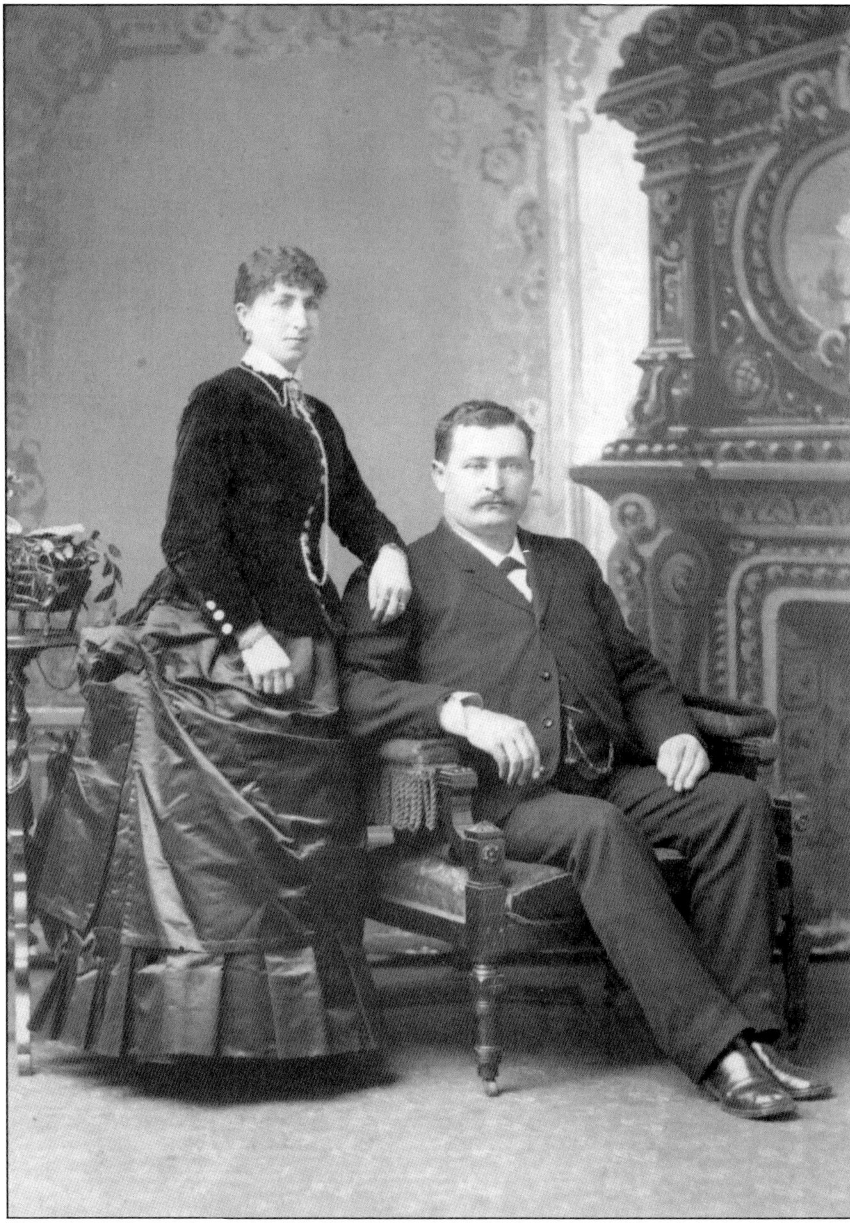

George Merritt Hoover, one of the "seven old timers" according to Wright, was born in Canada on August 8, 1847, and arrived in Dodge City on June 17, 1872, becoming the second settler after Henry Sitler. With business partner John McDonald, he set up a sod and wood-plank bar—the first Dodge City business—and sold whiskey for 25¢ ($20 today) a ladle full. Hoover first located his saloon south of the tracks, later moving to 36 Front Street (called Main Street in an early Hoover & McDonald Wines and Liquors advertisement) in 1874. By the time he died in July 1914, he had amassed an estate of at least $500,000, leaving $100,000 of it to Dodge City, in addition to thousands of dollars more for churches. Hoover was a devoted husband, entering McCarty Hospital on March 14, 1914, a week after the death of his wife, Margaret (Carnahan), whom he had married in 1875. The Hoovers raised a foster son, George Curry, who became one of the Roosevelt Rough Riders.

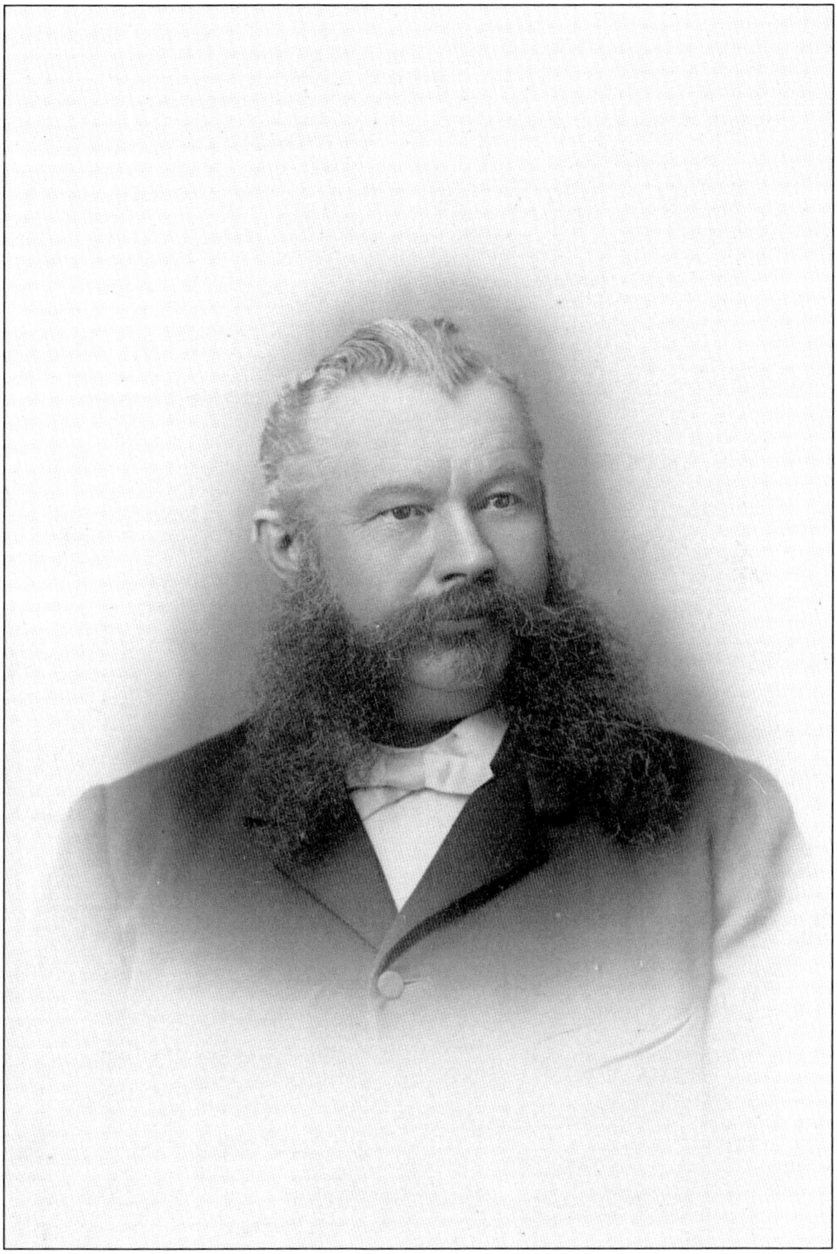

Frederick Carl Zimmermann was born in Saxony, Prussia, on December 29, 1833, and died in Dodge City on January 20, 1888. He arrived in the United States in 1863, after learning and practicing his trade of gunsmithing in Germany, Paris, and London. He married Matilda Messinger of New Britain, Connecticut, in 1865. He arrived in Dodge City in July 1872. Matilda arrived in September 1872, with their first two babies. When he arrived, there was only a sod house and two canvas buildings, and the Santa Fe tracks had not yet reached Dodge City. An experienced gunsmith was a valuable addition to the new town. Over the years, starting on Front Street in a building next to George Hoover's store, he built a hardware, general merchandise, and lumber business out of his gunsmith store. The F.C. Zimmermann Hardware store was one of the most profitable Dodge City businesses well into the 20th century.

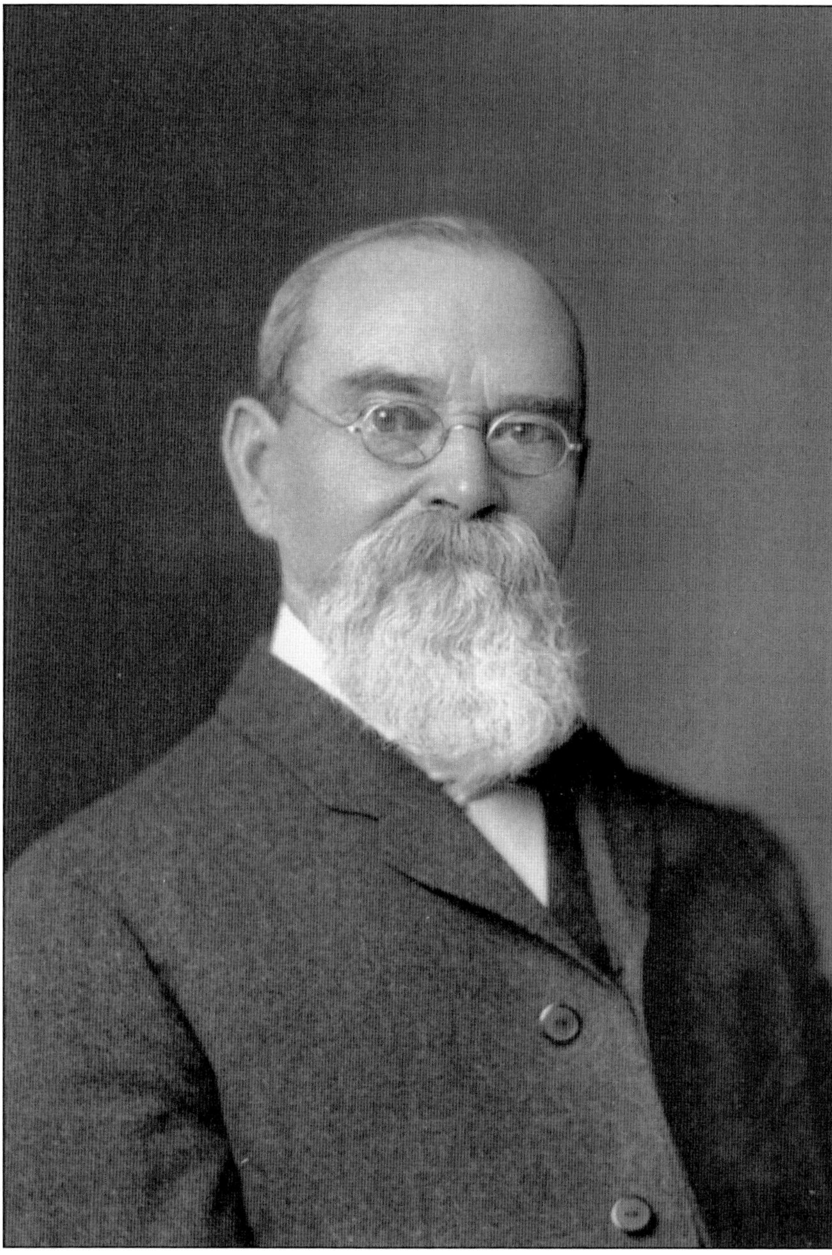

Judge H.M. Beverly was Rath's replacement at Wright's store, which became known as Wright, Beverly & Co. Beverly was introduced to Dodge City in the December 8, 1877 issue of the *Dodge City Times*, which announced, "The old familiar firm of Charles Rath & Company, has been dissolved by mutual consent. The business of the firm of Charles Rath & Company will hereafter be carried on with the same enterprise and energy as in the past by Hon. R.M. Wright, and Judge H.M. Beverly formerly of San Antonio, Texas, who has been with Rath & Co. for several years. The members of the new firm are men of known business ability and all have the confidence and esteem of the citizens of the community." Beverly had already brought cattle up from Texas, and the comfort of dealing with fellow Texans made him very valuable to Wright. Beverly started his own store a few years later; like most of Wright's partners, he branched out.

Charles Rath, born in Germany, was raised from age 11 in Sweetwine, Ohio. He was on the first Ford County Commission and was Robert Wright's partner. He set up Rath City, Texas, for the buffalo hunting that wiped out the southern herd. Known as "Plainsman Charley," by 1853, "he foresaw great possibilities in the opened market in the east, not only for buffalo hides, but for choice buffalo tongue, hump, and steak. As a boy, Charley Rath had been teased by other children because he wore his brother's outgrown suit, fully four sizes too large. If those children could have looked into the future, they would have seen a large man with a head of black hair topped with a fine beaver hat, clothed in a rich brown tailor-made suit and shirt. His button shoes were shining black and his gloves were white," according to Ida Ellen Rath in *Early Ford County*. He is pictured at right. The Rath house is shown below in 1877. From left to right are Alice Wright, Carrie Rath, and Carrie's mother, Katherine Markley. Carrie is expecting son Robert (born October 16, 1877).

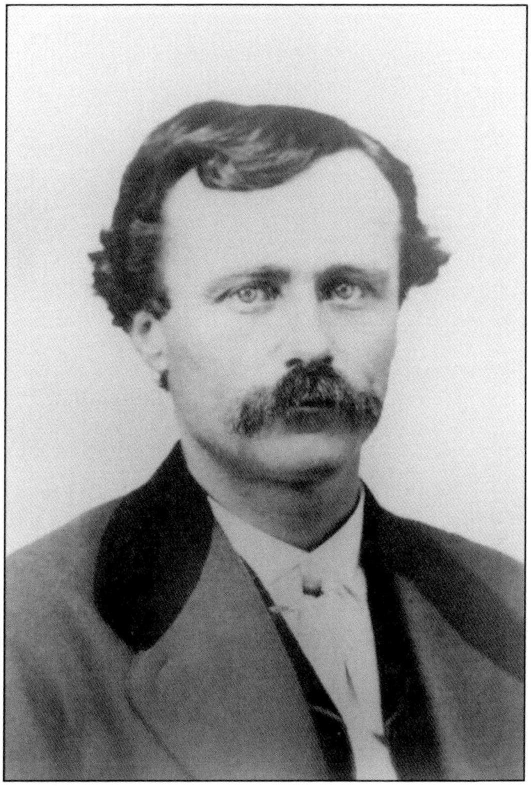

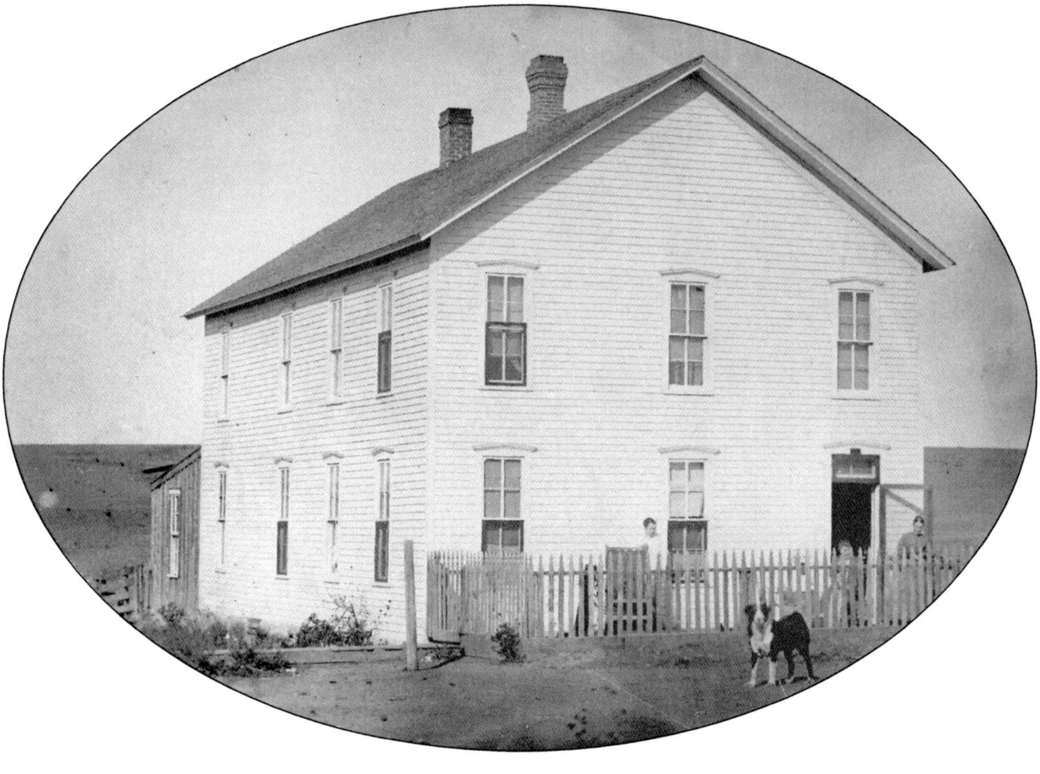

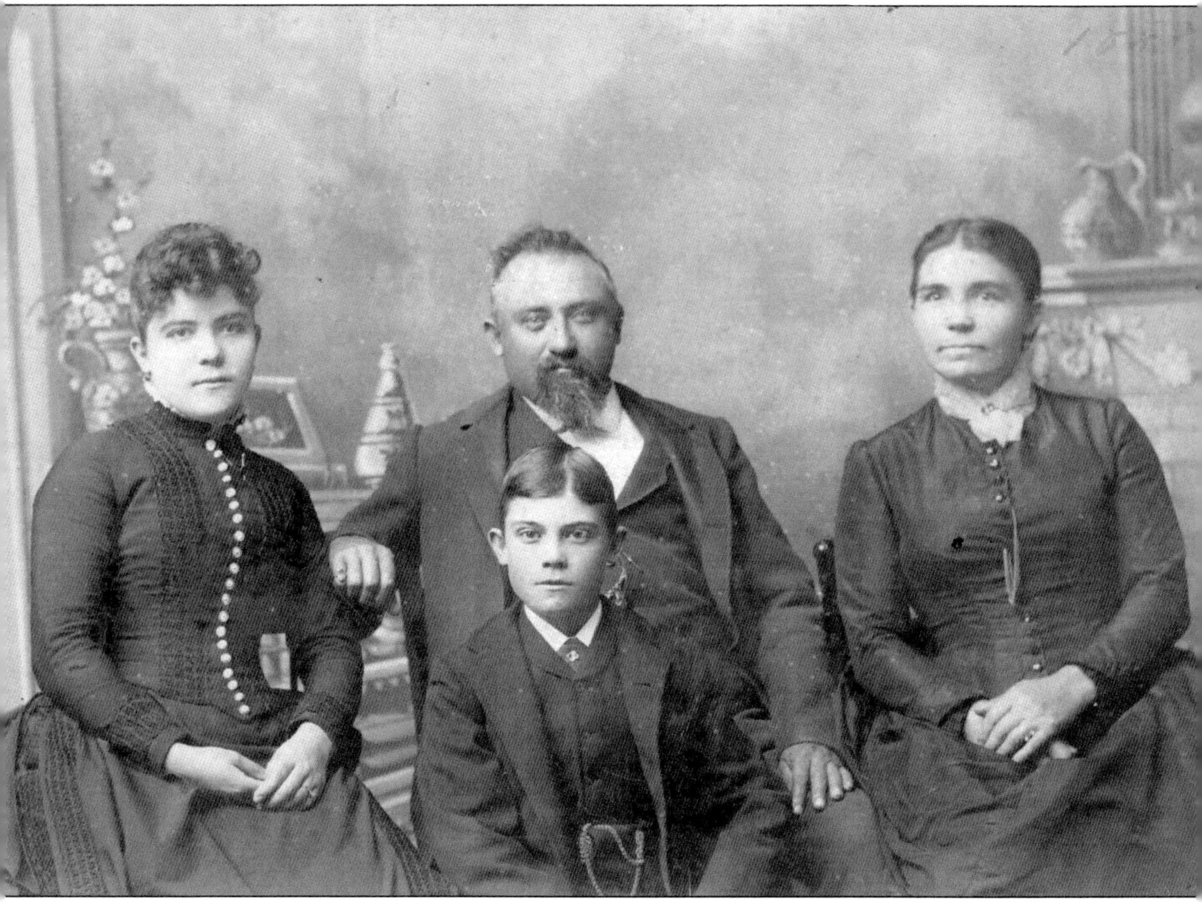

This 1889 photograph of the Mueller family was taken prior to the wedding of John Mueller's daughter Emilia. From left to right are Emilia, John, and his wife, Karoline. Son Henry is seated in front. John Mueller (originally Müller) was born in 1840 in Bavaria, Germany, and immigrated to the United States in 1855. He married Karoline Koch in St. Louis early in 1862. Karoline was born in Berweiler, Germany (Alsace-Lorraine). Like John, she immigrated through the port of New Orleans with her parents in 1850 and settled in St. Louis. John and Karoline had eight children, but only two survived, Emelia and Henry. By the time of this photograph, he had lost his wealth and cattle in the blizzard of January 1886. He moved back to St. Louis soon after his daughter's wedding, where he rejoined the army. He died in an accident a couple of years later, leaving Karoline and Henry with grandparents in Illinois.

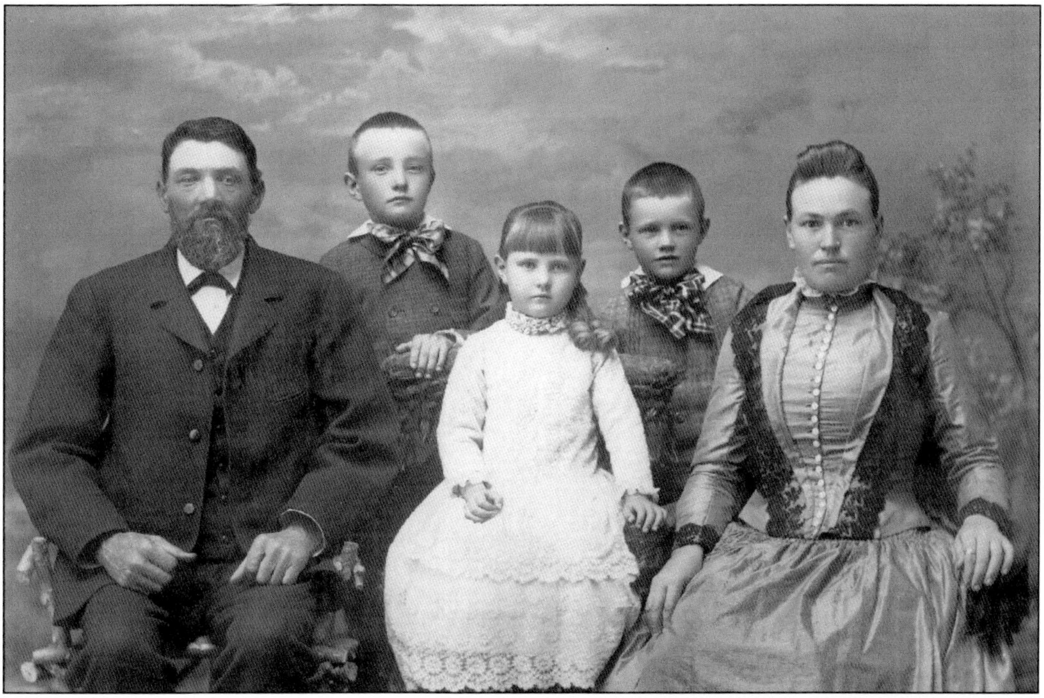

The Adam Schmidt family appears in the photograph above, which commemorated their move to their house, which they purchased from John Mueller. The three children, from left to right, with Adam and Elizabeth Berg Schmidt (flanking), are Heinrich, Elma, and Louie (the youngest boy). Adam's funeral notice read: "Mr. Schmidt had lived in Dodge City for thirty seven years. He was a native of Bavaria, Germany, and came to American at about the age of twelve years. He lived with relatives in St. Louis until 1874 when he came to Dodge City, then a frontier town, and established himself in the blacksmithing business which he followed industriously until about four years ago. He was 70 years and 4 months of age at the time of his death. He was a member of Co. B. of the First Missouri Light Artillery, and was with Siegel at Pea Ridge and Grant at Vicksburg." Pictured at left are Adam's sisters, Aunt Barbara and Aunt Kate.

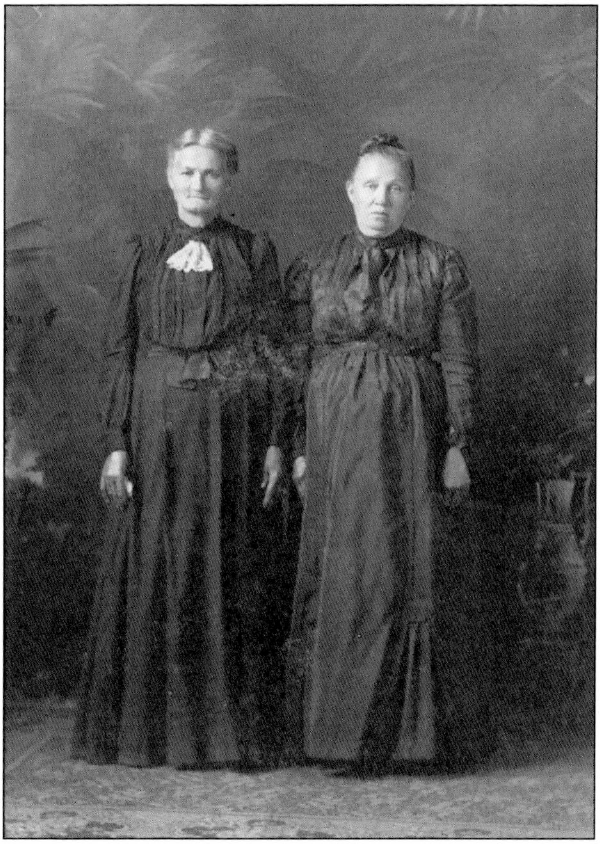

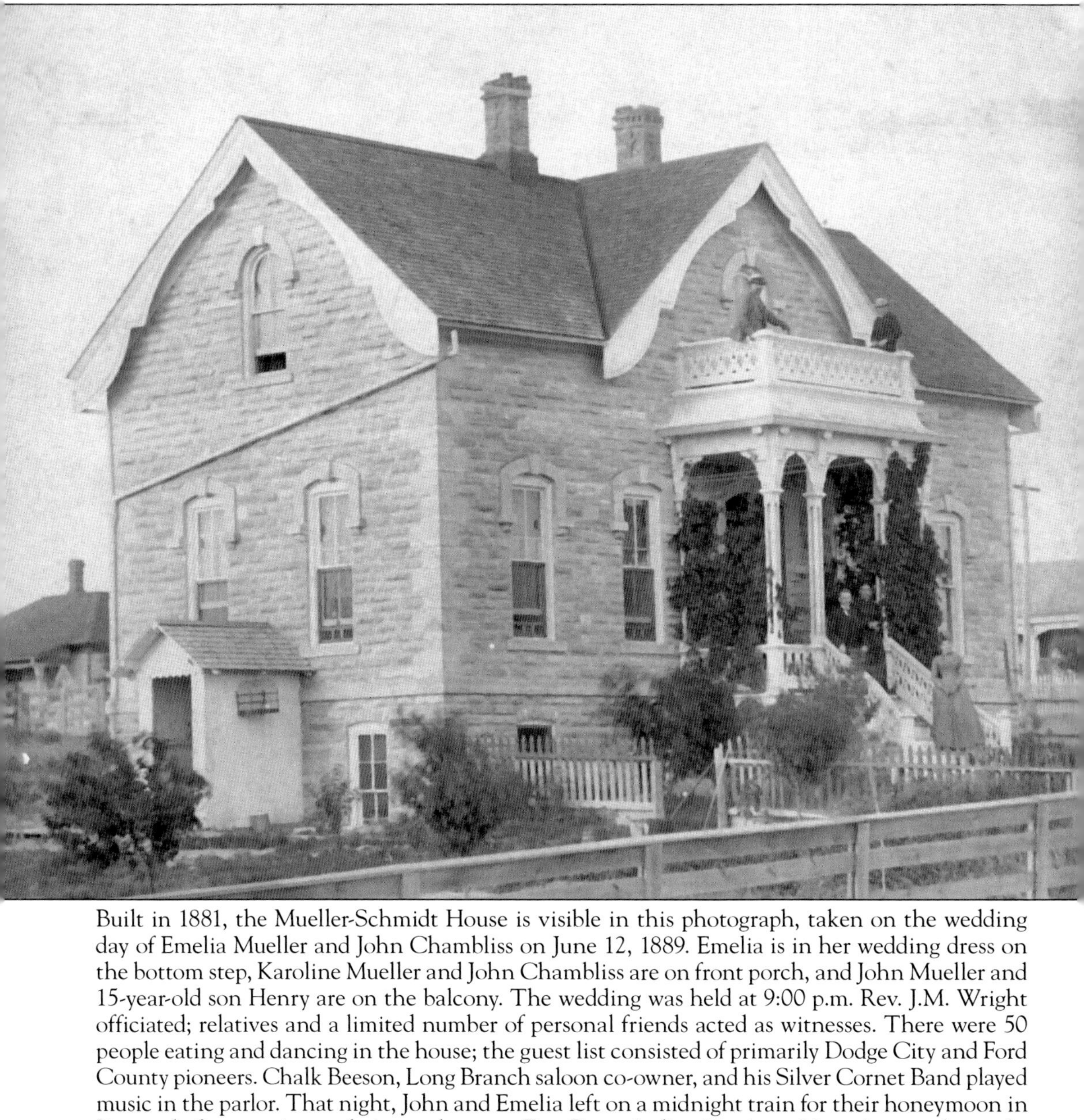

Built in 1881, the Mueller-Schmidt House is visible in this photograph, taken on the wedding day of Emelia Mueller and John Chambliss on June 12, 1889. Emelia is in her wedding dress on the bottom step, Karoline Mueller and John Chambliss are on front porch, and John Mueller and 15-year-old son Henry are on the balcony. The wedding was held at 9:00 p.m. Rev. J.M. Wright officiated; relatives and a limited number of personal friends acted as witnesses. There were 50 people eating and dancing in the house; the guest list consisted of primarily Dodge City and Ford County pioneers. Chalk Beeson, Long Branch saloon co-owner, and his Silver Cornet Band played music in the parlor. That night, John and Emelia left on a midnight train for their honeymoon in Denver before moving to their new home at Fort Reno, Indian Territory. Henry's carved initials, H.J.M., are still preserved on the right side of the window, visible behind John Mueller. Built with 22-inch-thick limestone walls, the home has true 2-by-12-inch floorboards on 14-inch spacing. It is the oldest house in Dodge City and the only one built in limestone.

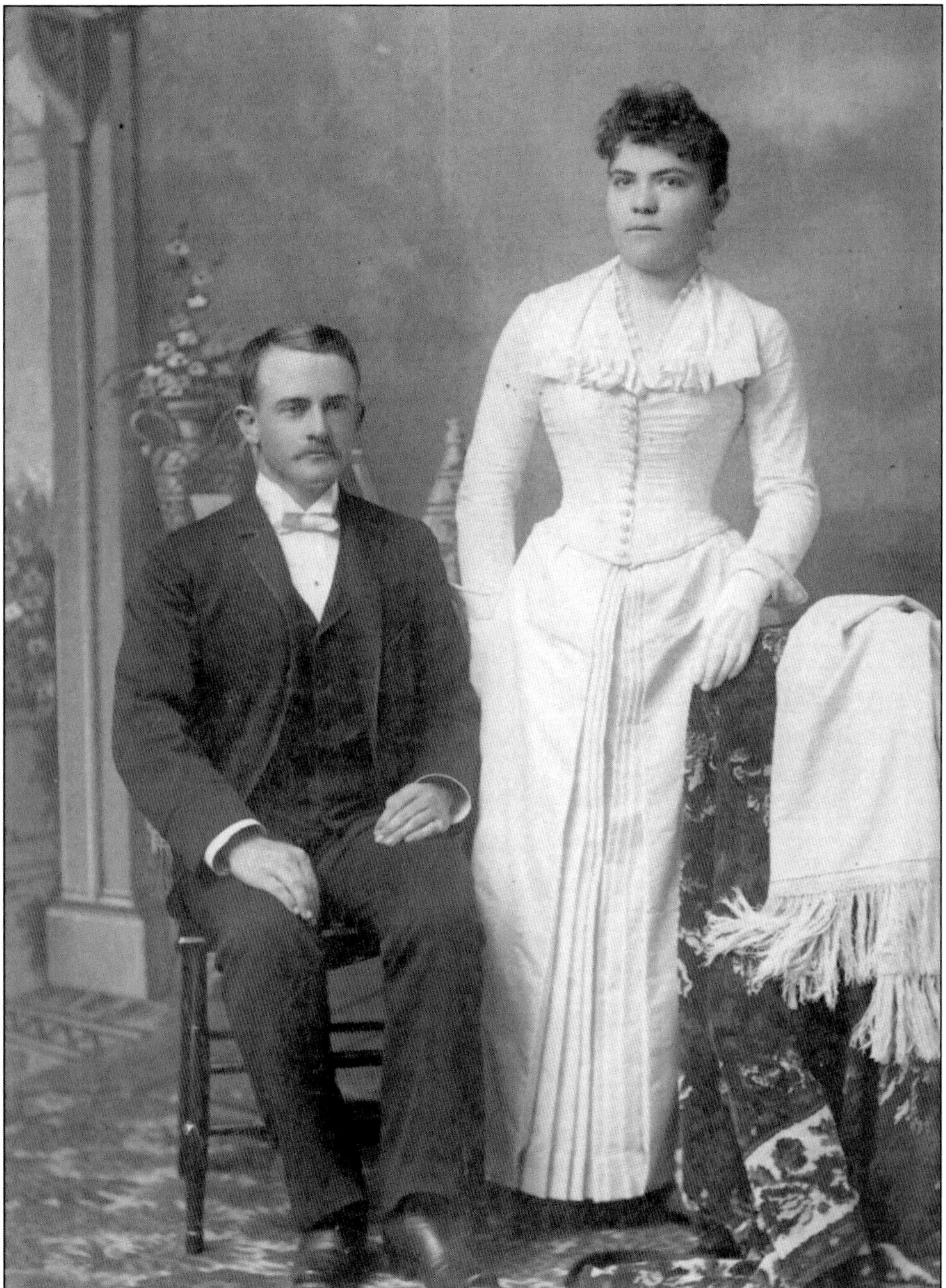

Emelia Mueller and John Chambliss pose for a wedding portrait. According to the June 13, 1889, *Dodge City Times*, "The bride was most handsomely attired in a white satin dress and ornaments, while the groom wore conventional black. The wedded pair was surrounded and received the hearty congratulations of the friends present after which an adjournment was taken and all proceeded to the dining hall where a sumptuous repast was awaiting them, where tables were found laden with many of the good things of this life. Fred Berg, the confectioner, again exhibited his superior skill in the art decorative as shown by the ornamentation of the bride's and groom's cakes, which exhibited the work of a genius."

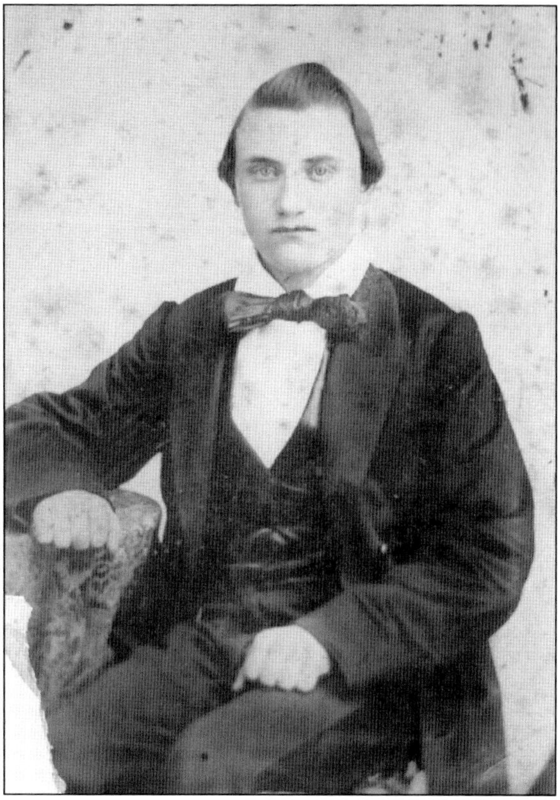

The portrait of John Mueller was taken in Germany, prior to his immigration to the United States. In St. Louis, Missouri, Mueller learned his trade of shoe- and boot-making. He was also among the first to join the Union Army in 1861 and was wounded twice before being discharged in 1865. In 1868, John moved his family to Kansas City, then to Great Bend in 1870, Abilene in 1872, and Ellsworth in 1873, as the cattle trails followed the expansion of the railroad tracks west. In November 1875, John purchased lot 10, block 2, on Dodge City's Front Street and opened his boot shop next to the Dodge House Hotel. His boots sold for what now would be from $400 to $600 and established the style known as the cowboy boot. Below, Karoline Mueller is pictured in St. Louis in 1873, before her arrival in Dodge City, where she moved with John and family from Ellsworth, Kansas.

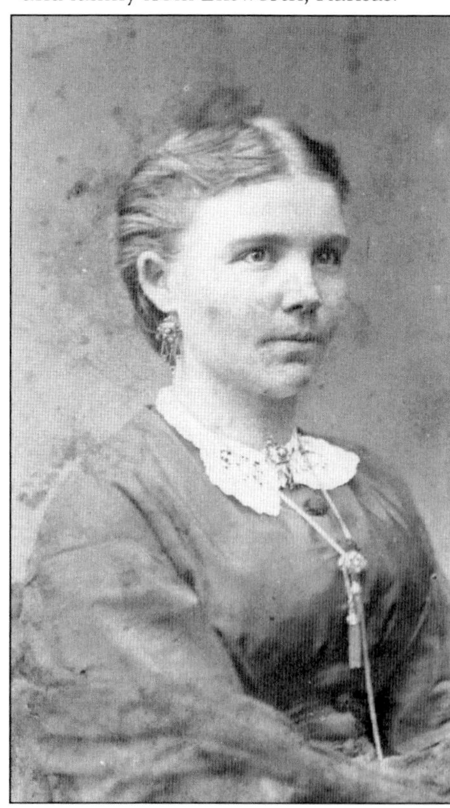

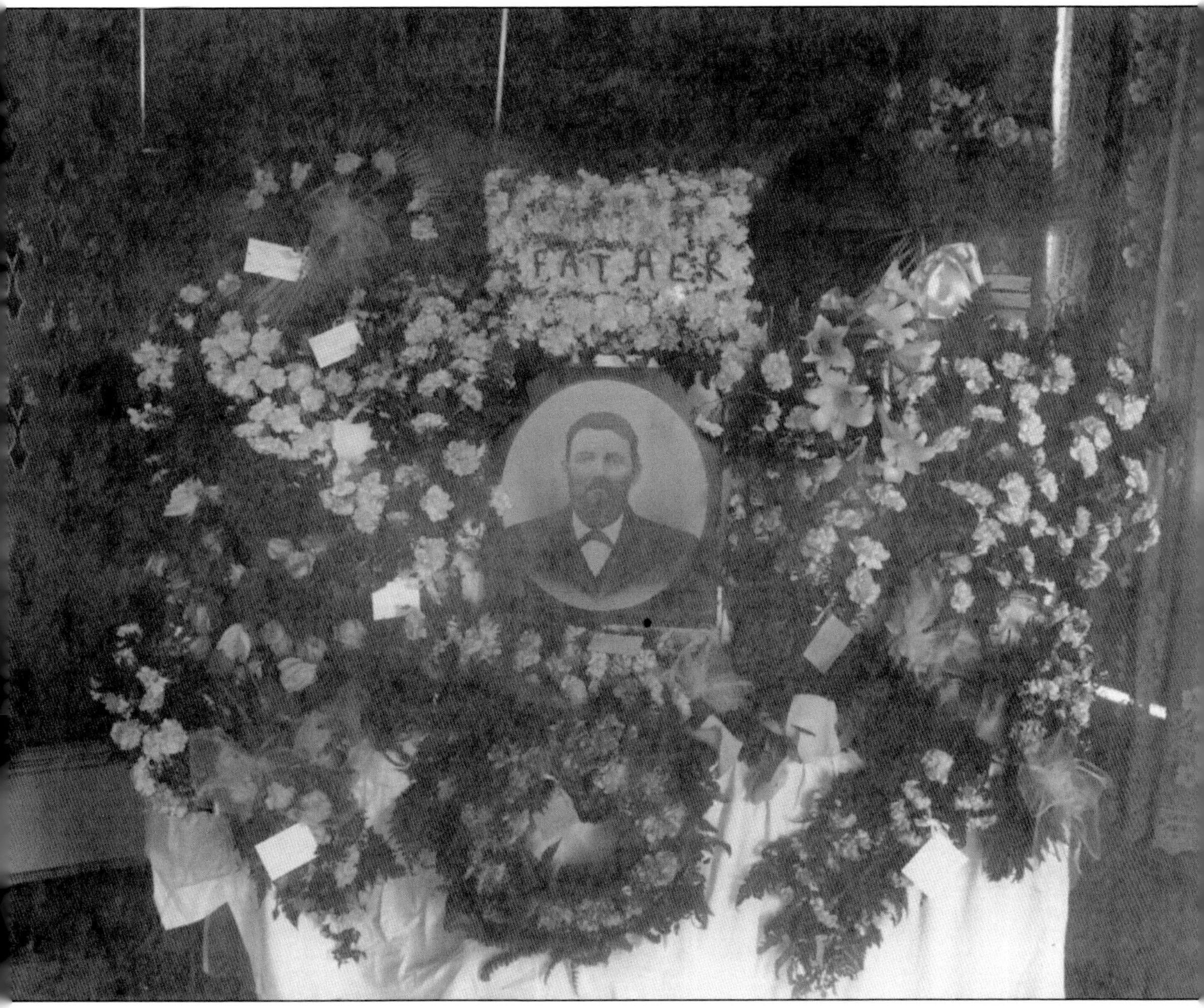

Adam Schmidt, pioneer blacksmith, died on May 1, 1911. The following is an excerpt from his obituary: "Mr. Schmidt was taken ill last November, and for a time his many friends feared that his life race was run, but that rugged constitution which had for so many years kept him free from ailment of any kind would not [let him] down . . . Saturday afternoon Mr. Schmidt was down town as usual greeting his friends, and said that he was feeling unusually well. But towards evening he was stricken with the same complaint that brought him low in the winter, and gradually he became weaker, till he fell into that sleep that knows no waking."

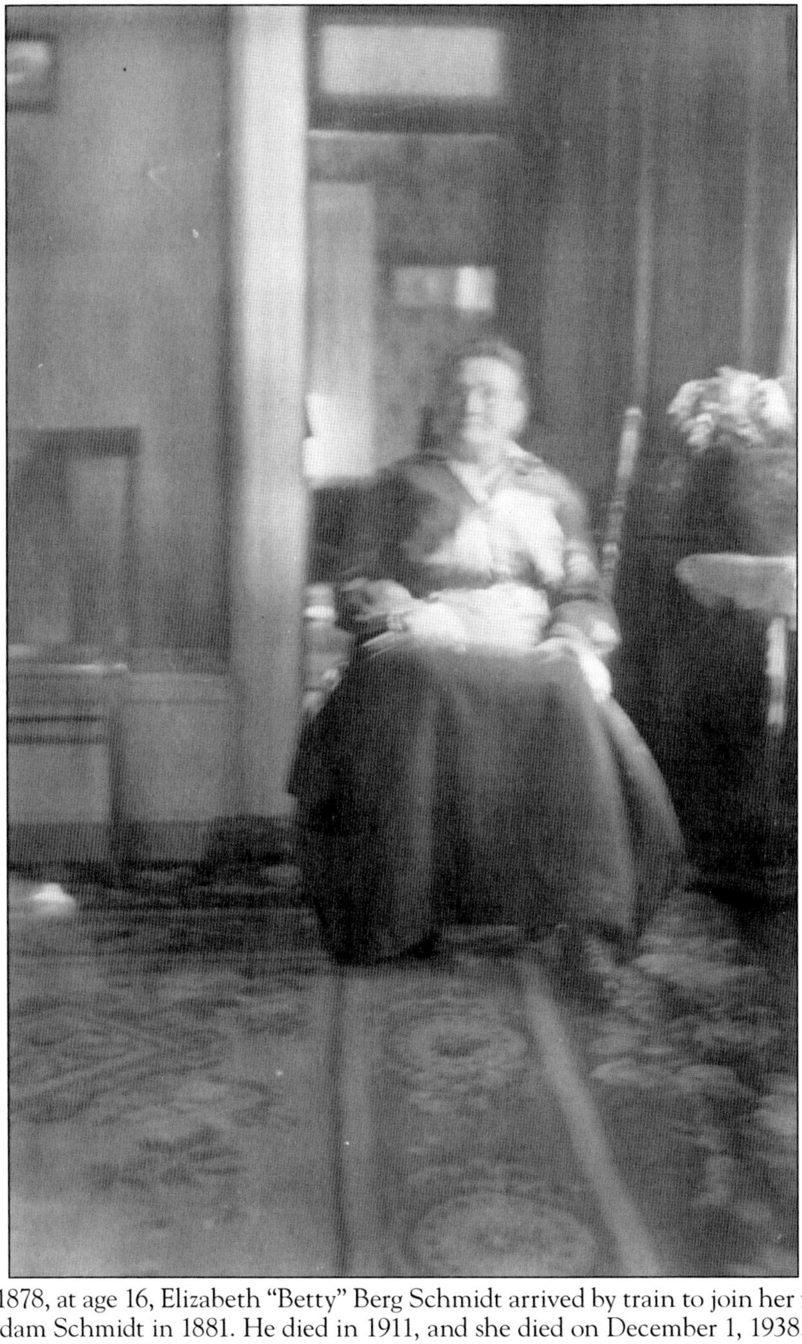

In March 1878, at age 16, Elizabeth "Betty" Berg Schmidt arrived by train to join her family. She married Adam Schmidt in 1881. He died in 1911, and she died on December 1, 1938. She was a short woman; much of the furniture in the house was lowered to suit her. There is no electricity yet in the house, nor indoor plumbing. Her children Elma and Heinrich added all the modern elements after Betty's death. They also changed her bedroom into a dining room and added a modern kitchen onto the back of the house, leaving the basement kitchen unchanged. Found in Elizabeth's funeral book, this c. 1938 photograph was the last one taken of Betty Berg Schmidt. It was taken from her bedroom, looking into the foyer and parlor of the Mueller-Schmidt House. She was the daughter of the first baker in Dodge City, Frederick Berg.

Pictured in 1893 is Henry Mueller at age 20. He visited Dodge City and the Schmidts until 1950, returning many of the photographs of his family. After his family moved back to St. Louis in 1890, his father, John, was killed in an Army accident (he had gone back in the service after losing all his cattle in 1886 blizzard), then Henry and his mother had to move to live with her parents in Illinois. Henry later returned as a barber at Fort Dodge and worked at Draper Clothes in Dodge City, where some charges arose concerning money. He died in Illinois in 1951. The Schmidt family always welcomed him to his old family home.

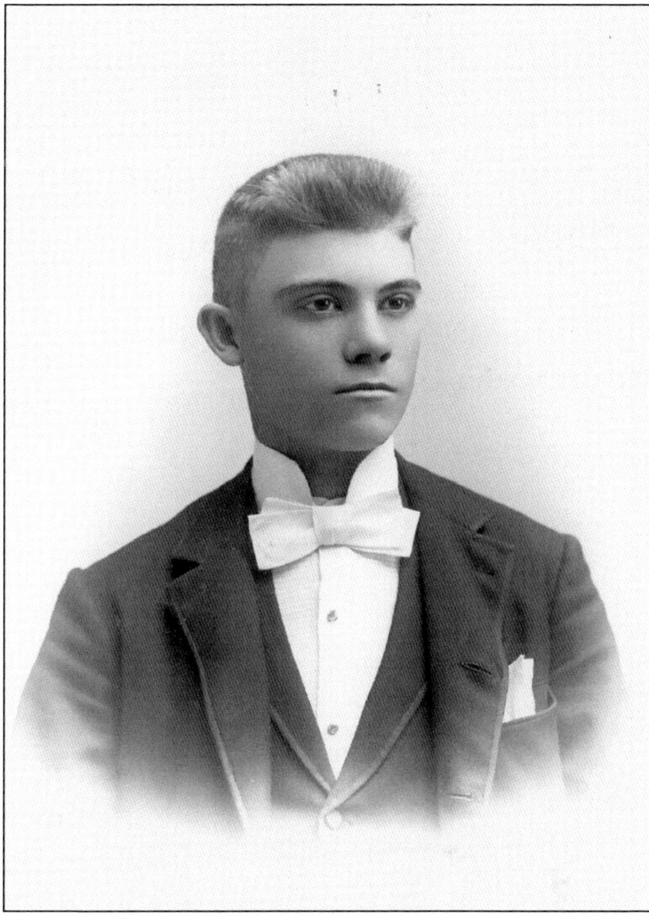

Henry J. Mueller

Born July 22, 1874 Died March 22, 1951

Funeral services will be held Sunday afternoon, March 25
at 2:00 o'clock in the Robert N. Smith Funeral Home

Friends are invited

Interment in the Masonic Cemetery
Nashville, Illinois

Lying at rest in the Funeral Home
after 7:00 p.m. Friday, March 23

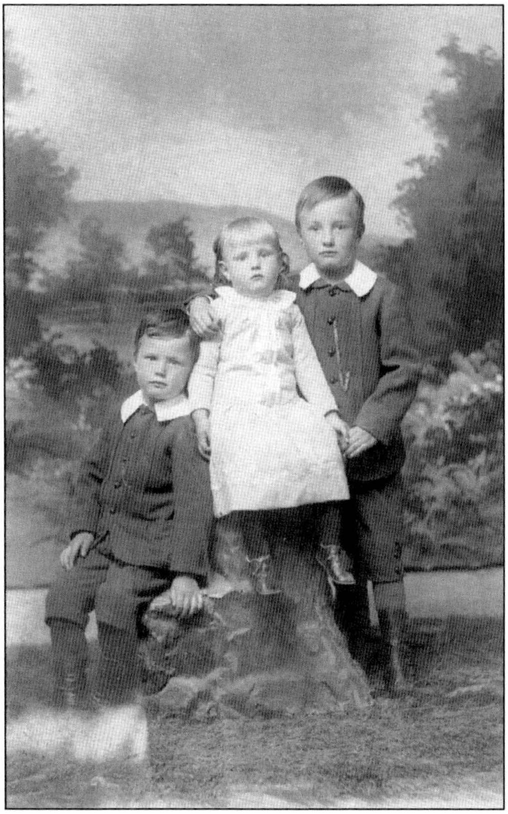

Louis "Louie," Elma, and Heinrich "Heinie" Schmidt are pictured around 1890. The photograph was probably taken to commemorate their move into the new, fully furnished house their parents purchased from John Mueller. This photograph has hung in the living room of the Mueller-Schmidt House since they moved into it. Below are cousins from the Schmidt, Berg, and Evans families.

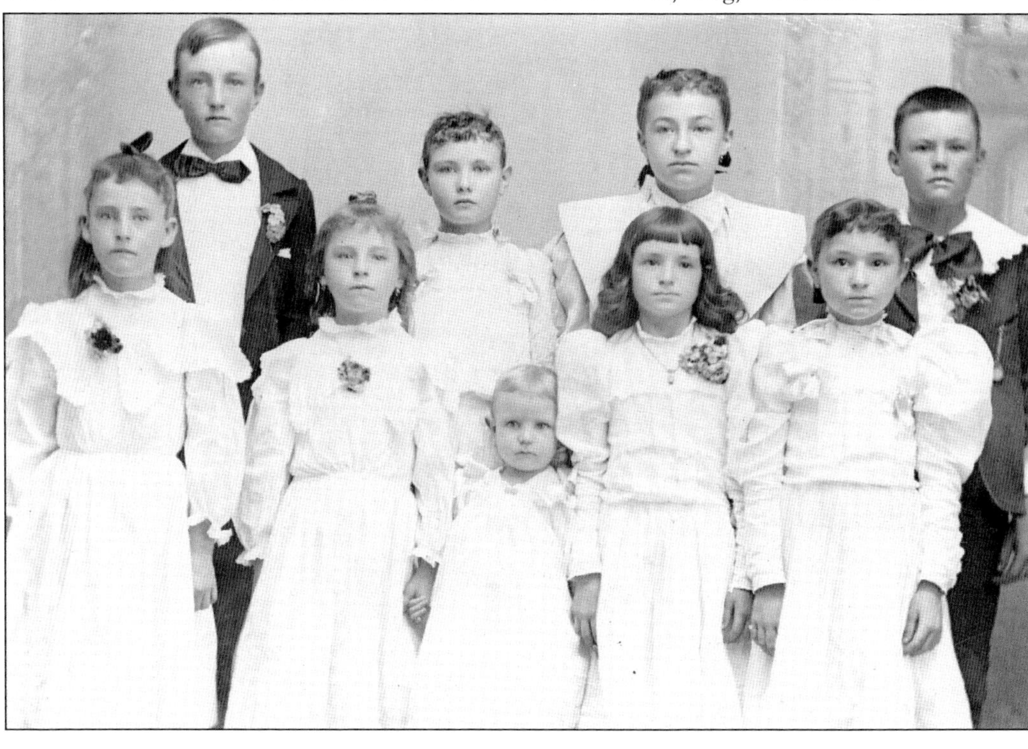

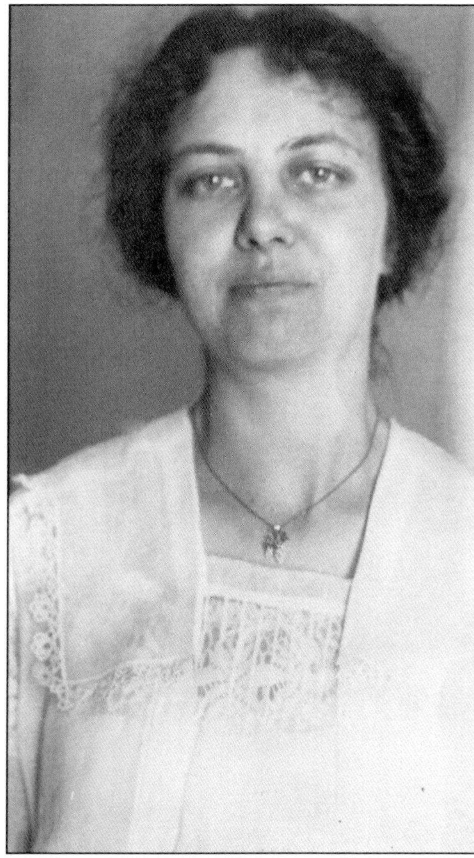

Elma Schmidt is pictured at right. Below, Elma appears with her aunts and cousins, the Bergs and Evans. The wooden stairs are the original ones at the Mueller-Schmidt House.

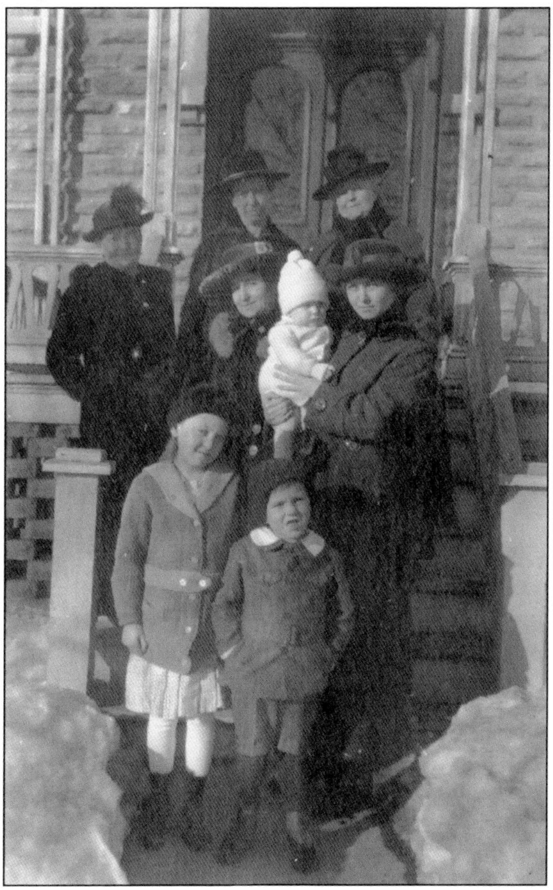

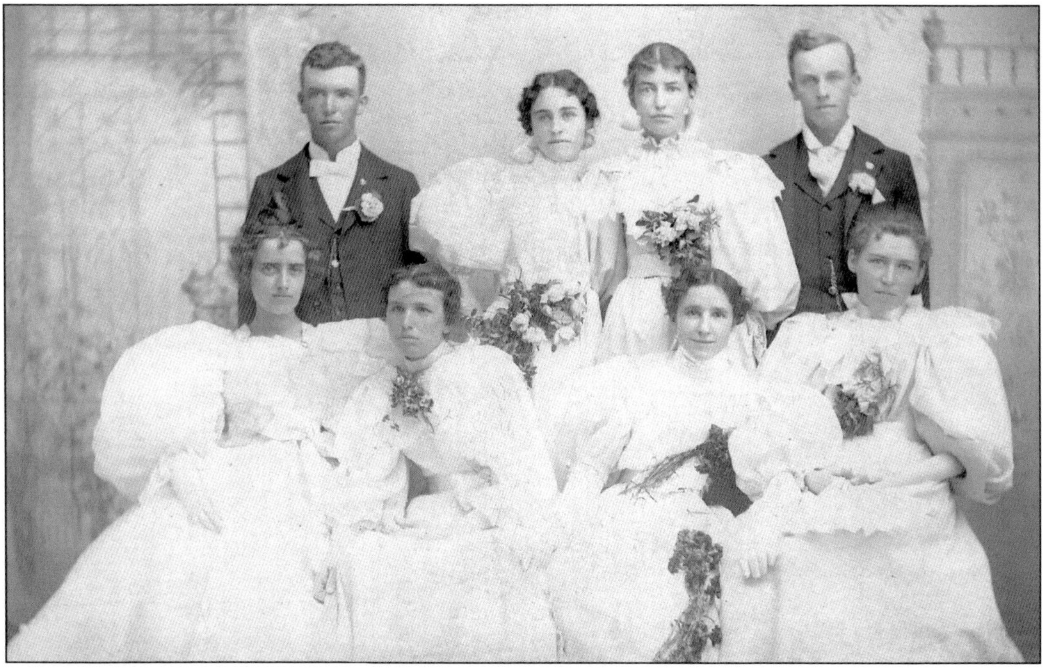

Robert Rath is pictured (second row, far right) with his sister Bertha and cousins, including Harry Markley (second row, left).

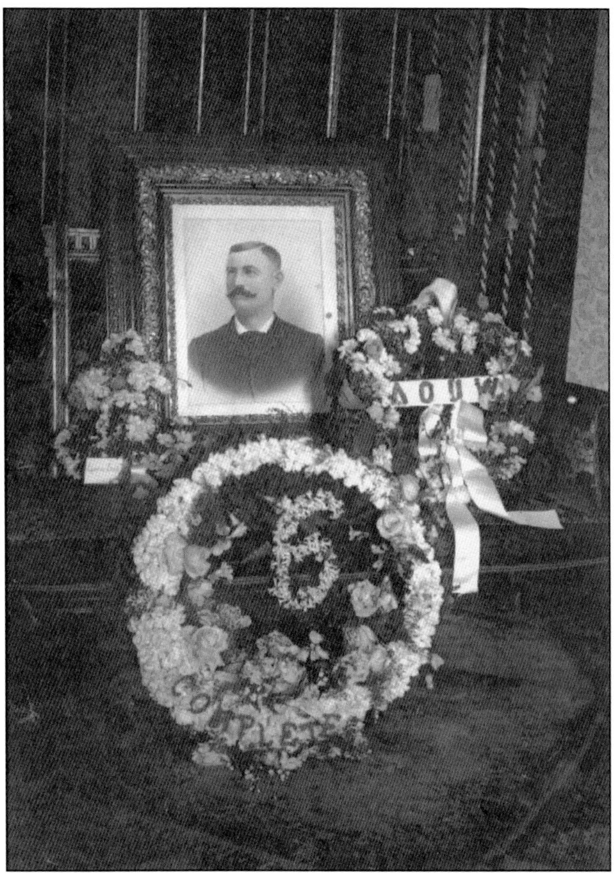

Pictured is the funeral presentation for Thomas Bainbridge, following his death in an 1899. He was killed by a mail crane near Holly, Colorado, on February 3, 1899. The display on the right is from the Ancient Order of United Workmen.

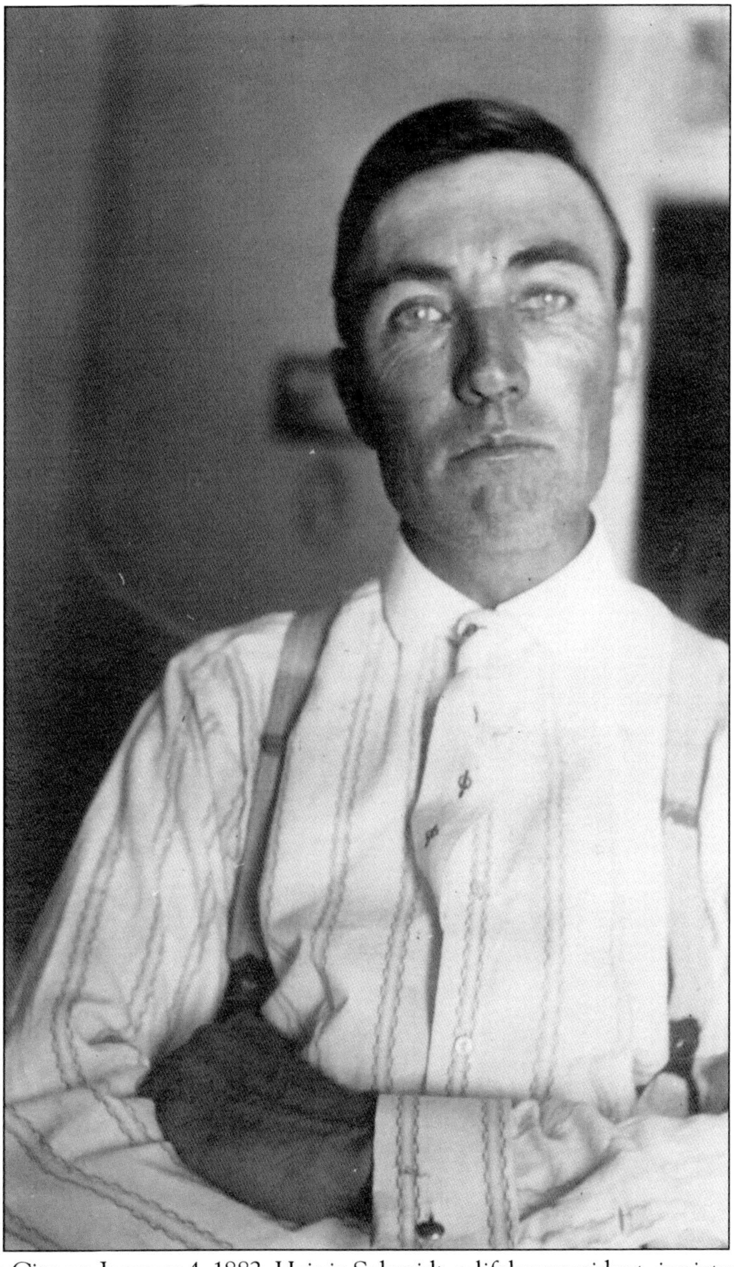

Born in Dodge City on January 4, 1882, Heinie Schmidt, a lifelong resident, is pictured here about the time of his run for register of deeds. He was elected in 1908 and served for two terms, a period of four years. He was later appointed postmaster on December 29, 1914. The following is a quote from *A Standard History of Kansas and Kansans,* published in 1919: "Heinie F. Schmidt, postmaster of Dodge City, has been active far beyond the average capacity in those duties that are closely connected with the public welfare, and for a man still under forty has achieved much that may properly have record in such a work as this . . . In a few brief years he acquired his education in the city schools. He was only a boy when he found a position in a local grocery store as a clerk. He moved from that job to a hardware store and remained in it in a clerical capacity for seven years. He has always been in politics and he exchanged a business career for one in public office."

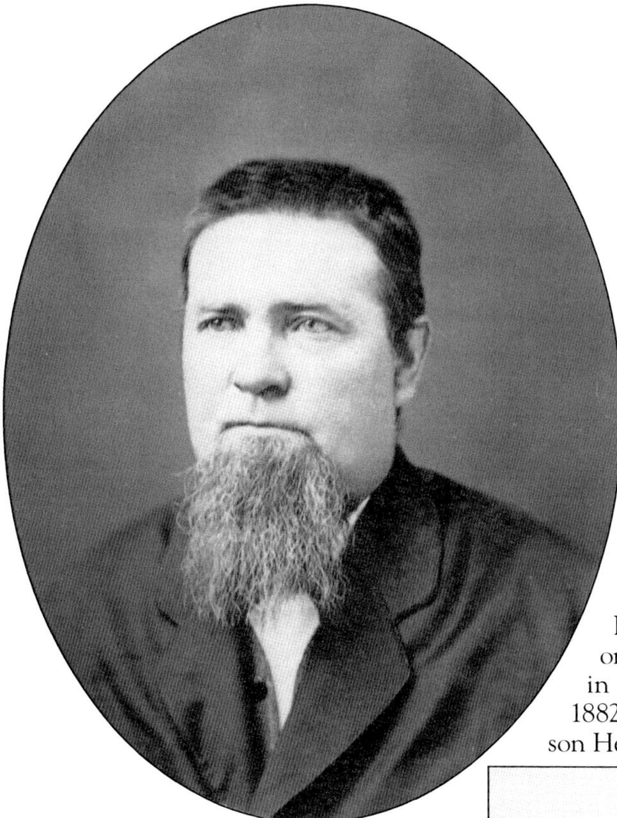

Elizabeth "Betty" Berg Schmidt's parents were Fred "Gran" Berg (left) and Elizabeth "Grama" Berg (below). They moved to Dodge City from Ohio in 1874, and Ohio-born daughter Elizabeth ("Betty" is the name she used on her wedding certificate) followed them in 1878. She married Adam Schmidt in 1882; she was 19, Adam was 41, and their son Heinie was a few days old.

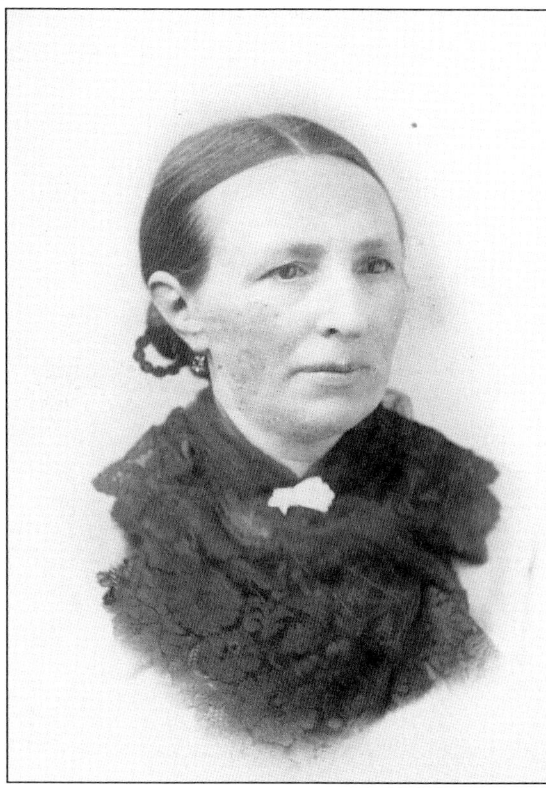

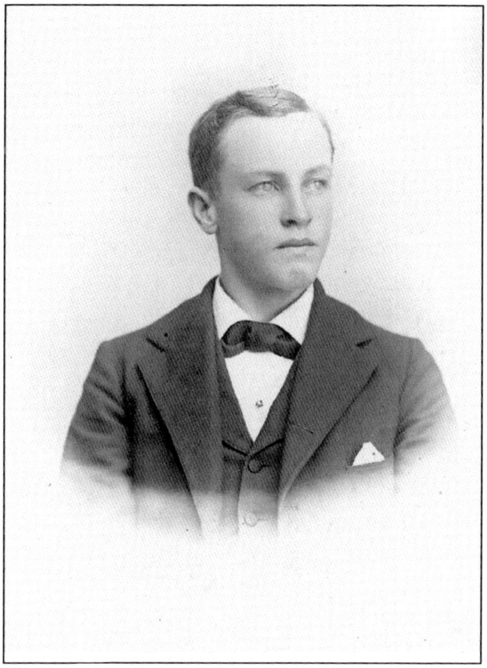

Pictured at right is Robert Rath. "The Nobel Trinity" is pictured below: Bert Hobble, Harry Taylor, and Robert Rath. Ida Ellen Rath wrote, "They staggered down Second Ave. on Sundays with plug hats on their heads and canes in their hands."

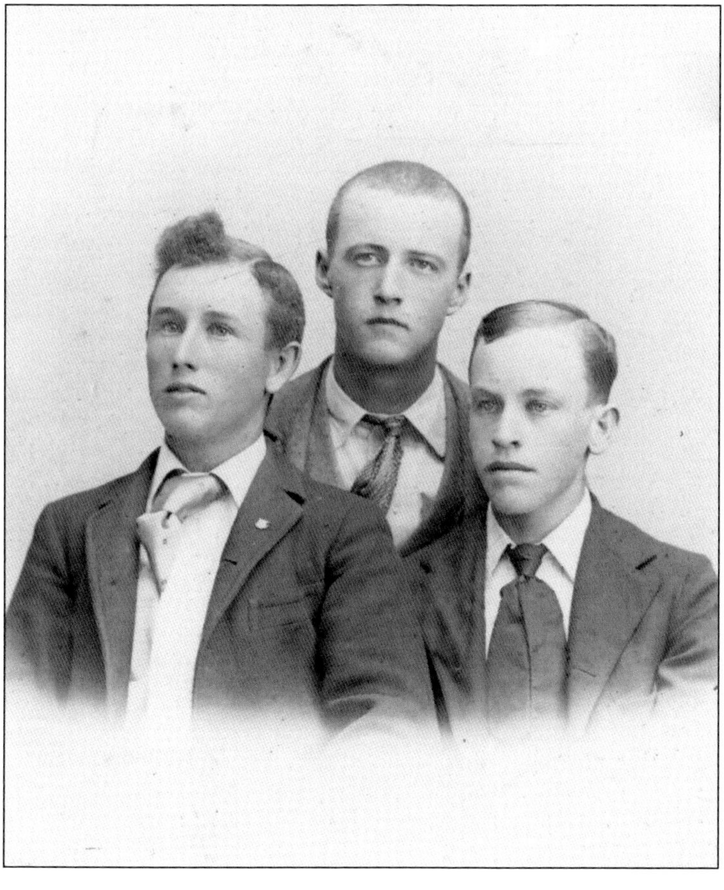

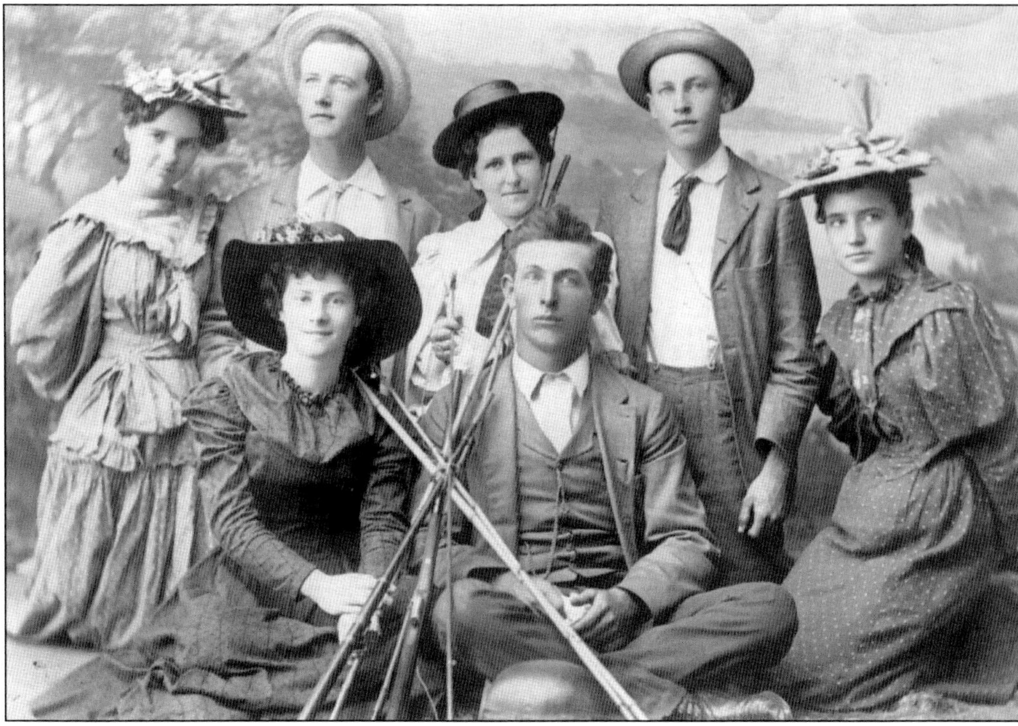

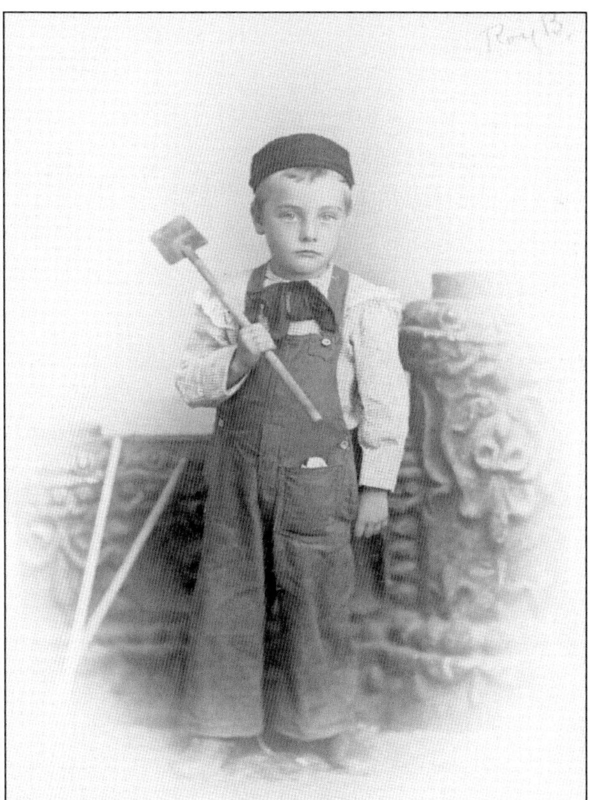

Above, Bertha Rath is at top left. The men in the back row are Bert Hobble (left) and Robert Rath (right). Harry Taylor is pictured center, and the others are unidentified. Roy Bainbridge is pictured at left. He was an early student at the University of Kansas School of Pharmacy, one of the first four state university pharmacy programs in the country. His father, Thomas Bainbridge, the stepfather of the Raths, worked on trains and was killed in an 1899 train accident. His mother built him a drugstore when he graduated; the building still stands in Dodge City.

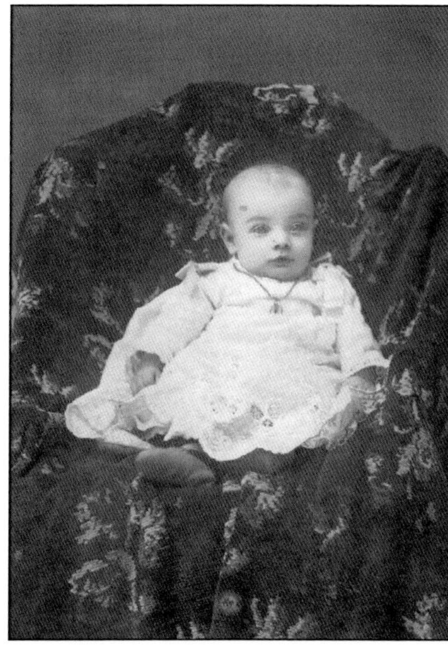

Roy Bainbridge is pictured on the right at nine months old and below at two years old.

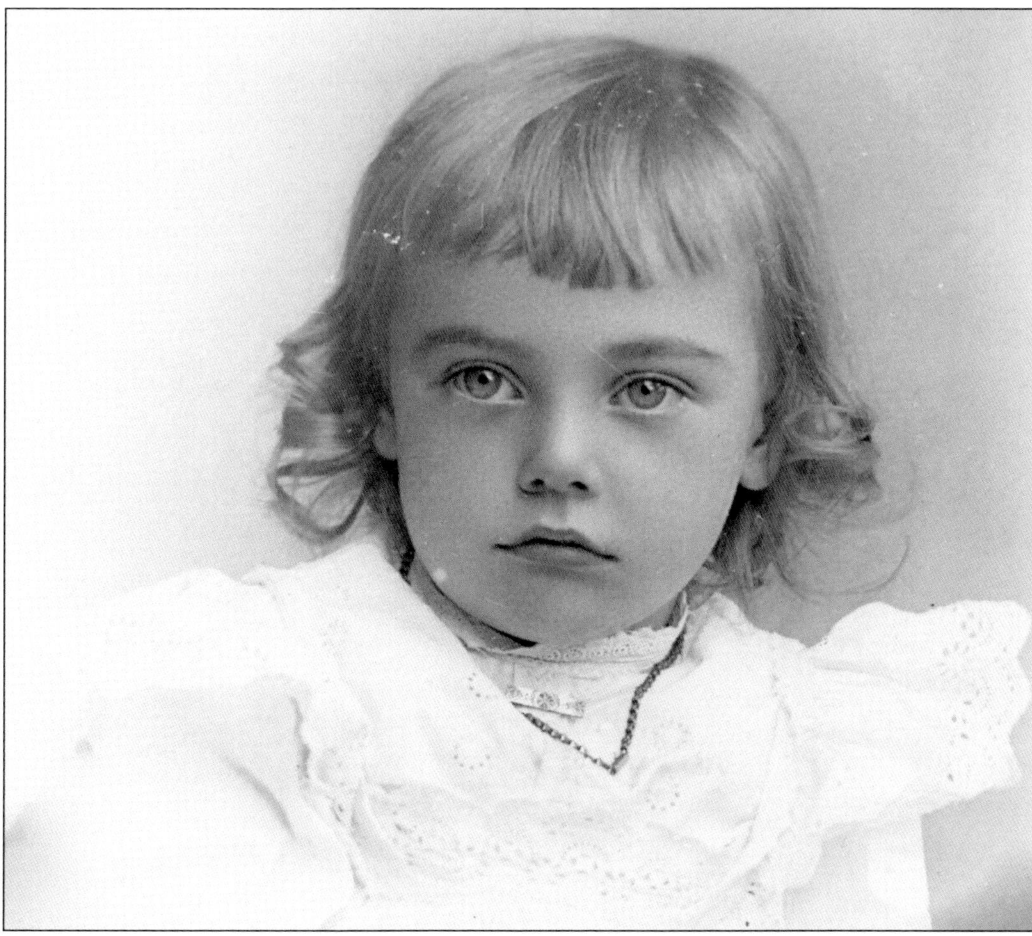

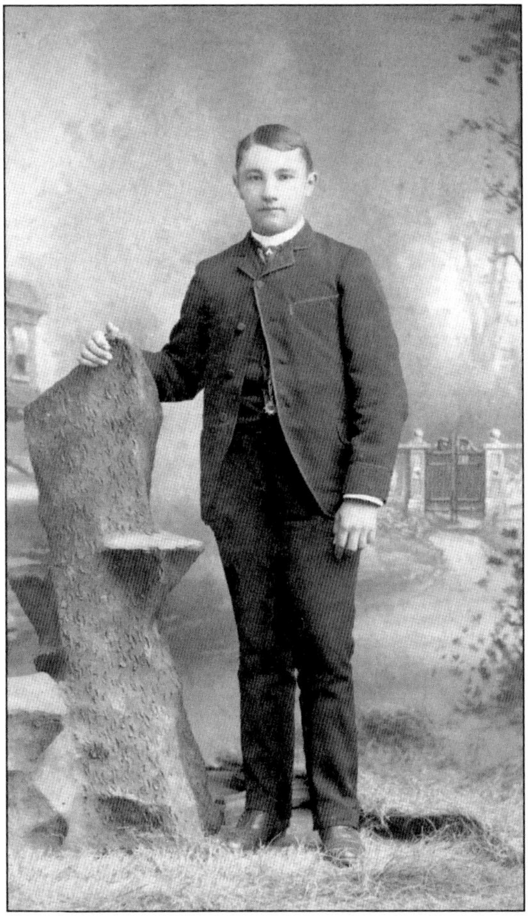

Arthur Zimmermann was a student at Washburn College for a full term when this birthday photograph was taken in Topeka, Kansas, in 1886. His parents—the gunsmith F.C. Zimmermann and his wife, Matilda—had five children, three of whom died in infancy. Arthur was killed in a horse accident at the end of June 1886, when he was 16. According to the June 29, 1886, issue of the *Globe Live Stock Journal*, "the horse fell over on its back, catching its rider [Arthur] and striking him in the breast with the pommel of the saddle." He died immediately after the accident. By his death, Arthur had already attended three post-grammar schools. His father was the owner of the leading gun and hardware store in Dodge City. Arthur's obituary states, "At the grove a beautiful hymn was sung by the church choir . . . and all that was left on earth of Arthur Zimmermann was consigned to the cold, cold grave." Below, Arthur Zimmermann and the Morris Collar boys are in front of the F.C. Zimmermann guns, pistols and ammunition store on Front Street in 1886. F.C. died on January 20, 1888. Matilda moved to Los Angeles, California, where she lived until returning to Dodge City in 1928 to live with her daughter Clarrisa. She died in September 1929.

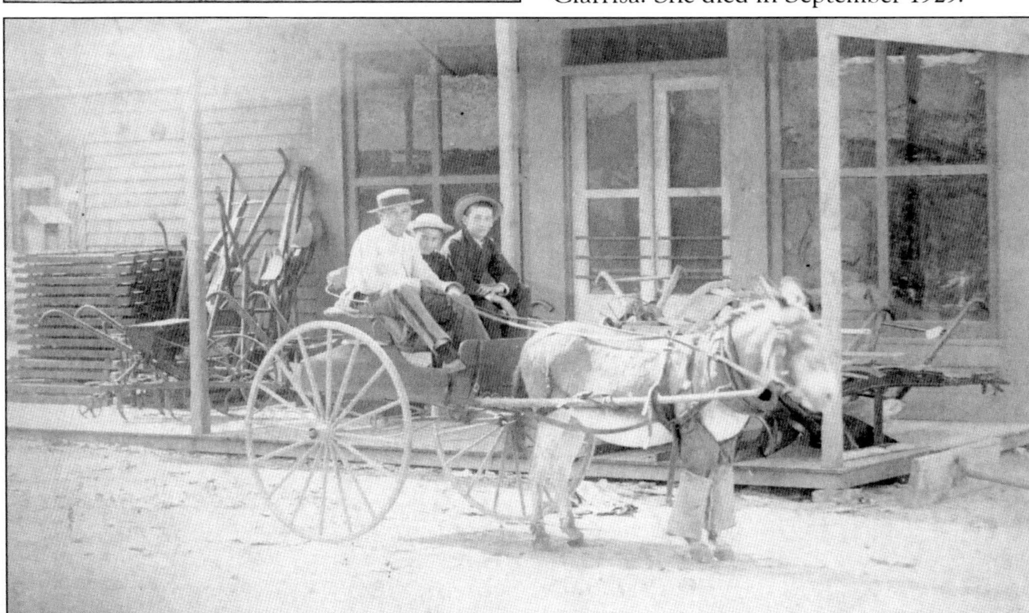

Richard Evans Jr., age 13, and his dog Rover are pictured on August 15, 1895. Born in 1882, his parents were pioneer settlers of Dodge City; his father, R.W. Evans Sr., being a member of the original town company and early-day banker, mayor, postmaster, and owner of a general mercantile store. R.W. Sr. had been postmaster of Hays City, Kansas, in 1869, before Dodge City was established. Young Richard was captain of the "First Super Bowl Champs," the football team that defeated a Dodge City team, 6-0. In 1904, he received a law degree from the University of Kansas. He returned to Dodge City to take care of his ill mother and opened his first law office at the corner of First Avenue and Walnut Street (Gunsmoke Street). He served as police judge in 1905 and was then elected county attorney for two terms. Later, he was appointed judge by Gov. Ben Paulen (1925–1929) and served as first district judge for Ford County for 23 years. He married Clara Sturgeon in 1904. She died in 1966; he died in 1971. They had no children.

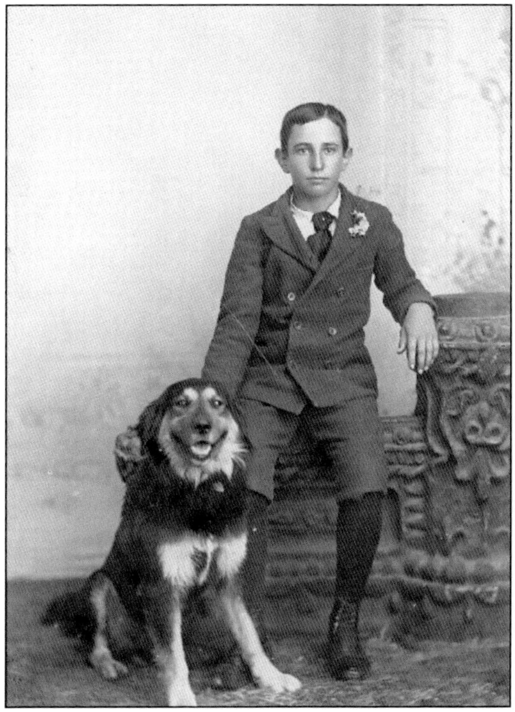

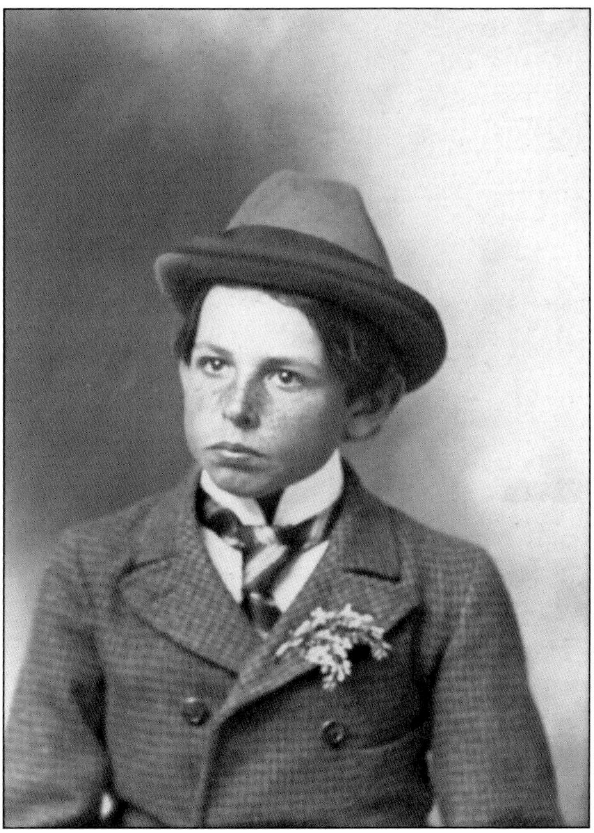

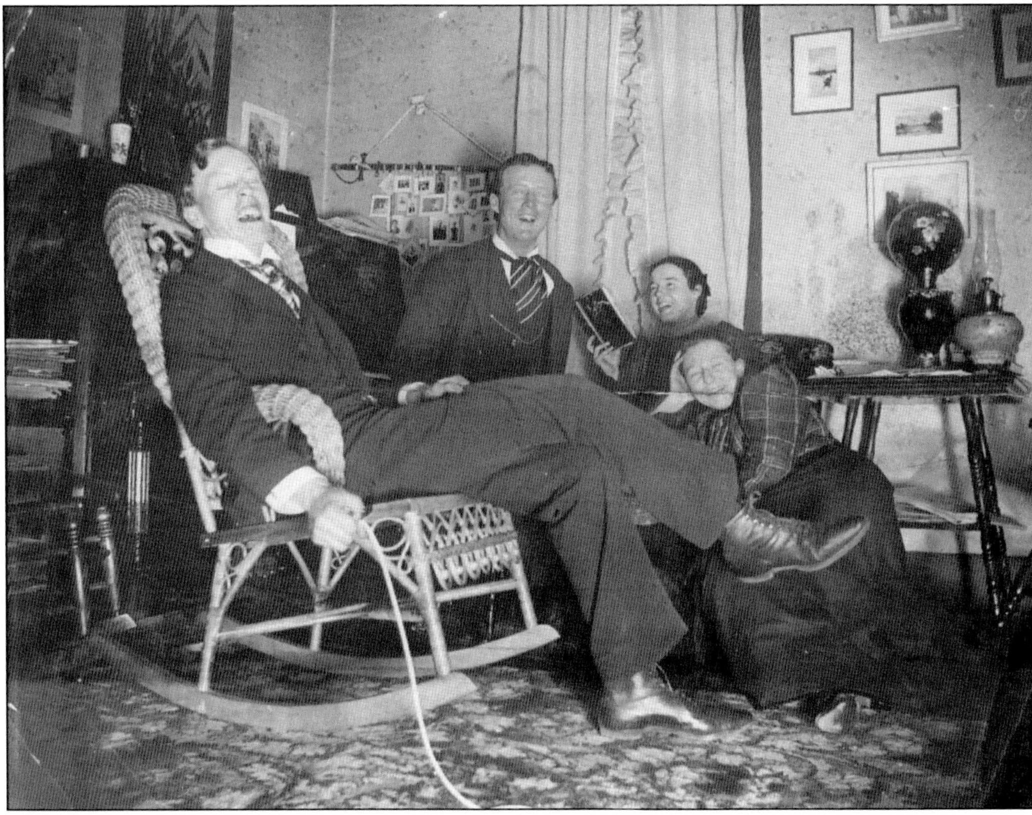

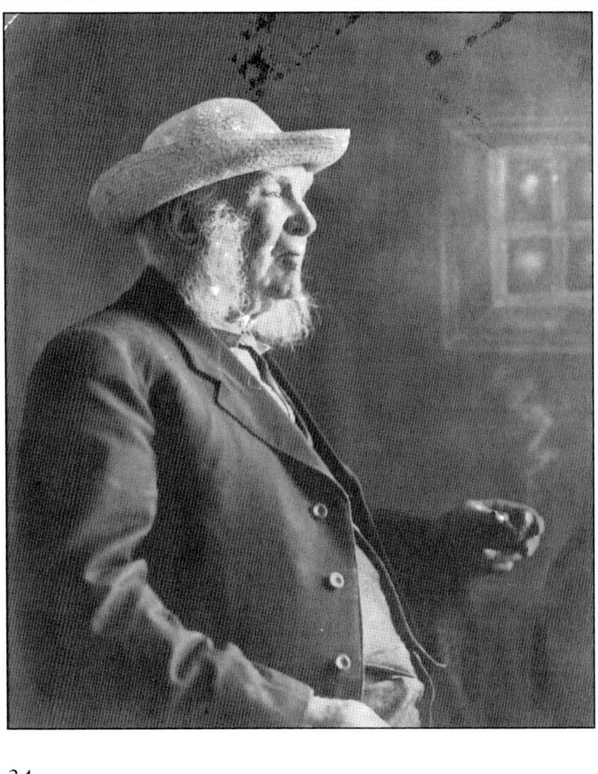

Charles Rath's 20-year-old son Robert appears on the left, holding a cable connected to his camera on Christmas Day 1897. Robert was a student at the University of Kansas. Mittie Wright, Robert Wright's daughter, who committed suicide in 1905, is in the back holding a book. Robert and Mittie are about the same age. Note the sword and the photographs hanging from it. Pictured on the left is Scotty Robinson, a longtime resident of Dodge City.

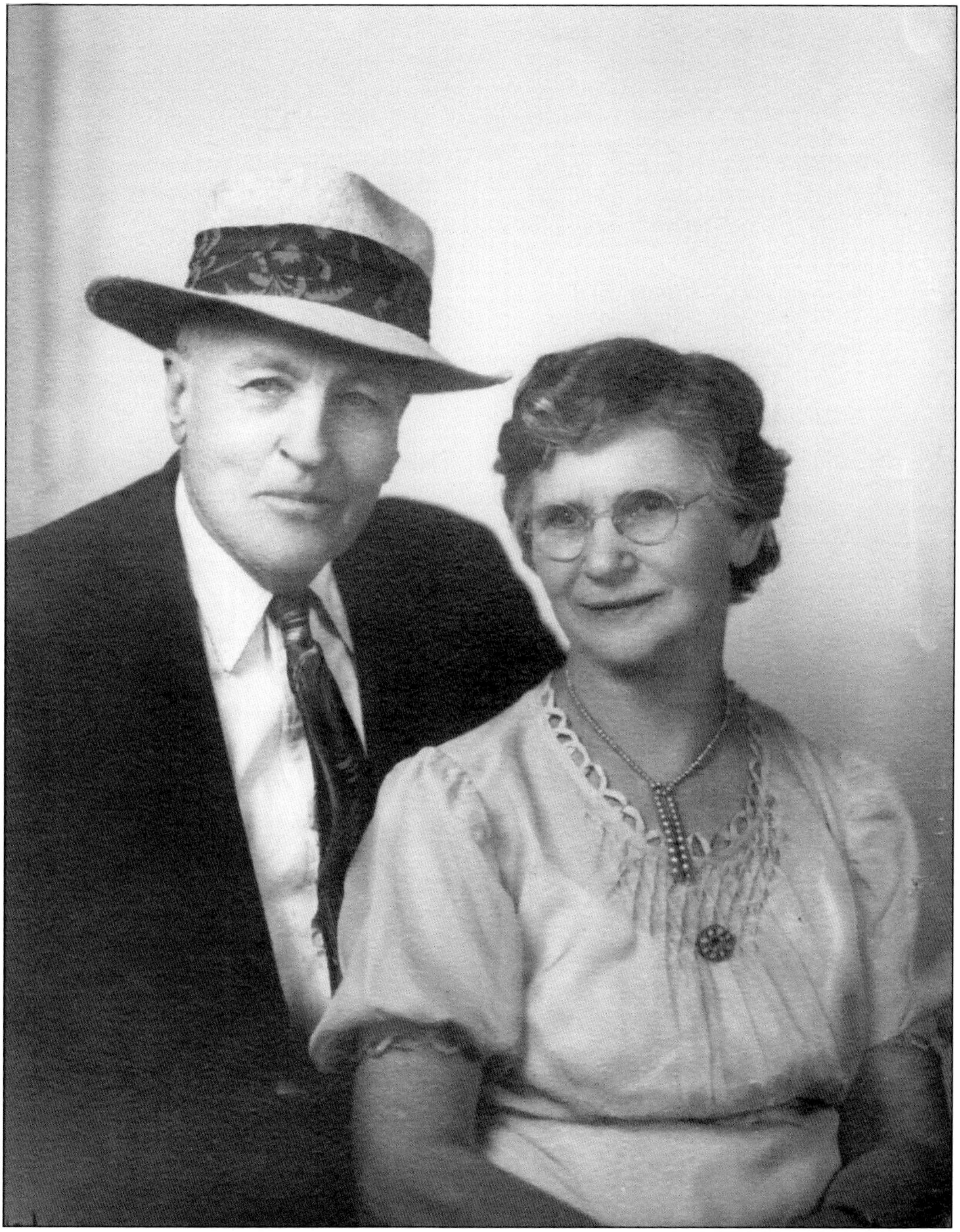

Robert M. Rath and Ida Ellen Cox Rath are pictured here around 1940. Ida Ellen married Robert Rath late in life. She raised a son, John Cox, who needed special care his whole life. Ida Ellen was a dirt farmer for 10 years in eastern Colorado after losing her first husband. She wrote books to support herself after Robert died, including *The Rath Trail* about Robert's father, buffalo hunter Charles Rath. Robert died on March 21, 1958, in North Fort Myers, Florida, while he and Ida Ellen were visiting Roy F. Bainbridge, Robert's half-brother. He is buried at Maple Grove Cemetery in Dodge City.

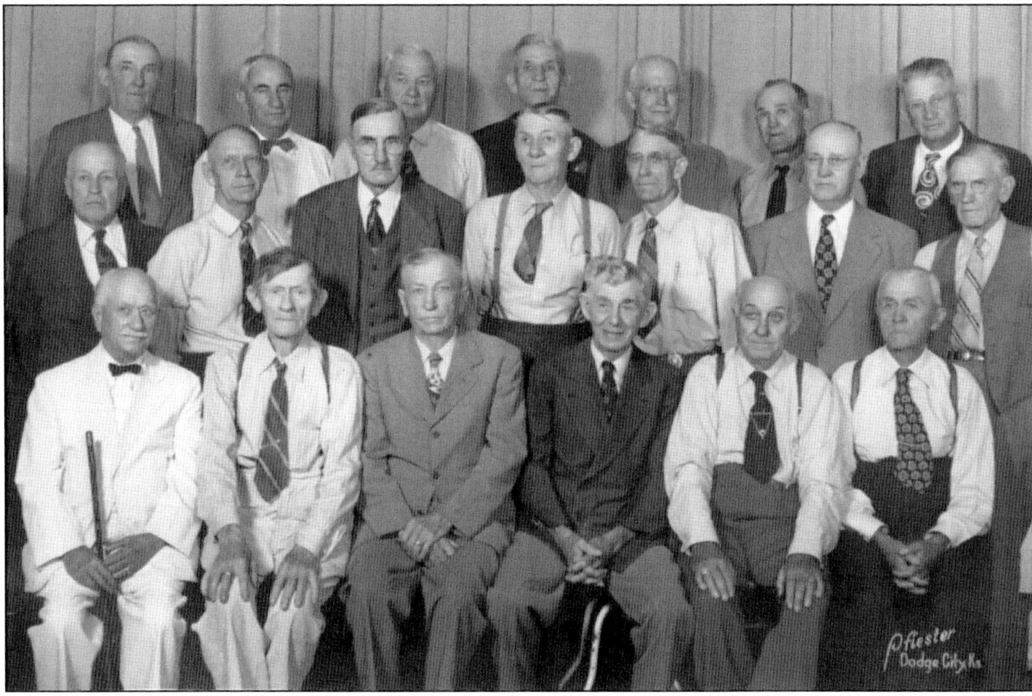

These men were first-generation Ford County residents, sons of the pioneers, all in Ford County before 1885. Their last names include Atens, Evans, Olive, Miller, Martin, Dowdy, Holfrisch, Riney, Straeter, Beeson, Cord, Rath, Trebilcock, Schmidt, Henry, Reighard, Crawford, and Bell. Below, an even smaller group of men were residents of Ford County prior to 1880 is pictured here on September 8, 1949. From left to right are (first row) Herman Straeter, H. Holtfrerich, and Bud Riney; (second row) Frank A. Hobble, Charles M. States, Robert M. Rath, and Merritt Beeson.

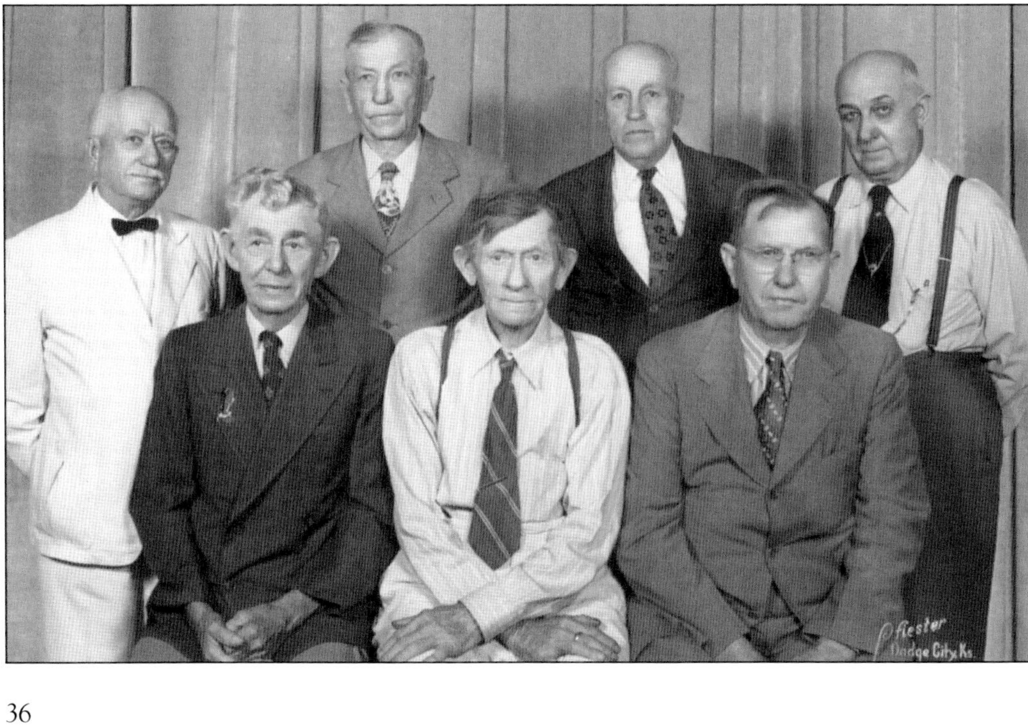

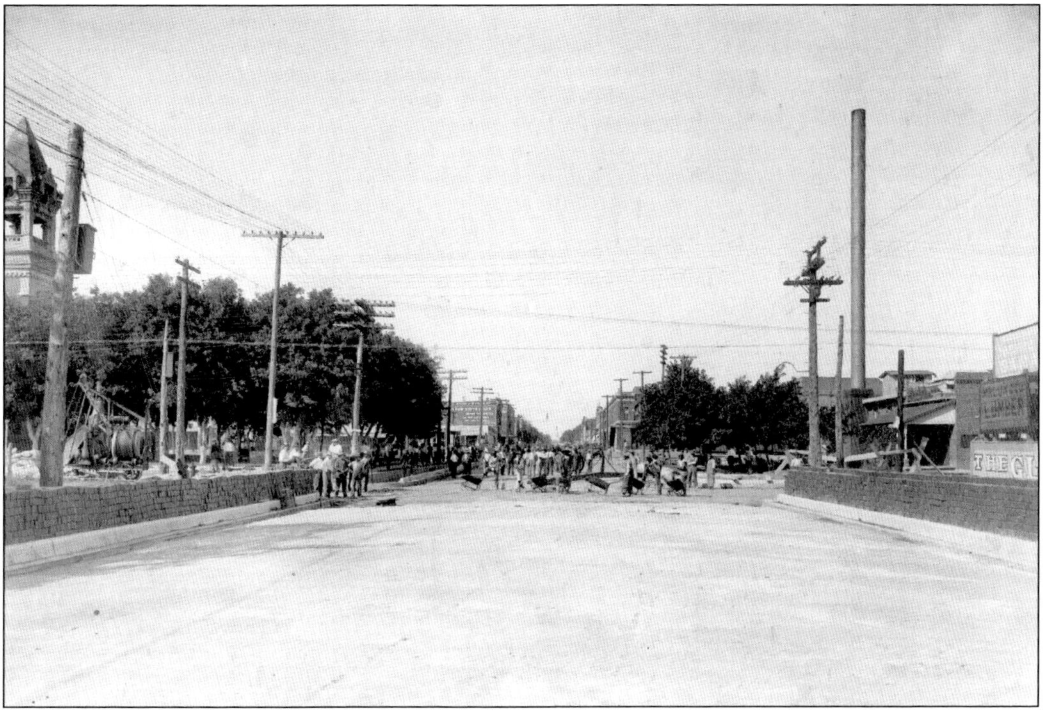

By 1912, the Dodge City Commission voted to brick the dirt streets of the city. The first city blocks bricked included Second Avenue at the corner of Trail Street, south of the railroad tracks by the then city hall. The top photograph looks north up Second Avenue. In the back center can be seen Dodge City mayor Hamilton B. "Ham" Bell with Dodge City commission treasurer George E. Laughead and other city officials. Below is a group of hunters. Hunting was a necessary task and a hobby on the plains. There was always something to eat on the prairie.

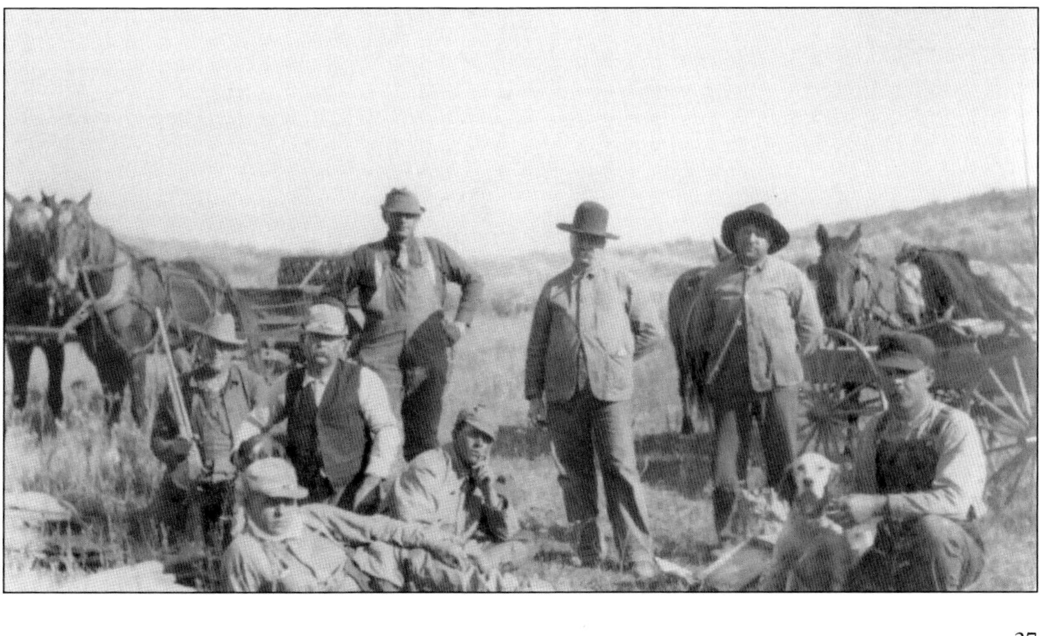

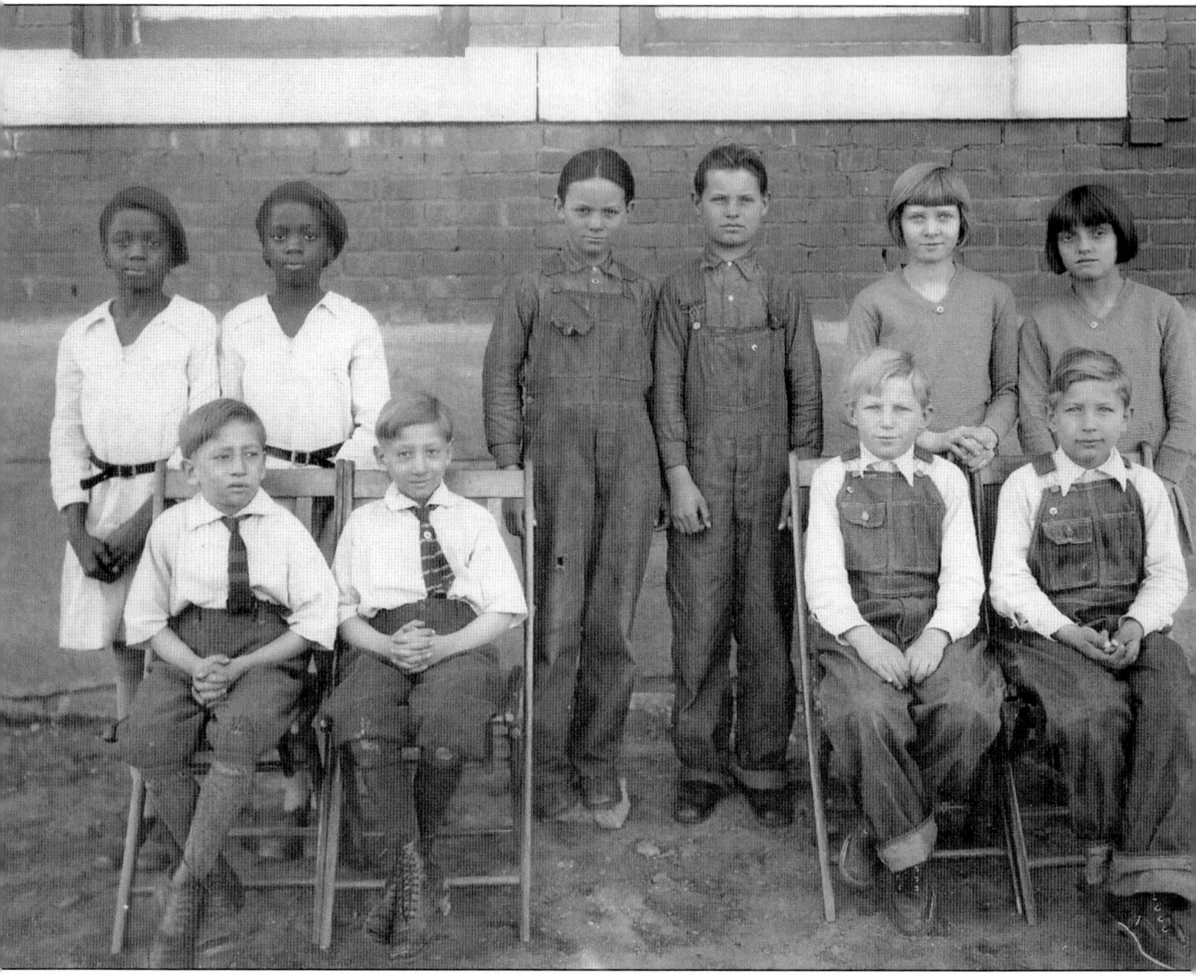

Twins appear in this c. 1905 photograph.

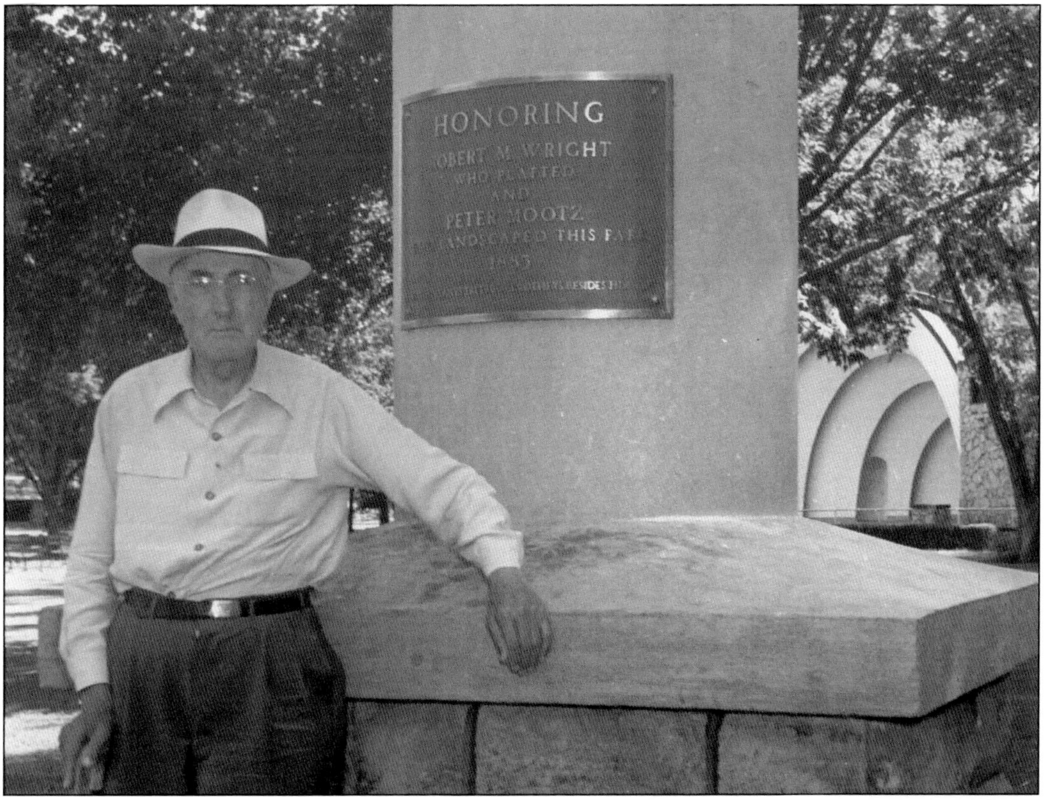

Heinie Schmidt stands by a memorial to Robert Wright in Wright Park around 1950. When Robert Wright donated the land, he also sent around 1,000 trees. The water table by the Arkansas River was very high, and the huge trees that grew from Wright's days as a Kansas state arborist in the early 1900s lasted until after the late-1960s drought in Dodge City. Pictured at right is Sally Wright, the final wife of Robert Wright. She lived from 1875 to 1966.

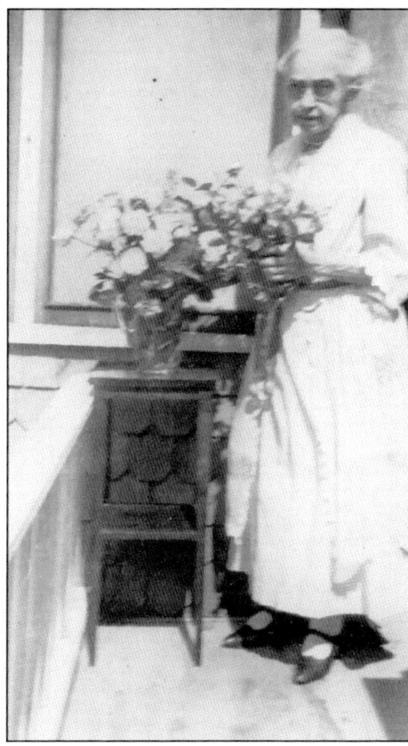

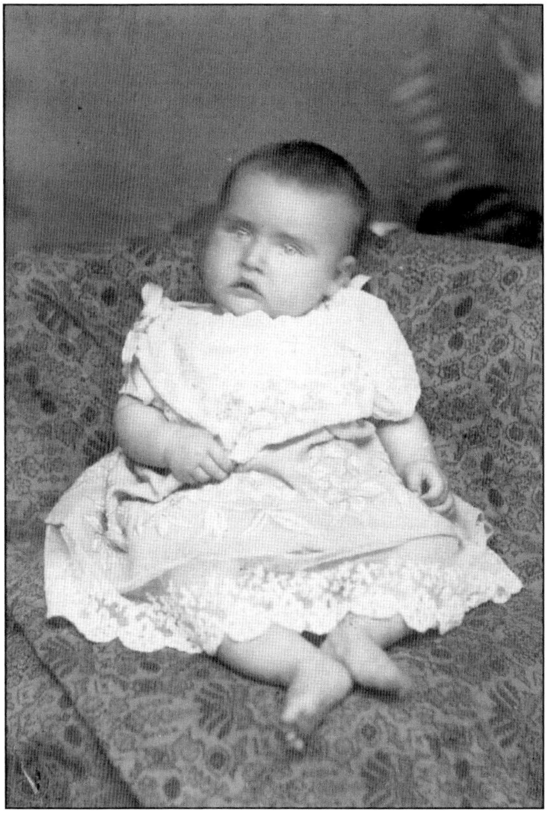

Baby pictures of the Schmidt children show Heinie (left), born in 1882, and Louie (below), born in 1884.

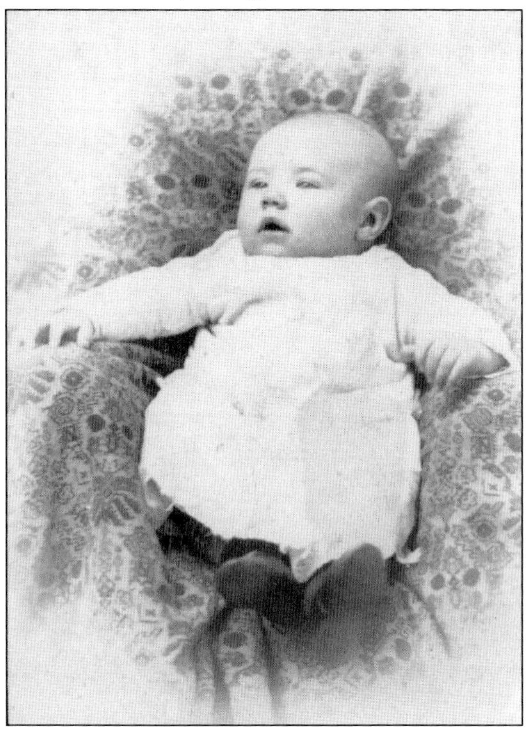

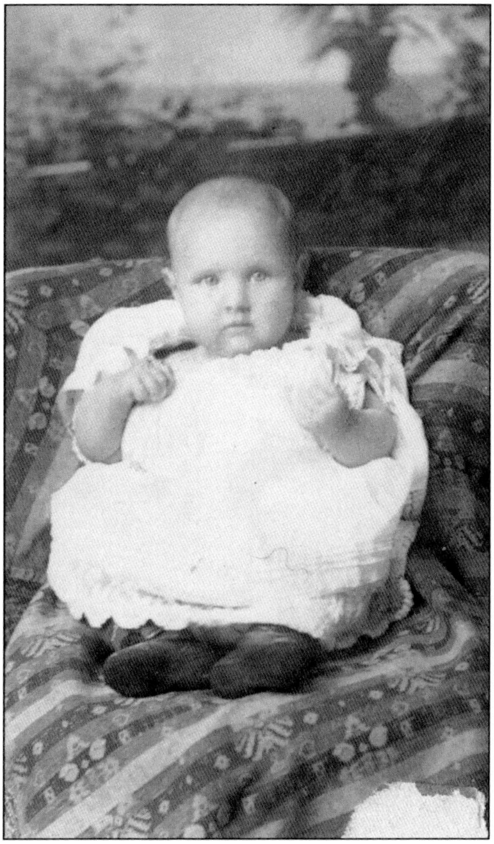

Pictured on the right, Elma Schimdt was born in 1885. Henry Mueller is shown below around 1889. Henry moved to St. Louis with his parents but sent back photographs and artifacts to Heinie Schmidt for the rest of his life.

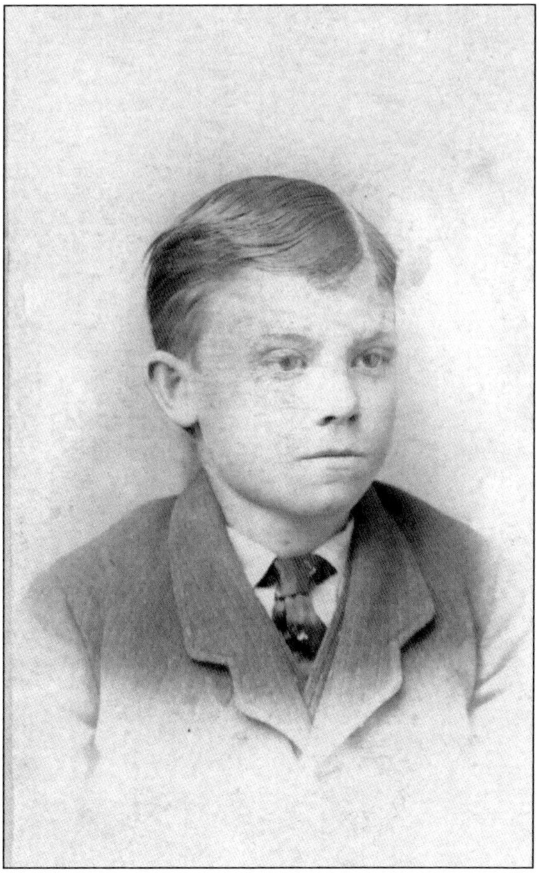

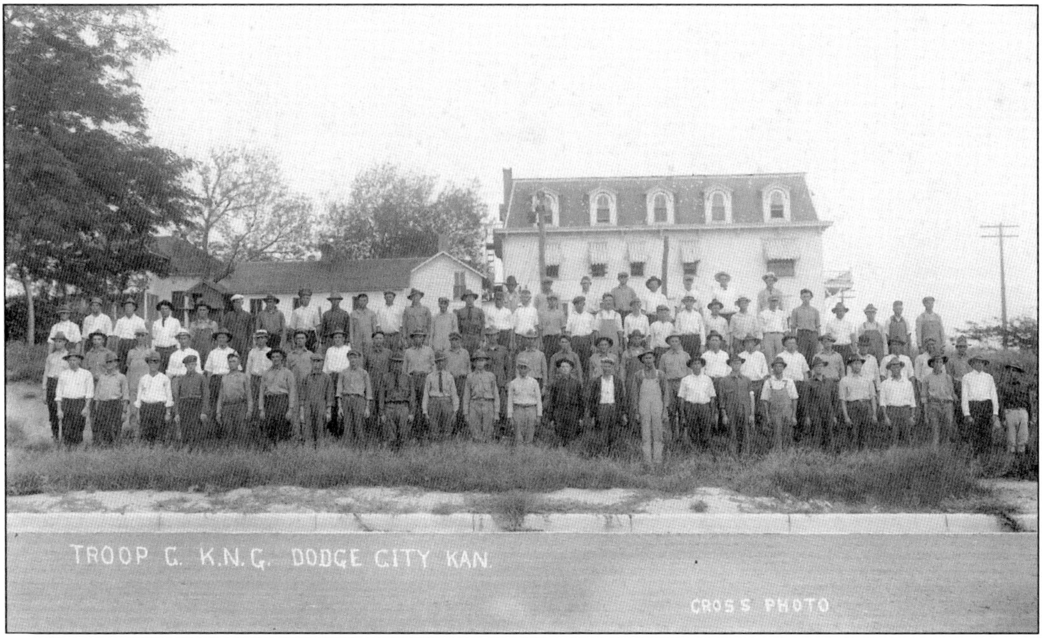

Civic organizations, including the Masons, the Knights of Columbus, and the Grand Workers, were active in Dodge City. These photographs show members of such local organizations. Pictured below, members of the Ancient Order of United Workmen are at a 1901 funeral.

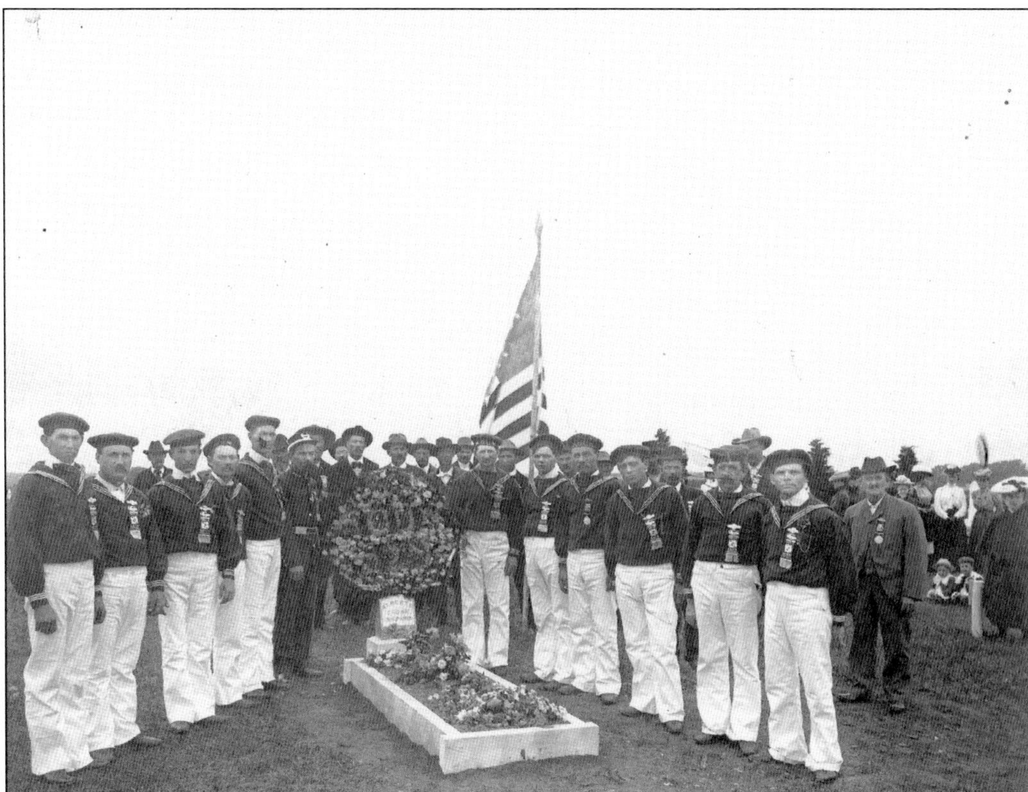

Two

Pioneer Civilization of Dodge City

In a long study of documents from both Dodge City and Ford County, Kansas, one certain fact that shows up in the public record is the same people, all men, remain part of the civic process until they are unable to do so due to poor health or death. The financial bonding required in the 1890s and 1900s to run for some political offices, especially city and county treasurer positions, meant that friends and associates had to put up thousands of dollars personally for a candidate—a great deal of money at the time. The same names show up over the decades, including Charles Rath, Robert M. Wright, F.C. Zimmermann, Morris Collar, John McDonald, and George M. Hoover, all appearing on legal forms into the 20th century.

Dr. C. Robert Haywood, from southwest Kansas, was known as the "Dean of Kansas History." He stated that to the modern eye, early Dodge City would have looked like a 24-hour-a-day carnival. By the late 1880s and 1890s, the main drive of the community was to be as cultured, educated, and aware as any persons outside of major cities. This means the pioneers of Dodge City required each resident to help in any way necessary to get a train out of the snow, build a theater, become educated to national standards, and support schools, libraries, churches, and stages.

The past violence was not discussed much until author Stewart Lake made Wyatt Earp famous in the 1930s. According to Earp's journal, from the Glenn Boyer Collection of the Ford County Historical Society, Wyatt's last wife, Josephine, stated, "From Bat [Masterson—he had met her in Denver and later wrote 1907 magazine articles about Earp and the West], I learned much of my husband's history for the first time for Wyatt would never talk of himself. In fact, in all our years together, he never described a gun battle to me. He considered it a great misfortune that he had lived in such a time and under such circumstances that guns had figured at all in his career."

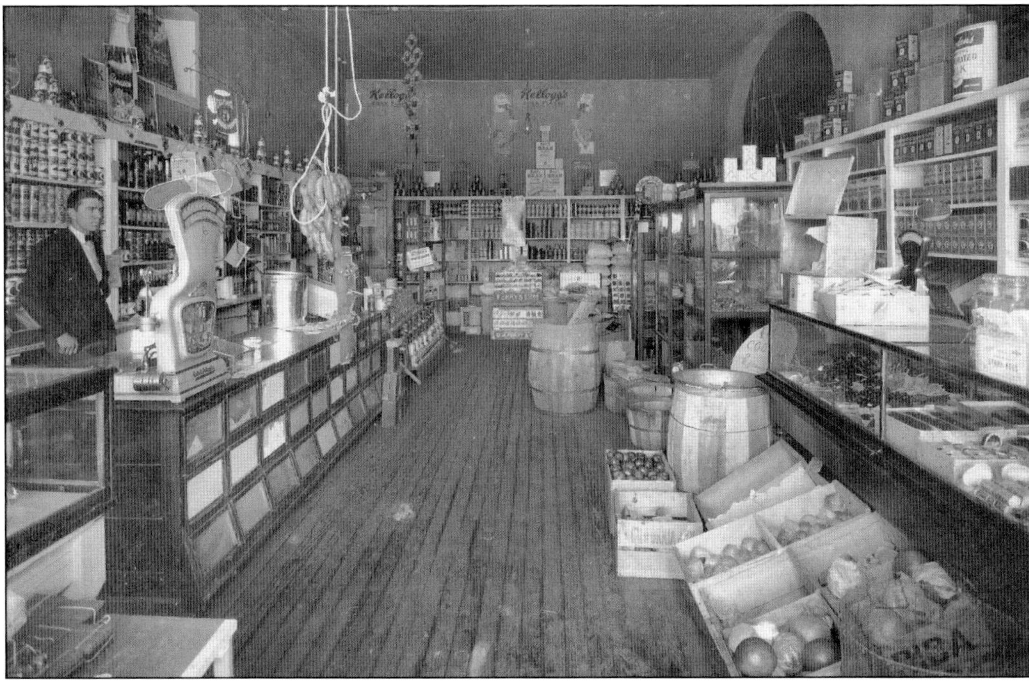

The first person to open a business on the site of the future Dodge City was George M. Hoover. Although a small sod home had been built at the edge of the Fort Dodge reservation (marked with a large stone that still exists), Hoover came to where the railroad was being built in order to sell whiskey. The Masterson brothers came from the Wichita, Kansas, area to provide both buffalo meat for the railroad workers and to work a team of animals grading the roadway for the railroad tracks; the Atchison, Topeka & Santa Fe Railroad had to have tracks reaching the Kansas-Colorado border under its agreement with the government. The railroad loading area, roundhouses, and cattle trails stayed in Dodge City for a decade until the cattle were killed off by the blizzard of January 1886. Millions of dollars of food, equipment, horses, clothes, guns, bullets, and liquor moved through Dodge City from 1872 to 1886, an amount that matches other boom towns built around mines. The Santa Fe Trail was a commercial roadway and Fort Dodge was charged with the protection of that business and later, the movement of money from Dodge City to Leavenworth, Kansas. (Town founder Robert Wright had an account at the German Bank of Leavenworth.) Since Dodge City did not have a bank for the first 10 years, the shipment of money required both soldiers and lawmen.

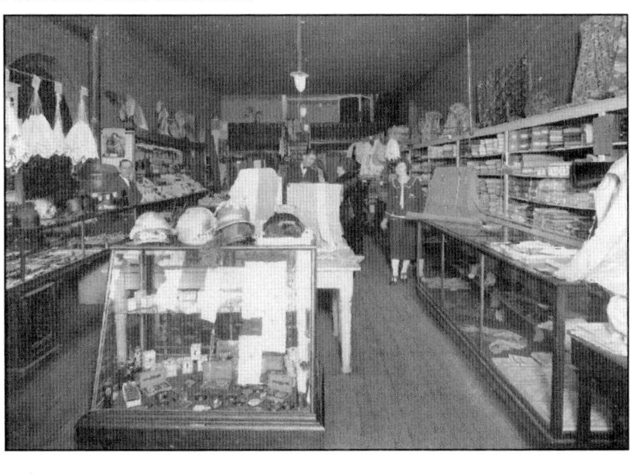

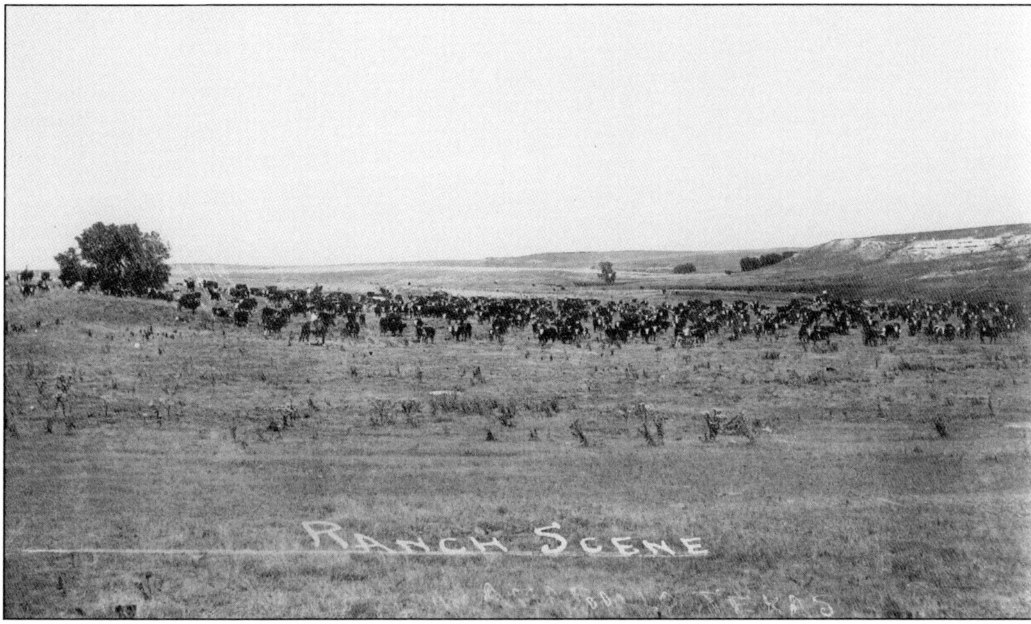

In *Dodge City* Robert Wright wrote, "The cattle drive to Dodge City first began in 1875–1876, when there were nearly two hundred and fifty thousand head driven to this point. In 1877, there were over three hundred thousand, and the number each year continued to increase until the drive reached nearly a half million. We held the trade for ten years, until 1886, when the 'dead-line' was moved to the [Colorado] state line. There were more cattle driven to Dodge, any and every year that Dodge held it, than to any other town in the state, and Dodge held it three times longer than any other town, and, for about ten years, Dodge was the greatest cattle market in the world."

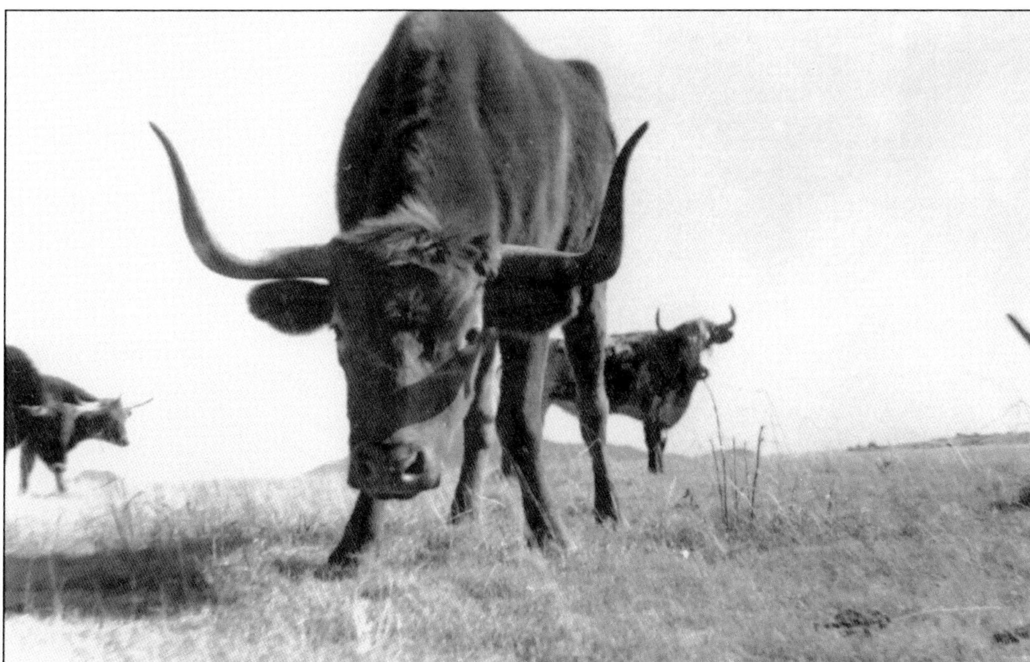

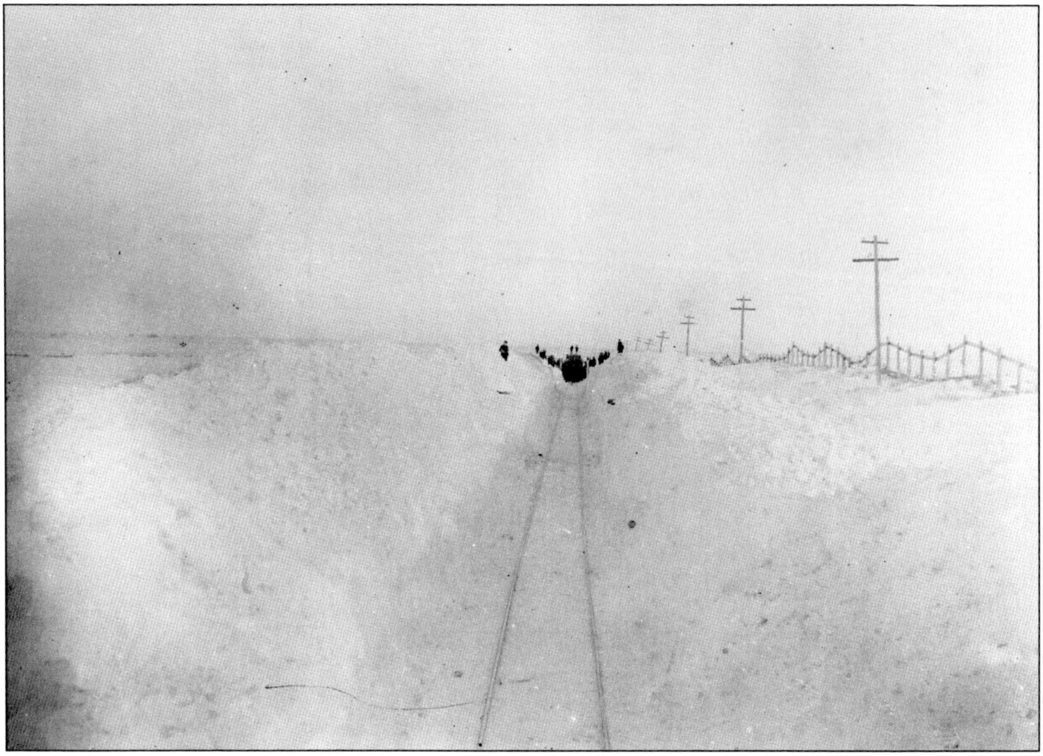

It snowed for days during the blizzard of early January 1886, which had 80-mile-per-hour winds. The train pictured here was snowed in for five days east of Dodge City. The weatherman wrote that during the storm he could not find the weather station. Barbed wire crossed the plains, and the cattle, trying to go south, reached the barrier and subsequently froze. After the snow cleared, 10 miles of cattle were found dead on the ground. The cattle industry ended that month for Dodge City, and the quarantine line, which kept wild Texas cattle from giving a tick illness to domestic cattle, was moved to the Colorado border.

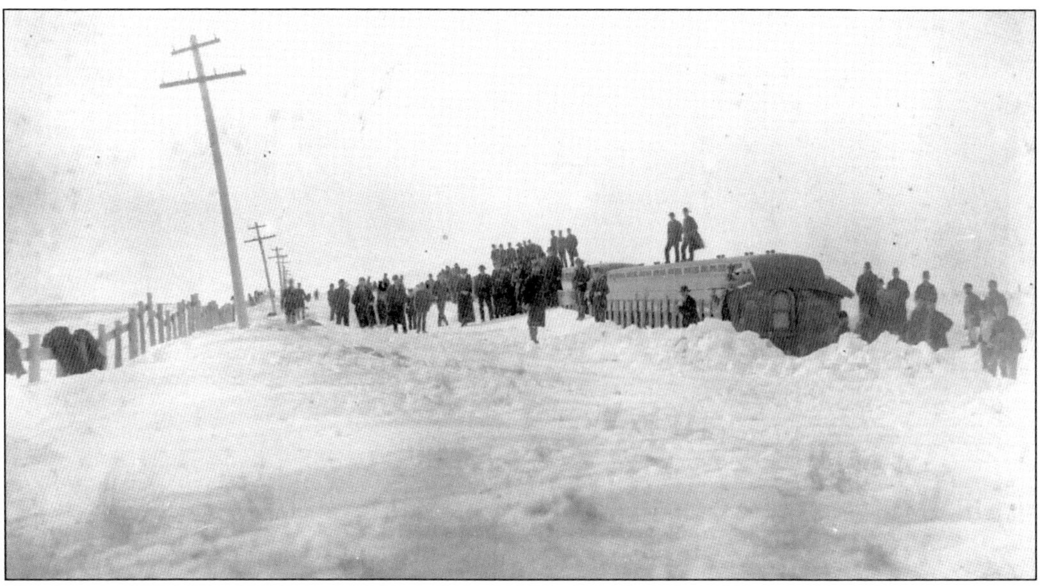

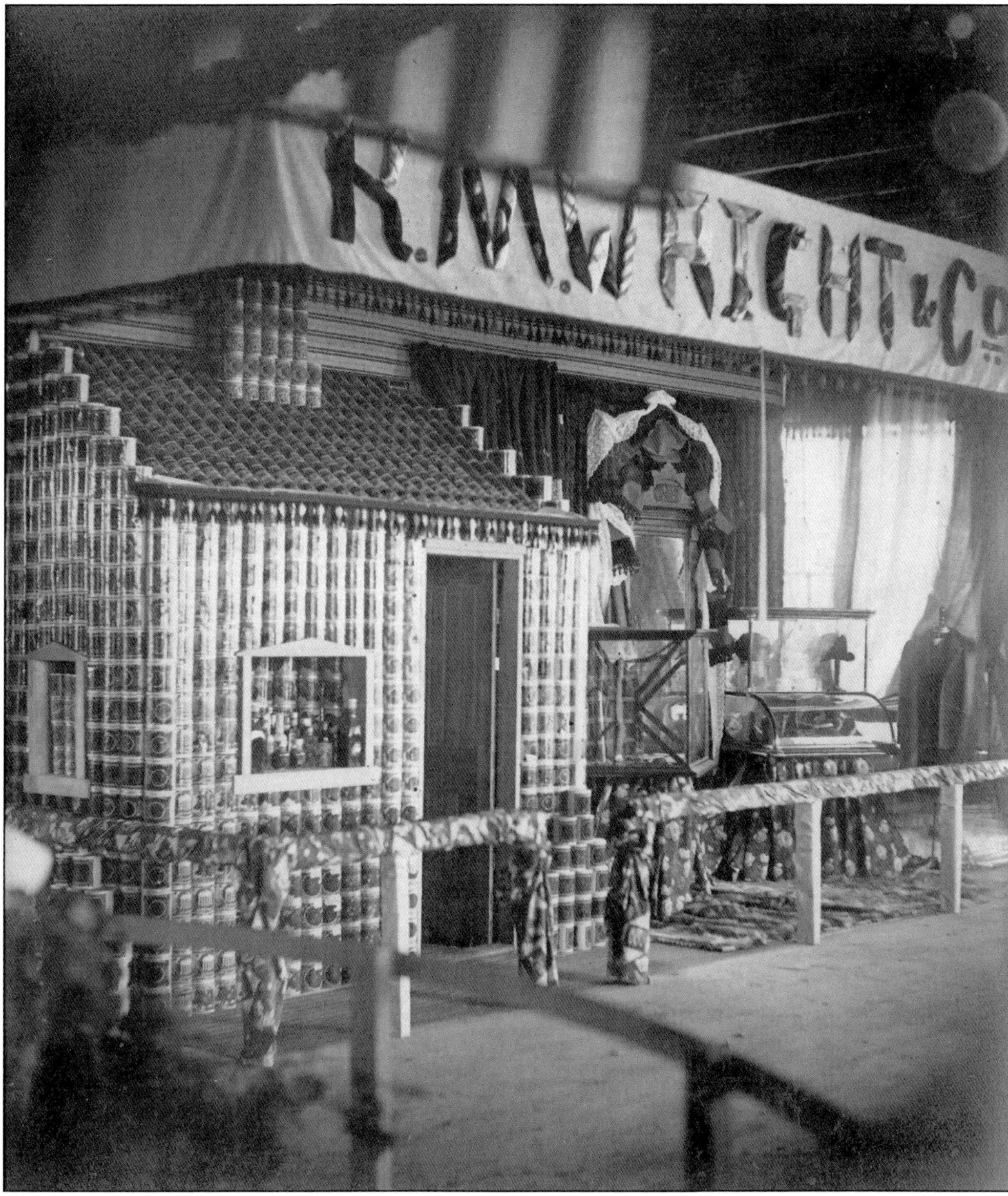

Robert M. Wright's display at the Kansas State Fair is pictured here around 1886. His display, a store built from tin cans, proudly showed the varieties of crops grown in Southwest Kansas, the quality of the goods sold in Dodge City (hats included), and promoted Wright's name. Wright always promoted Dodge City and even as president of the Kansas State Historical Society, his speeches and articles focused on frontier and pioneer living. Wright was the first person to own and sell the land of Fort Dodge when it was closed; Wright's addition includes the east portion of the downtown area of Dodge City, where Military Avenue ends in front of the Santa Fe depot. In Wright's final days, he owned almost no land or cattle and had to sell all of it in 1906 after treatment for drug addiction. During a stint at the Keeley Institute for the treatment of alcohol, drug, and tobacco addiction in Kansas City, Missouri, he wrote, "I was out of my head part of the time and full of morphine part of the time."

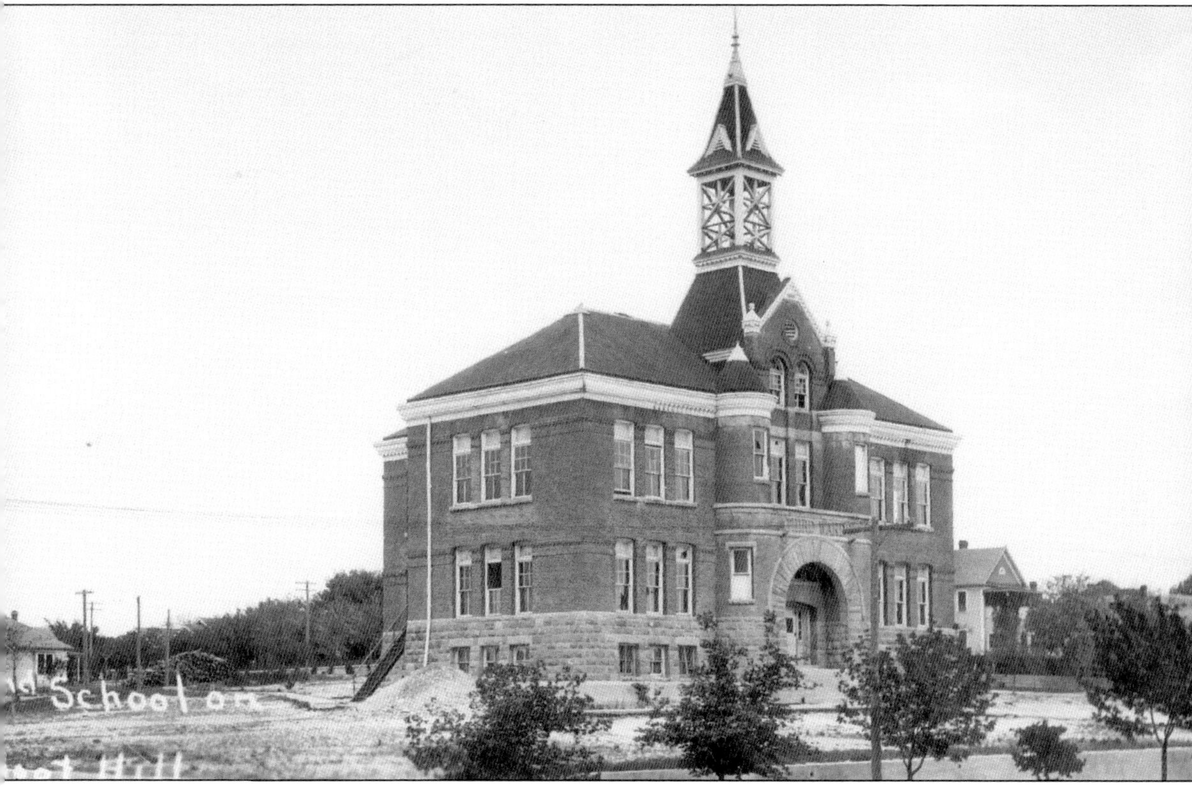

On Boot Hill, an 1879 school building was torn down, and the Third Ward School was constructed in 1890, pictured here nearly complete. The first building's bricks were soft. Bodies buried on Boot Hill were found during construction of both buildings. The 1890 school served as classrooms until 1927, when it was torn down for a new city hall. The city had to vote twice whether to buy back the land from the school district. This was in a decade that the town chose to reject the old West history. Finally, a new city hall opened in 1929, along with a cowboy statue.

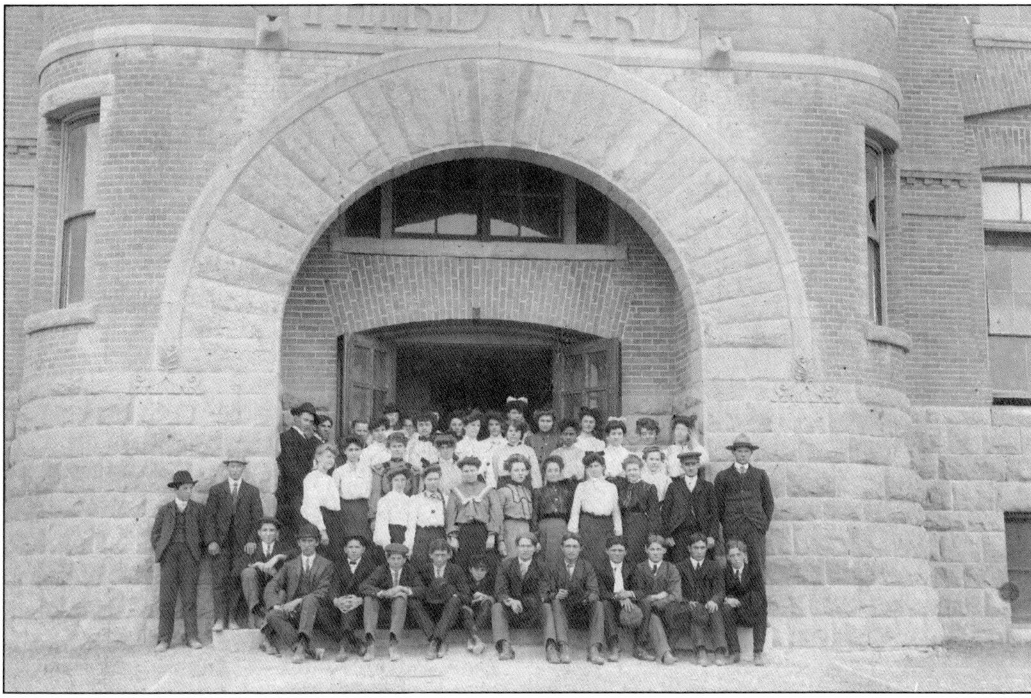

Students gather in front of the Third Ward School building around 1890. The students in both photographs are wearing their very best clothes.

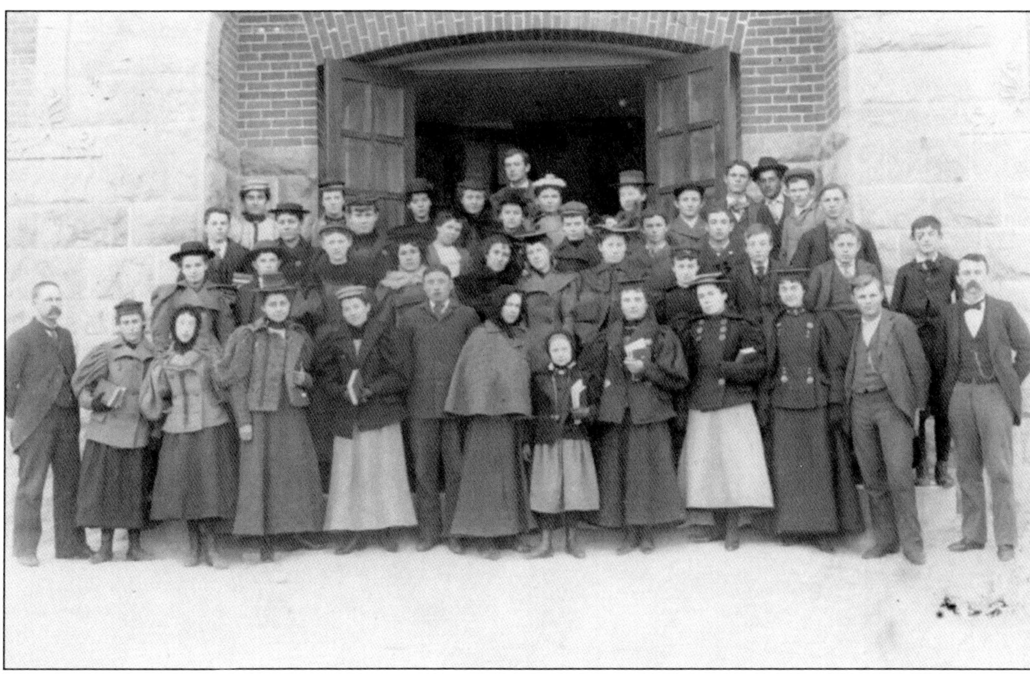

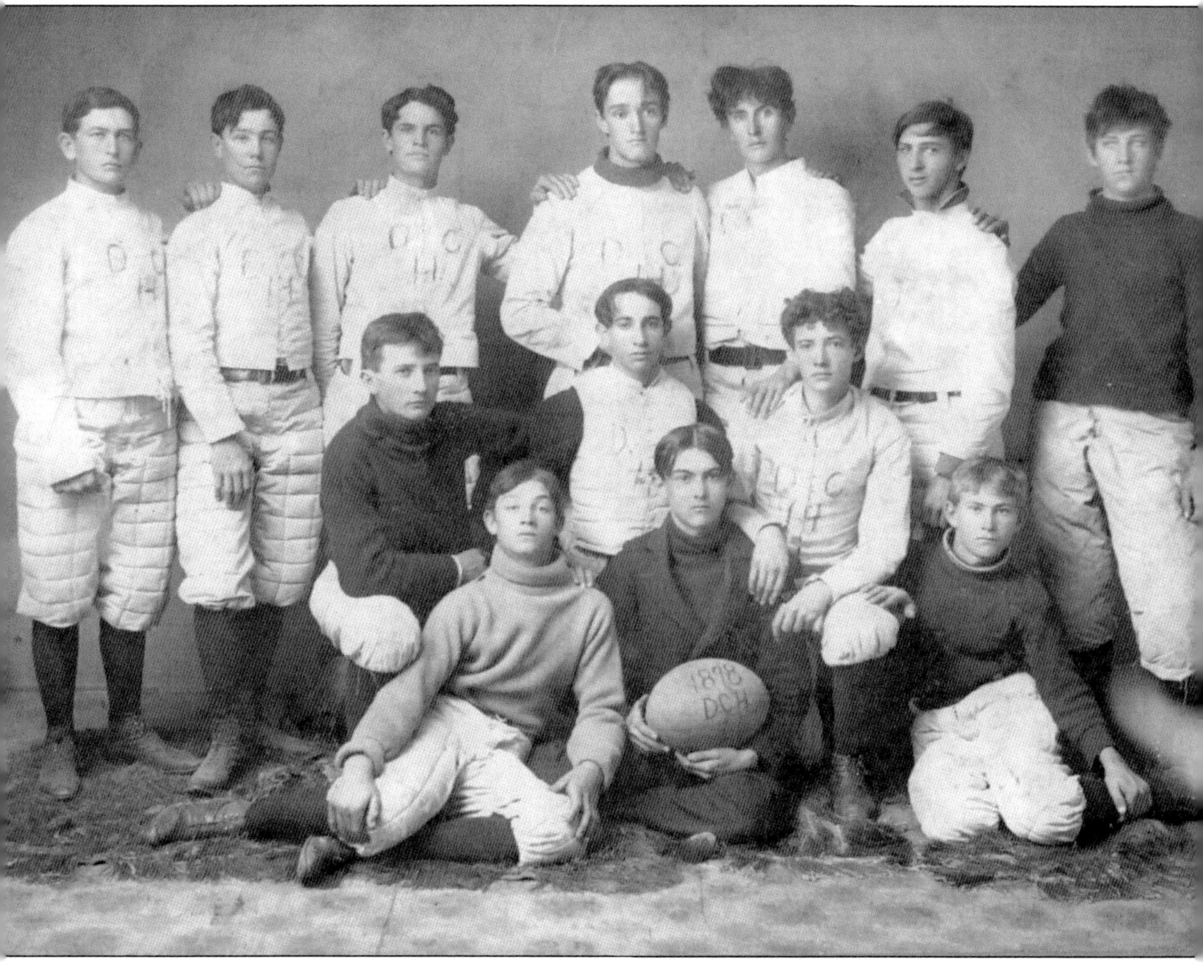

The first Dodge City High School football team (1898–1899) is pictured here. The football team members are, from left to right, (first row) Edward Stubbs, Charles Milton (team manager), and Oliver Stubbs; (second row) W.B. Bill Miller, Richard W. Evans, and Fred Straeter; (third row) Art Riney, Roy Kirkpatrick, Charles Imel, Carl Van Riper, Waldo Tarbox, Charles Kampf, and R.G. Baird. Evans and Van Riper become lawyers and judges in Dodge City. The coach was Presbyterian minister Dr. William Westwood.

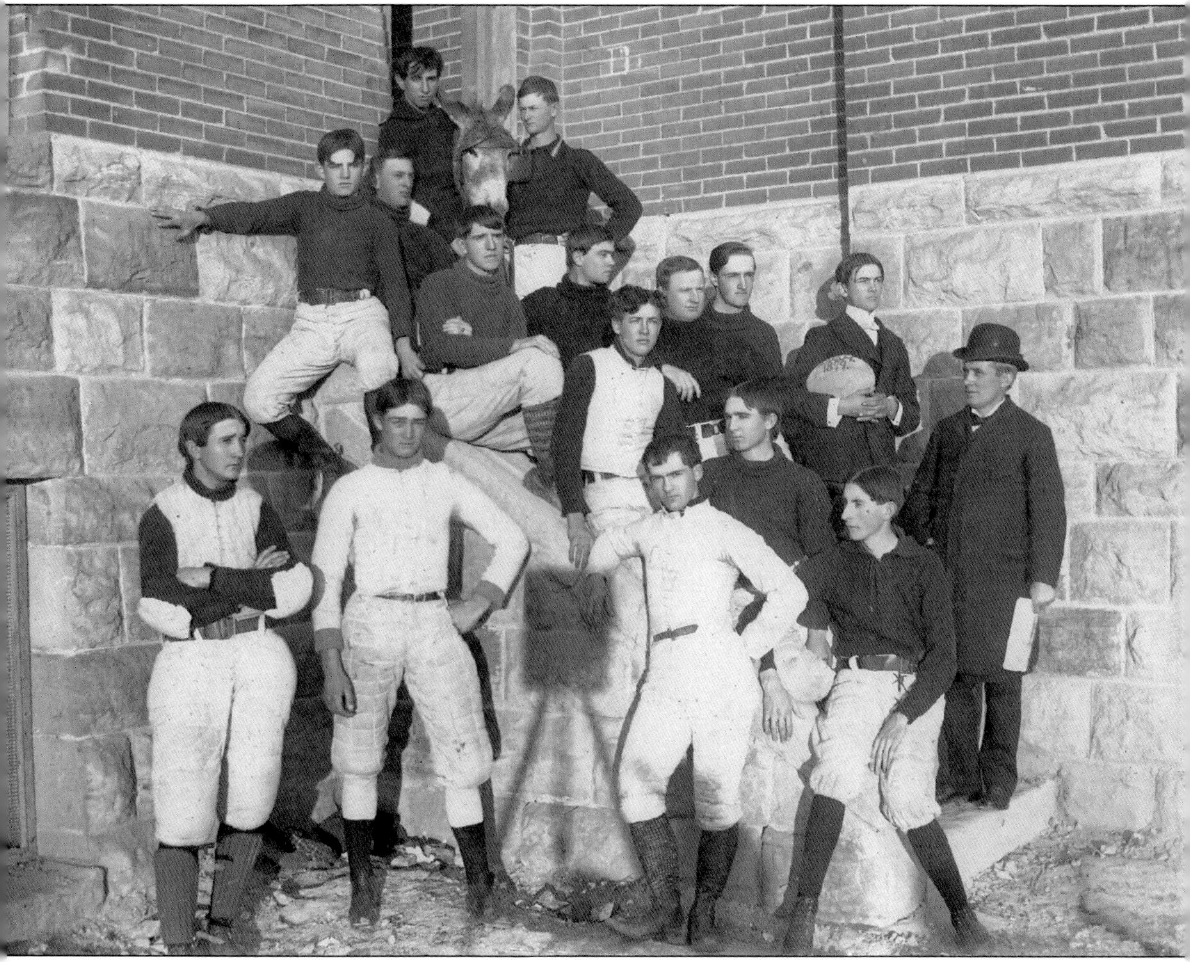

Pictured in an 1899 photograph is a larger football team, although not identified; one student is holding an almost rugby-shaped football. Note the donkey at the top of the stairs. According to a 1950 Dodge City High School athletic history booklet edited by Doral Grose, a mid-century coach, there were no football teams from 1899 to 1902. By 1903, teams were started again and football remains the major high school sport in southwest Kansas. The October 8, 1903, issue of the *Dodge City Daily Globe* stated, "The football team under Professor Smith as coach is performing feats which absolutely alarm the bystanders. Mr. Mill's smelling apparatus has been perceptibly enlarged of late, and something less than 17 bbls. of arnica, 8 gals. of witch hazel and numerous other applications have been purchased by him in the last week."

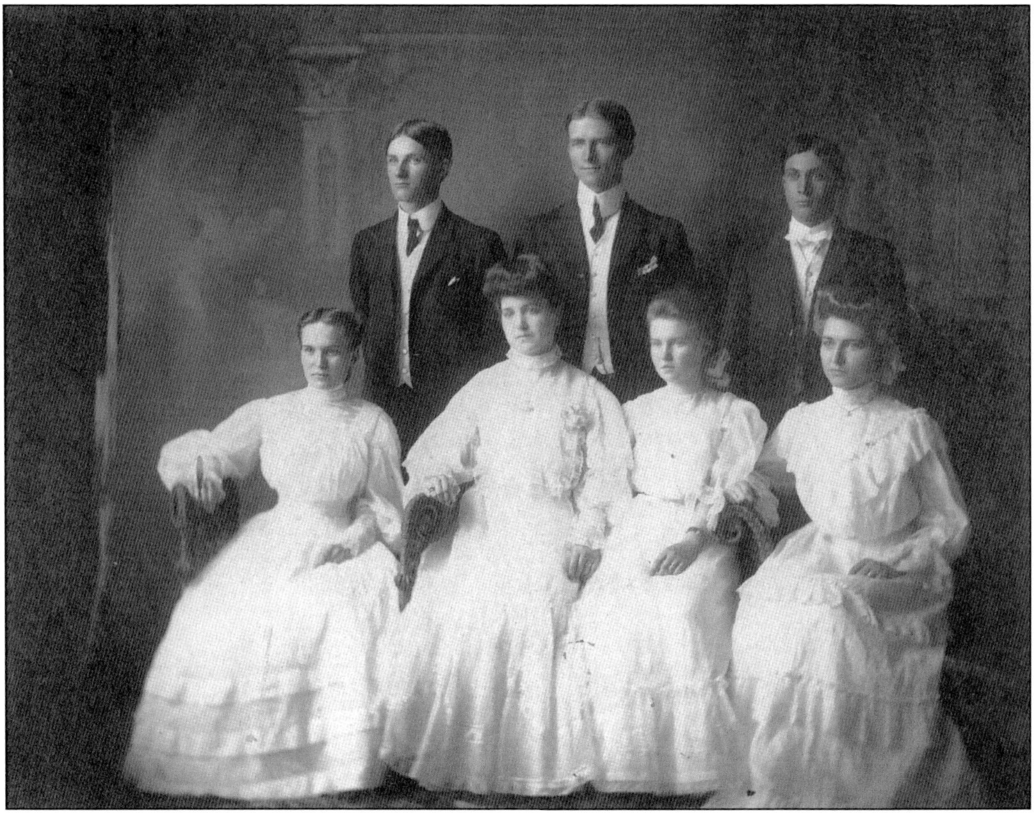

The 1905 Dodge City High School (DCHS) class is pictured above and the 1911 DCHS graduating class is visible below.

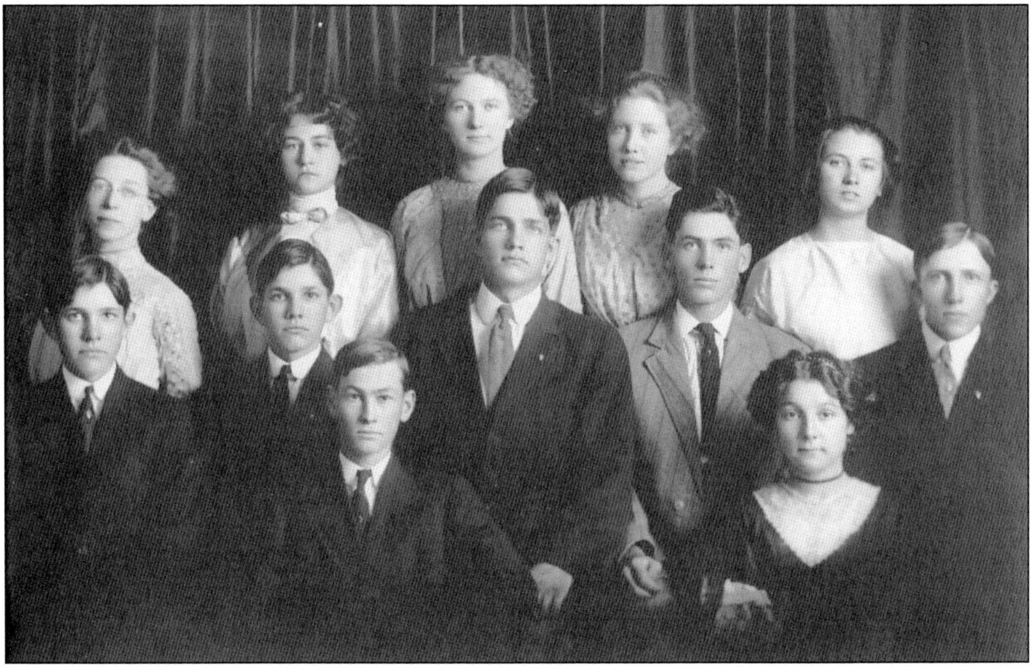

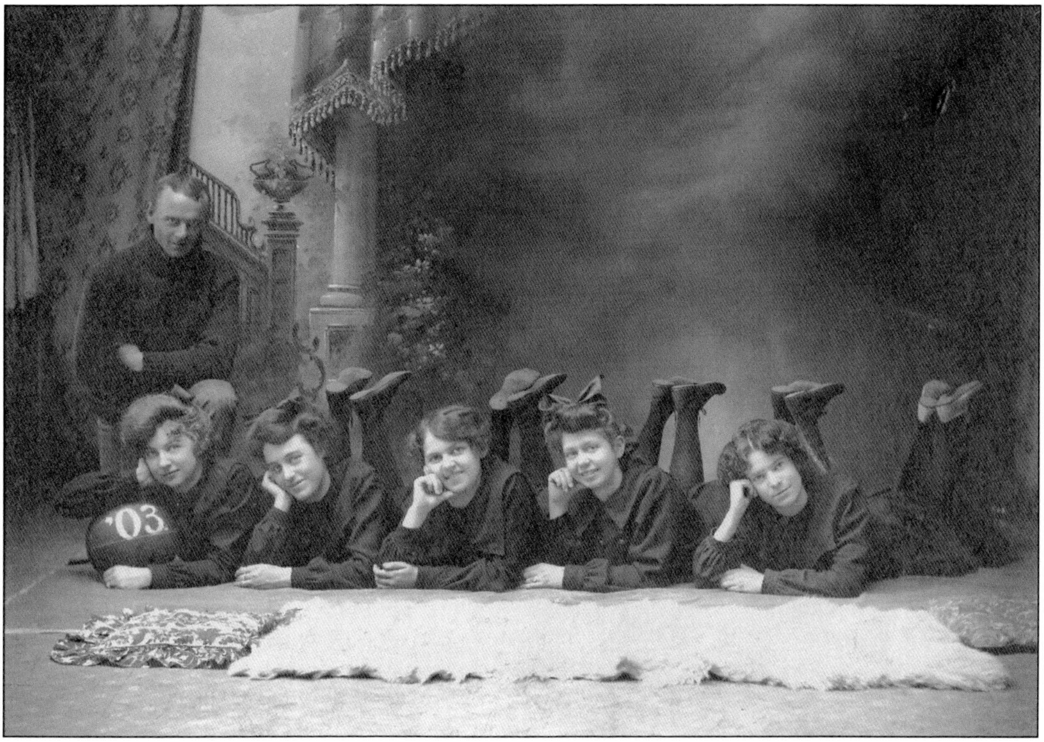

The first Dodge City High School basketball team is pictured above in 1903. The members are daughters of lawmen and early merchants; they introduced the boys to the game in 1905. The girls' basketball team appears below, in 1907.

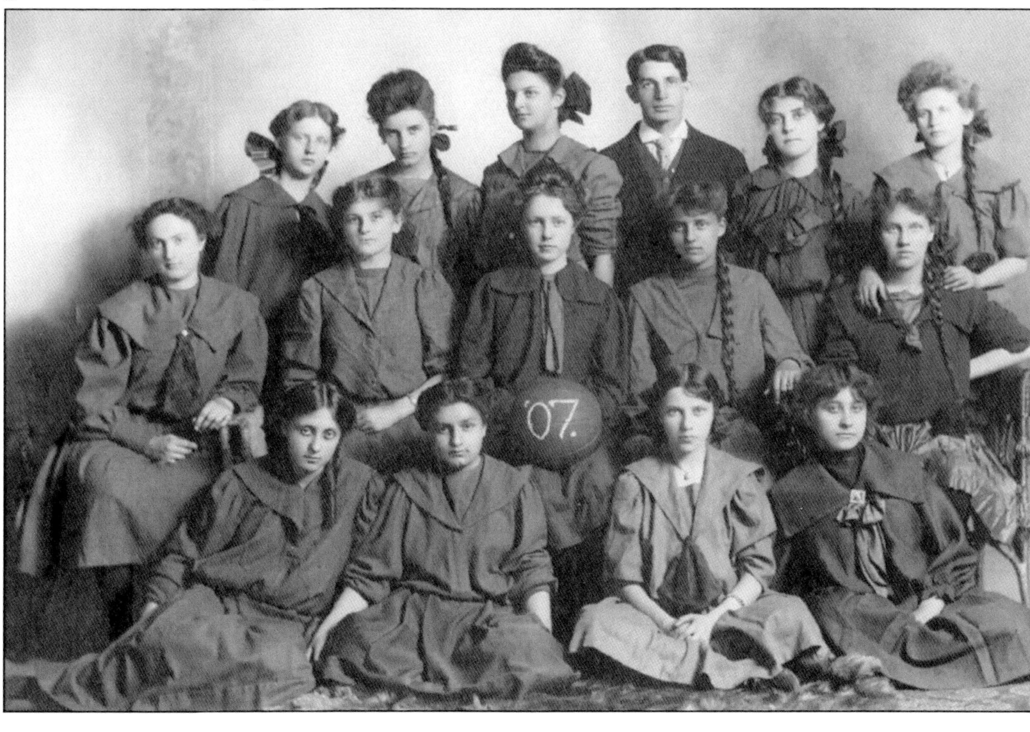

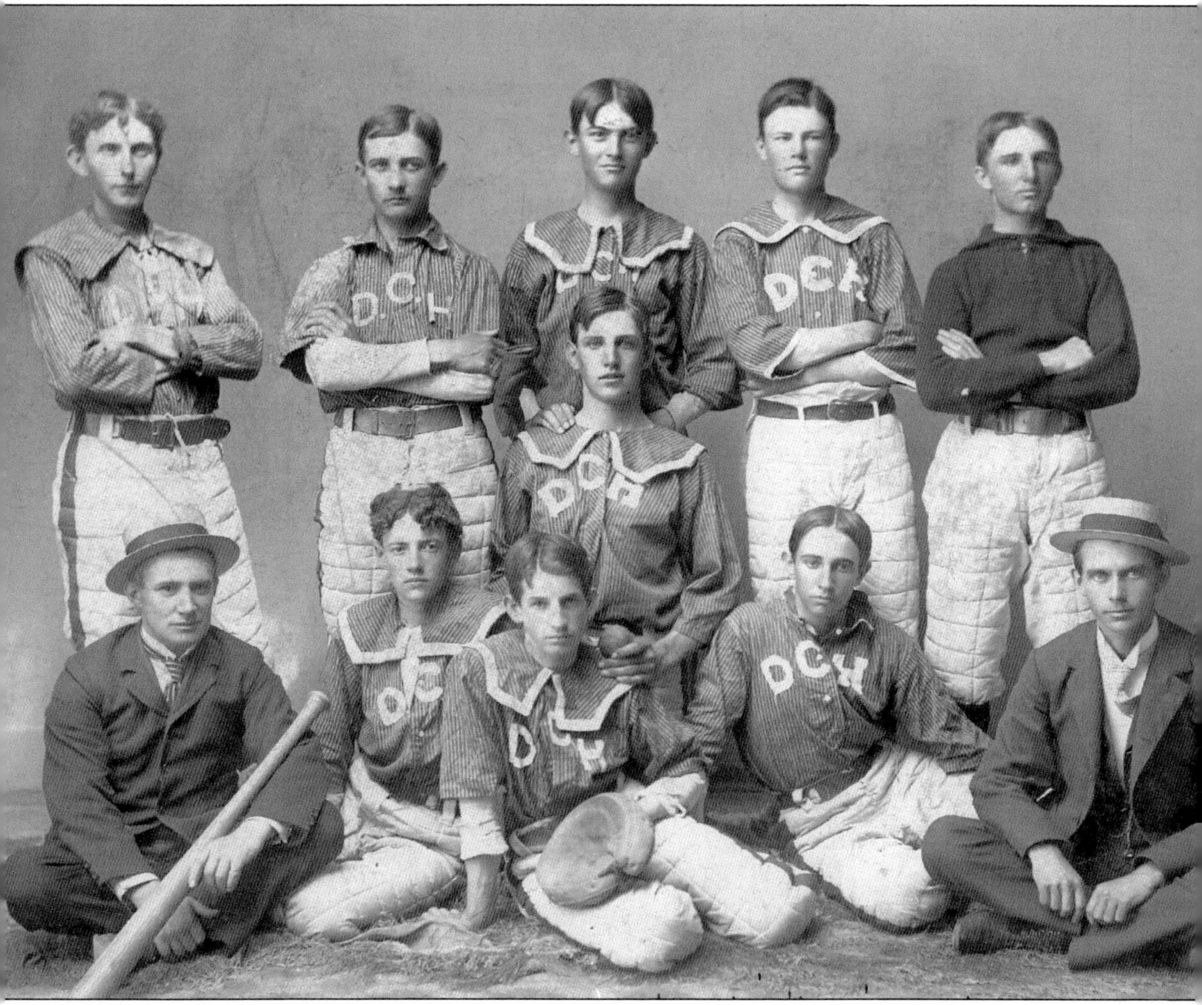

The First Dodge City High School baseball team appears here in 1898. Louie Schmidt is in the back row, second from the right. Baseball became popular during the Civil War, and buffalo hunter H.H. Raymond writes of playing it with Bat Masterson. All of these players were born after 1880, the first generation of pioneer children in Dodge City. Dodge City High School beat Jetmore 10-7 on July 4, 1899.

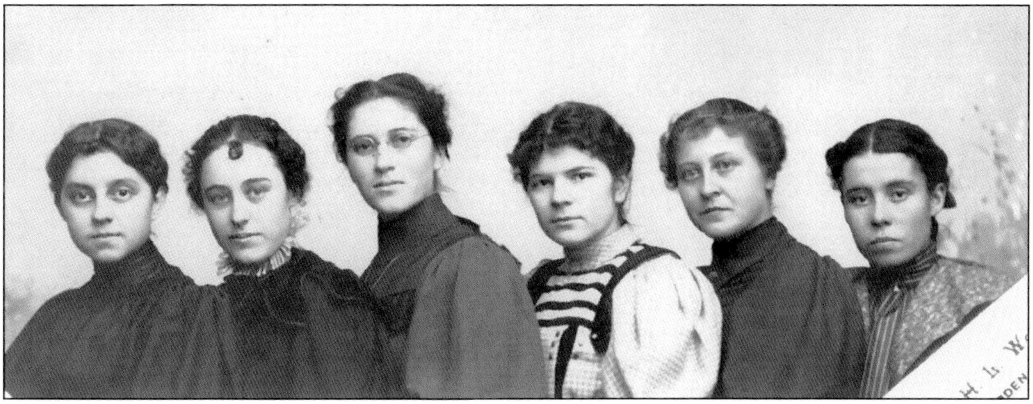

Above, a Dodge City High School girls' church group visits Garden City around 1904. Bertha "Bertie" Rath, buffalo hunter Charles Rath's daughter, is second from left. Below are friends and relatives. Karl Miller, an early judge, is on the far right and Richard "Dick" Evans Jr., also a judge, is on the bottom left. Evans set up the post office at Fort Hays City, Kansas, and was the first merchant there before moving to Dodge City.

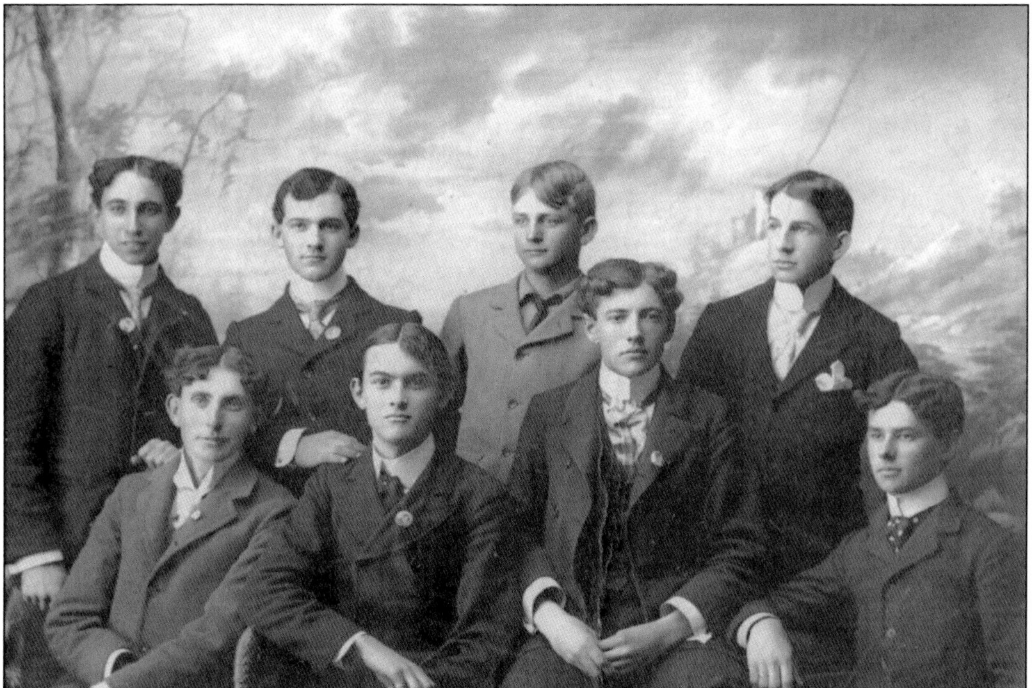

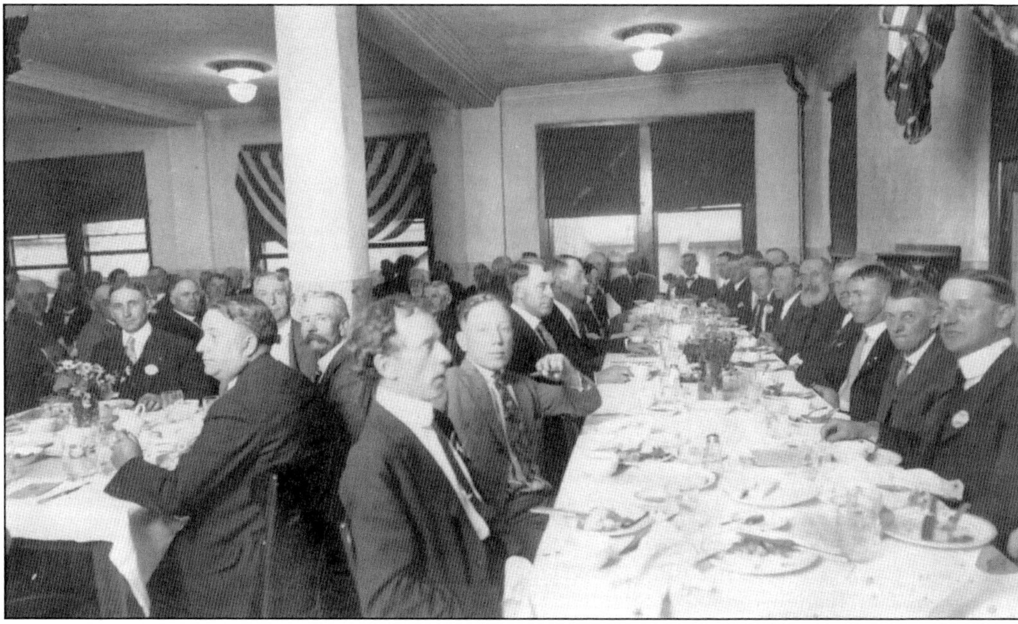

Above, a major business lunch is held at the O'Neal Hotel in 1916. Jess Denious, publisher and editor of the *Dodge City Daily Globe*, is seated far right, with a badge on his lapel. Below, Ida M. (Chalk) Beeson's birthday party takes place around 1926.

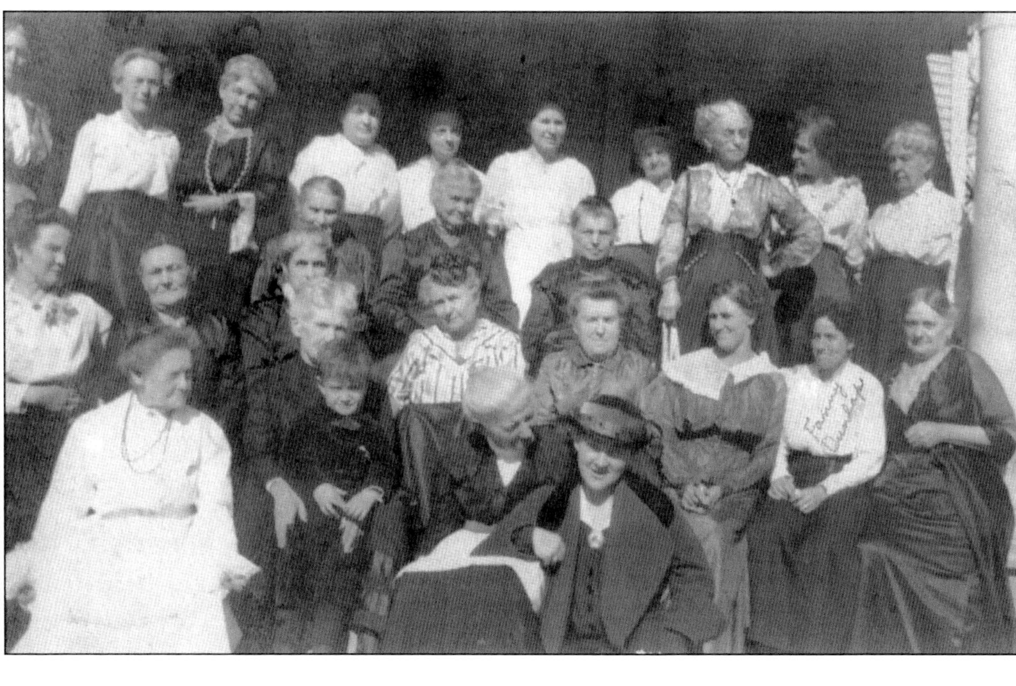

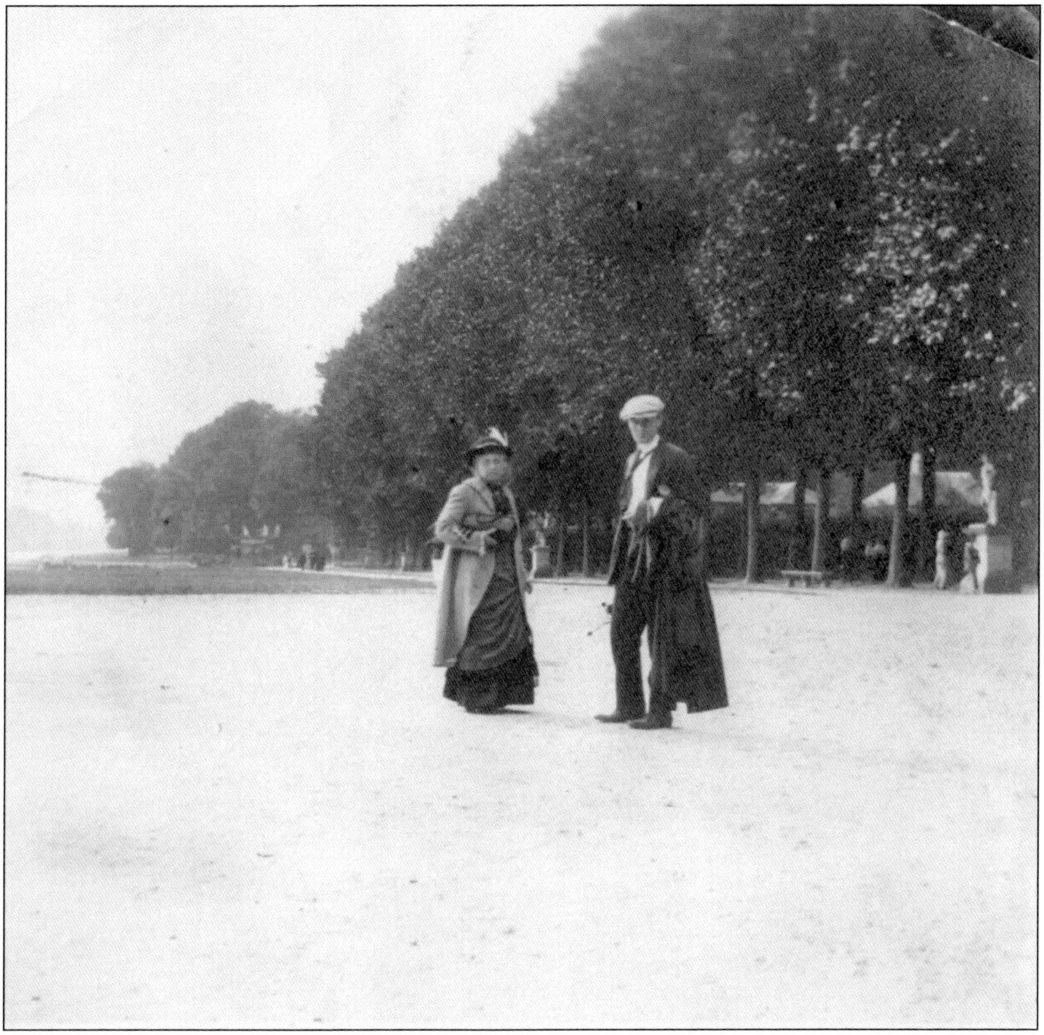

Carrie Markley Rath Bainbridge is pictured with her son Roy Bainbridge in Versailles, France, probably before World War I. Carrie died on November 27, 1923, at age 63. Roy died on February 5, 1969. Children of the town's pioneers, such as Roy, survived in Dodge City through the 1970s.

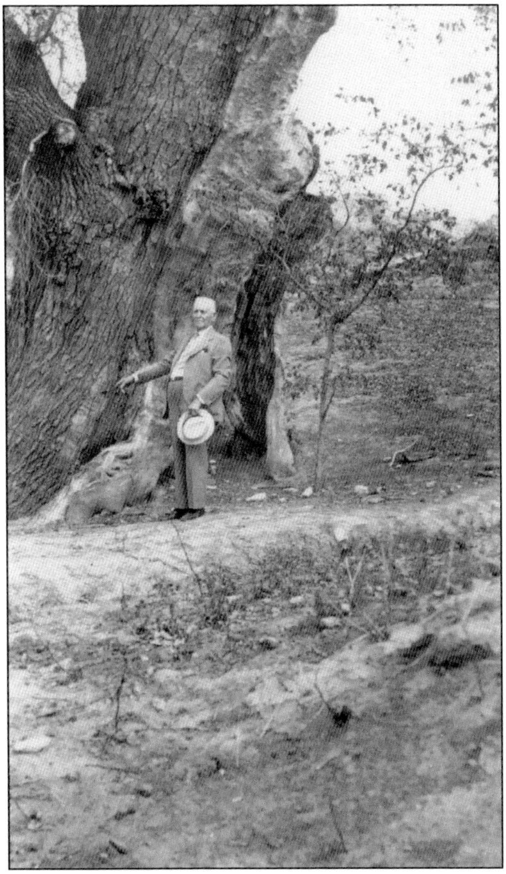

On the left, Ham Bell stands by graves where men were buried in 1884. The following is written on the back of a photograph postcard in Bell's hand: "The largest cottonwood tree in Kansas on the Harry Reekie farm. From the projecting limb on the left two horse thieves were lynched in 1884. In the foreground, H.B. (Ham) Bell, last surviving famous frontier US Marshall & Sheriff at early day Dodge, points to the graves." Below, Bell stands by his Boot Hill memorial, topped with the first bell of the Union Church.

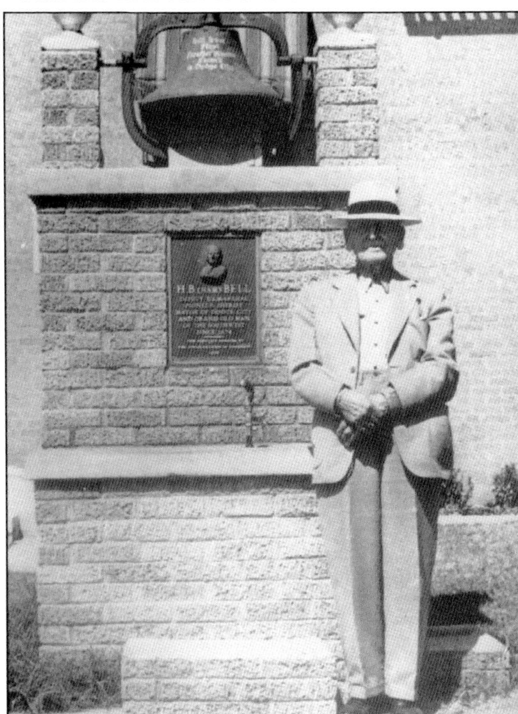

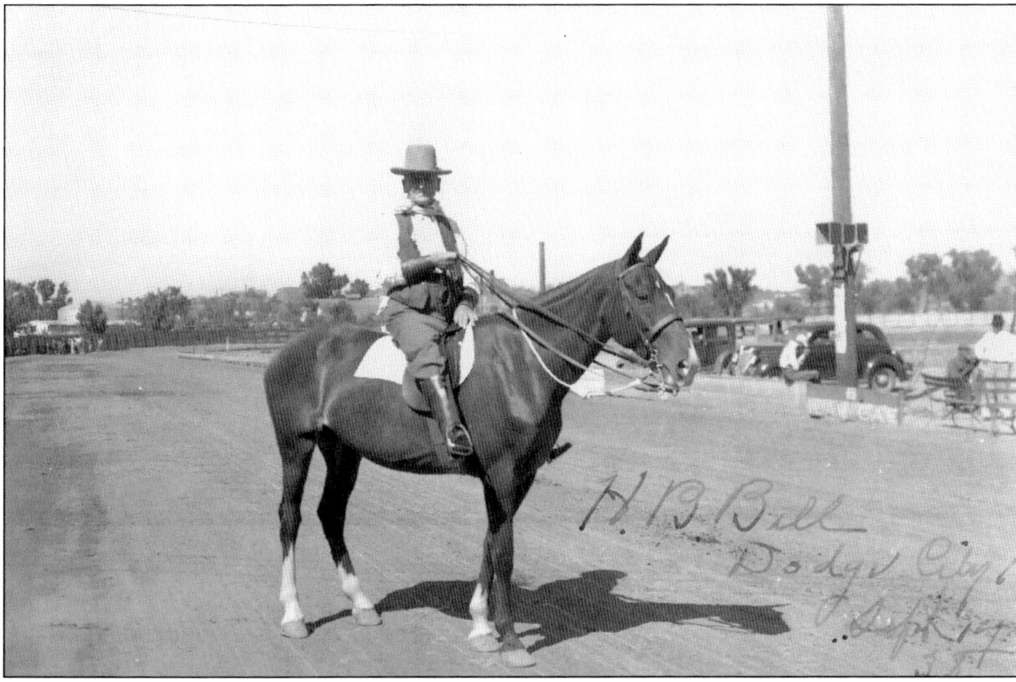

Ham Bell is on horseback at an Old Pioneer Days event at the racetrack in Dodge City's Wright Park in September 1938. Ham outlived most of his generation. His formal portraits were always facing the camera so that his, as Ida Ellen Rath called it, "Roman nose" was not visible. Ida Ellen also hints in her handwritten notes that Bell's name may have been Hannibal Boettler Beltz. Bell was orphaned young and came west when he was 17 years old.

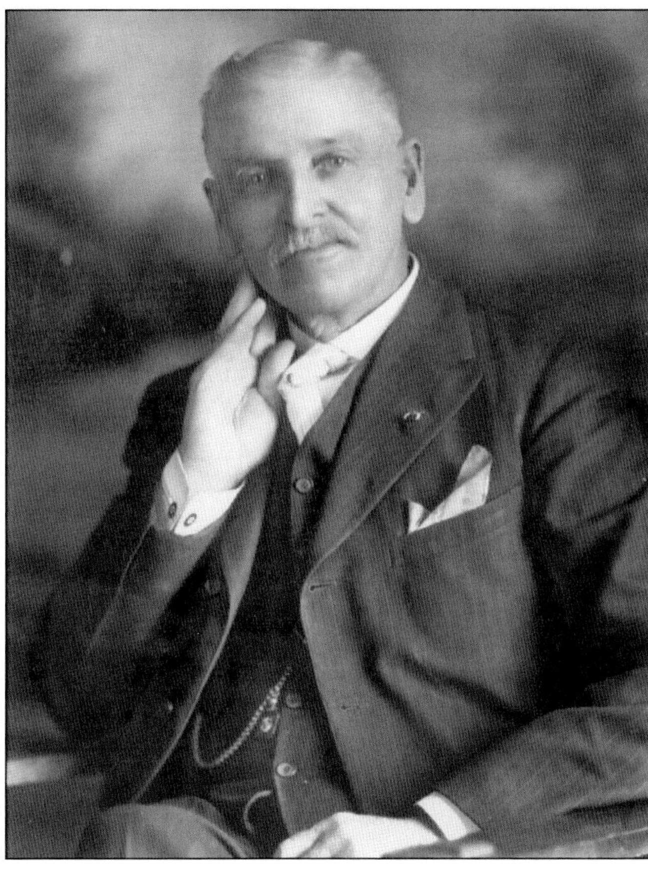

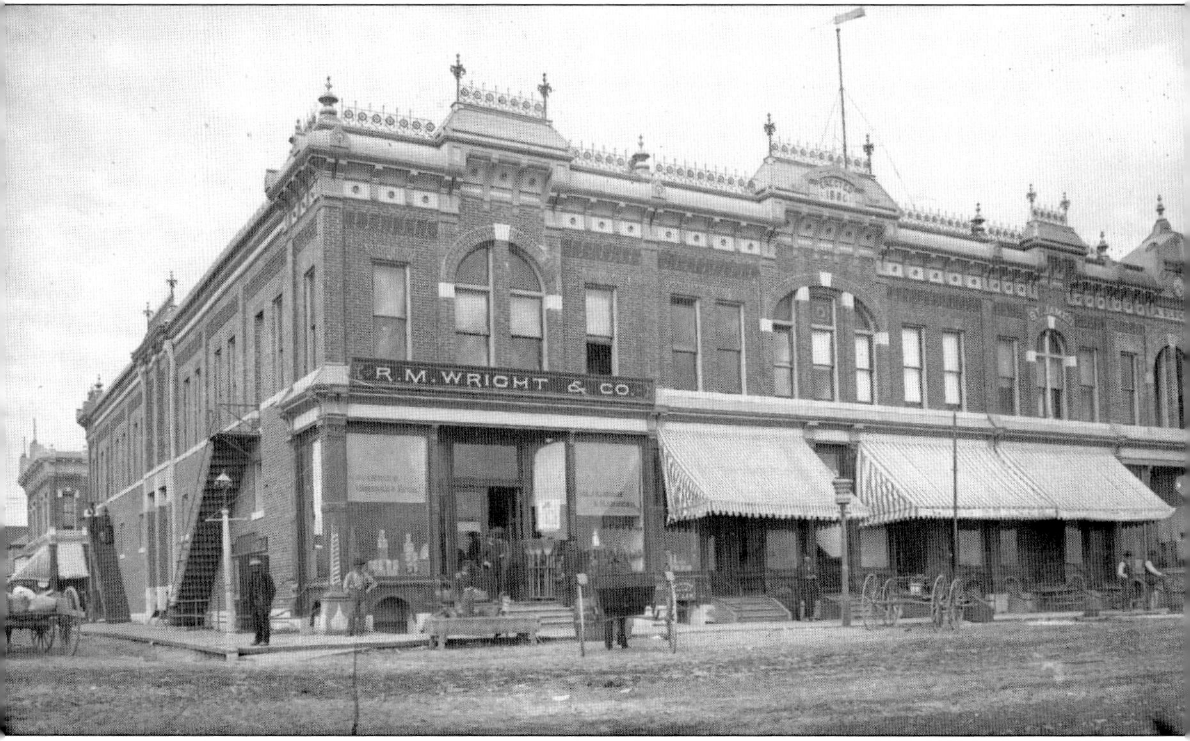

The final version of Robert Wright's store and the block built after the fire of 1885, dated 1886, is visible in this photograph. Standing at the bottom left corner of Wright's is Robert Rath's cousin Dick Silver, an early stage driver. Note the horse trough in front of Wright's, the lawyer's office next door, and former mayor A.B. Gluck's shop farther to the right. This is the location of the first block north of the railroad tracks in 1872. The Long Branch saloon is the third building from the left. Wright's shop stands in its original location, but buildings beside it were replaced over the years, including the Long Branch saloon.

Three

Merchants and Commerce in Dodge City

The growth of downtown Dodge City continued from the 1890s, when the economy and the city almost disappeared, to the post–World War I boom. The Dust Bowl stopped that growth, but World War II initiated a new expansion, including a US Army airbase west of Dodge City.

Judge Gene Penland, raised in Dodge City, listed all the downtown businesses and entities that he remembered from his youth, including Anderson's Cleaners; a Christian church; a Methodist church; Johnny Malo's small café; the *Dodge City Daily Globe* building; KGNO radio; the Moose Club; the Carnegie Library; Pop Jenks's popcorn and candy stand; First National Bank; the bus depot; the White Buffalo Café; the Pollock & Beck Shoe Co.; Hoffman Jewelry Co.; Eckles Department Store; Kuhn Drug Store; Mosher & Cochran Drug Co., where Doctors Klein, Melencamp, Alderson, and others had their offices upstairs; A&A, Campbell, May, Keller, Hoffman, Lubbers, and Reynolds drugstores; the jewelry shops, including Morgan-Penland, Arvin Heichen, Bangs, and Walkers and Clark's; the Taskers; Gwinner's Palace of Sweets; Fidelity State Bank; Warshaw's Clothing; Palace Drugs; Duckwall; Montgomery Ward; Woolworth; McLellan's; Virtue; and J.C. Penney. Other blocks included businesses such as the Dodge Theatre, the Loral-Locke Hotel, the O'Neal Hotel, and a dozen restaurants and bars.

Dodge City had a complete downtown until urban renewal in 1970. It even had a pizza place, called Paisans, which offered 12 types of pizza in two sizes and kosher sandwiches in the 1950s, long before Pizza Hut opened. With cowboys drinking European wine, bootleggers in the 1950s, and the Lamplighter Club, which featured jazz acts traveling across the county, such as jazz great Count Basie, there was always an edge to the entertainment.

Robert K. DeArment writes about Bat Masterson's last visit to Dodge City in July 1910, when he journeyed to Reno, Nevada, to cover the heavyweight title fight. After reporting the action on the Fourth of July, Bat started back to New York. He rode over the Santa Fe line from Colorado into Kansas. From the window of the coach, he looked out over fields that had reverberated to thousands upon thousands of buffalo and the boom of his Sharps Big Fifty before the steel of the railroad. He wrote about the experience after his return, published in the *New York Morning Telegraph* on July 31, 1910, "In coming down the Arkansas Valley from Pueblo to Dodge, I could not help wondering at the marvelous change that had come over the country in the last twenty years. As I looked from the window after reaching Kansas, I saw in all directions groves of trees, orchards and fields bearing abundant crops of corn, wheat and alfalfa . . . Dodge City is now a thriving little country village, surrounded by a thrifty farming community. There are many of the oldtimers still living there and it is doubtful if they would care to live elsewhere. They are well-to-do and happy. And may they live long and continue to prosper, is my sincere wish."

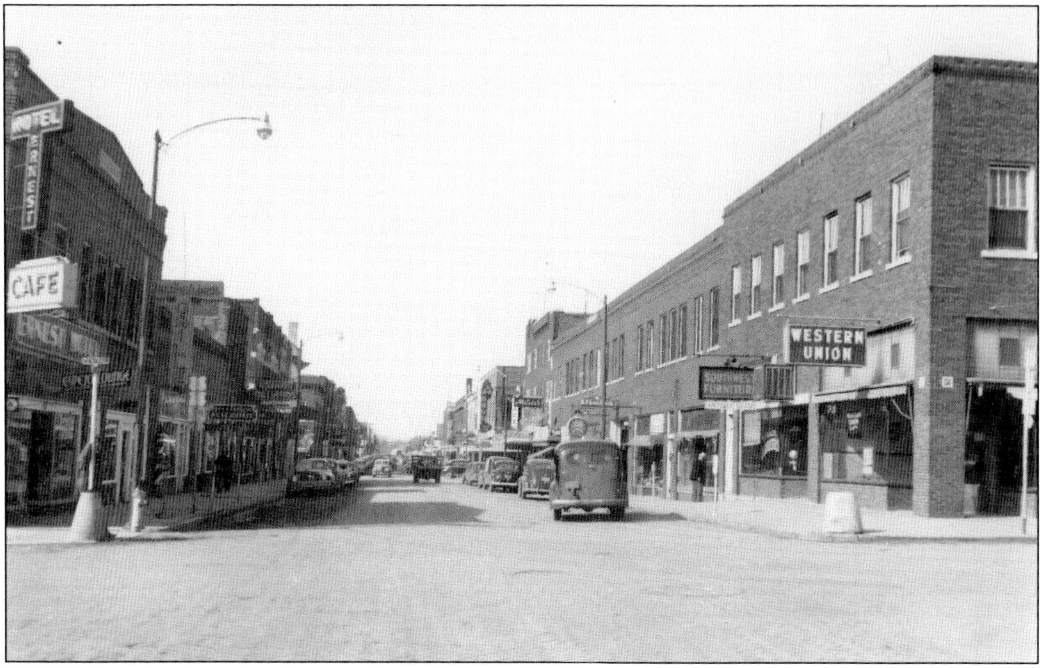

Busy modern Dodge City streets scenes are pictured in both of these c. 1945 photographs. Below, is the O'Neal Hotel, which was one of a number of downtown hotels that depended on the Atchison, Topeka & Santa Fe Railroad workers for tenants. There were also many passengers that stayed overnight for trains or buses.

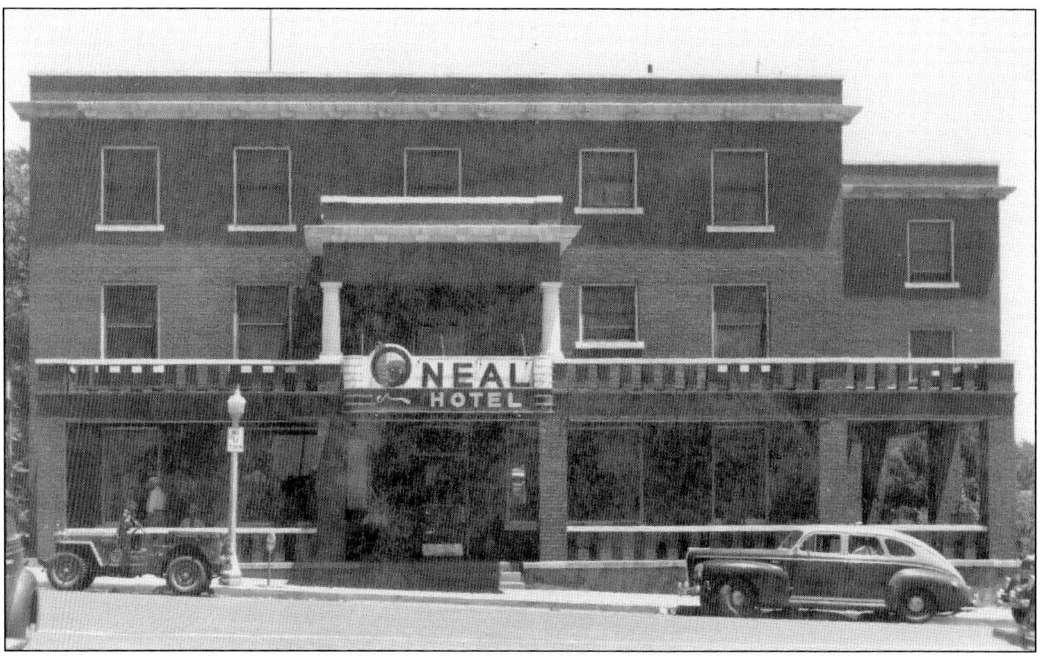

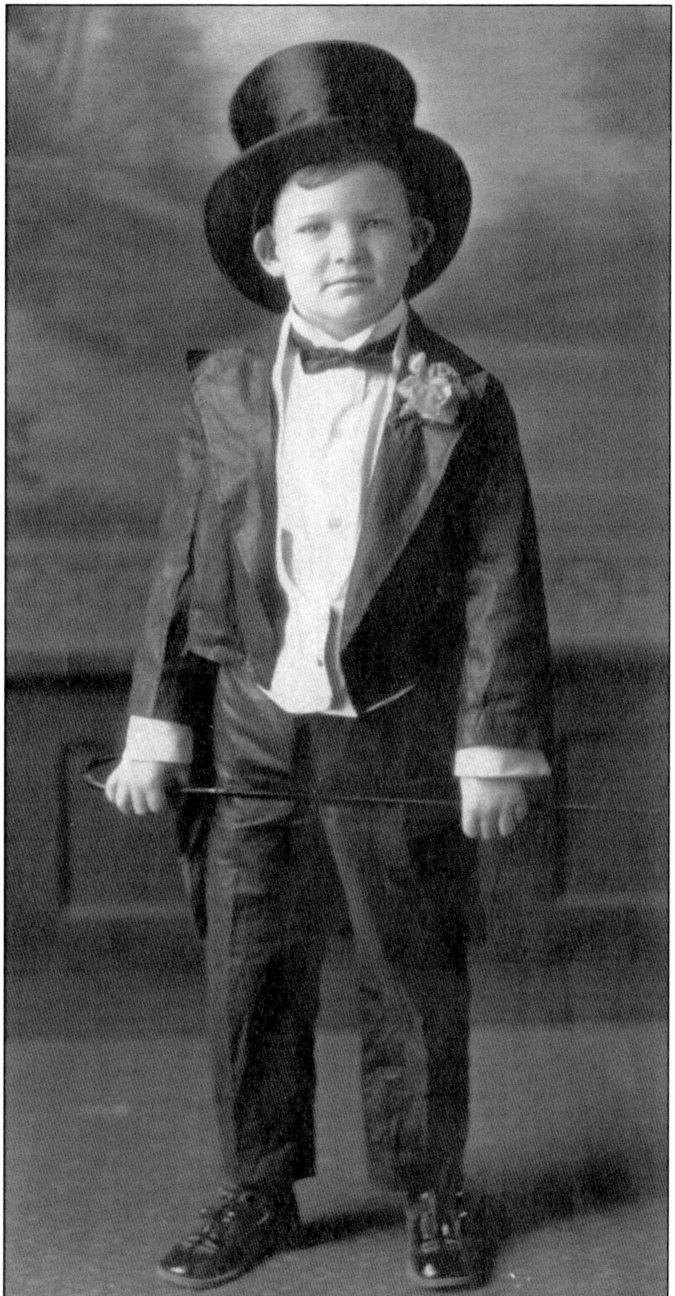

Entertainment always played a major role in Dodge City, whether live music for cowboys or live theater for the town, an event occurred every week or more often. The Beeson Theatre was built in honor of Long Branch saloon owner Chalk Beeson by his sons. Beeson was the father of the Cow Boy Band of 1880s fame. The Beeson Theatre was the venue on February 24–25, 1927, for the Business and Professional Women's Club presentation of *Springtime*, "A Sparkling Musical Comedy." Seven-year-old George R. Laughead Sr. played Master Jack in the production, which was a story that "deals with the blighted romance of a scion of 1868 aristocracy and the daughter of the maker of Brewster's Pills."

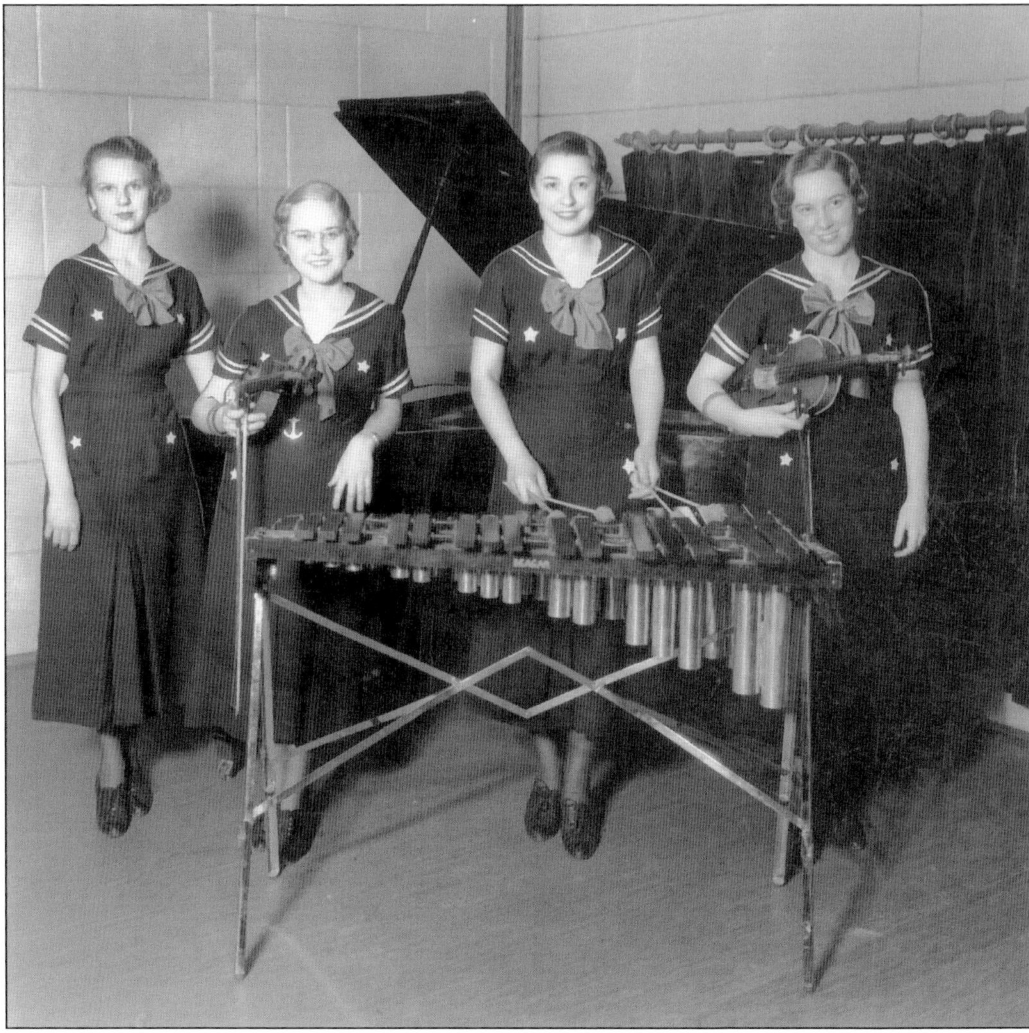

High school musicians in the band Rhythmic Four appear with a piano, violins, and a marimba around 1934. The third from the left is Anna Marie "Murry" Stark (Mrs. Jack Eckles), an entertainer who continued to play music on the marimba past her 90th birthday. The marimba shown here cost her family $500 at that time; they now cost around $10,000.

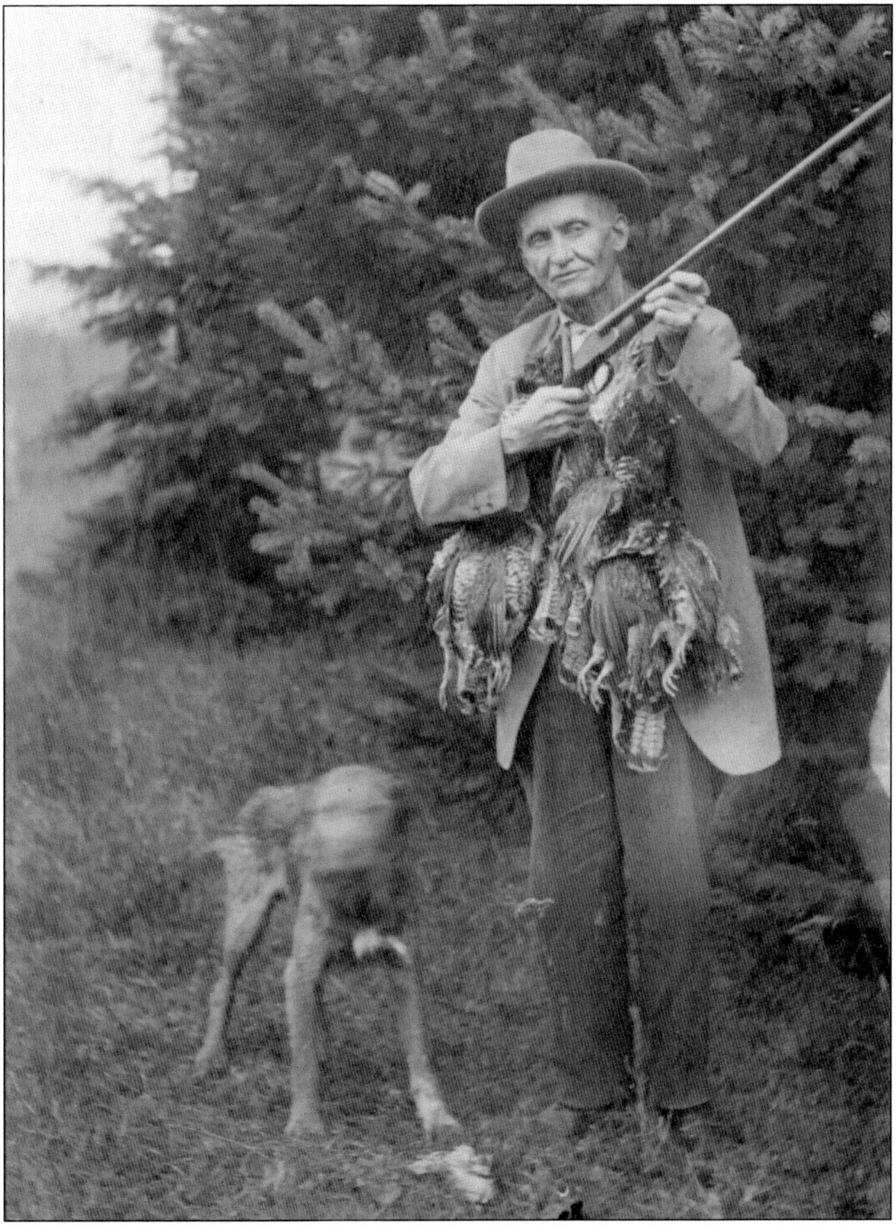

O.A. Bond, nicknamed "Brick" for his red hair, killed 6,000 buffalo from November 1, 1874, to January 1, 1875. He was allowed to leave Adobe Walls during a battle to get help, because the Native Americans respected him. Later, after Kansas Liquor Prohibition in the 1880s, Brick and A.B. Weber, mayor of Dodge City and later bank president, started the Palace Drug store in 1883 in order to sell medicinal liquor, which was legal. Brick owned a farm on Buckner Creek in Hodgeman County. The *Dodge City Daily Globe* reported the death of Brick on Monday, May 9, 1927: "The sudden death of the aged freighter, buffalo hunter, peace officer, cowman, and druggist this morning brought sorrow to a community in which he was universally loved for his positive but unobtrusive personality." Brick was born in New York on March 21, 1849. He moved to Dodge City in the spring of 1872, after coming to Kansas from Minnesota in 1871. He is shown with prairie chickens that he shot.

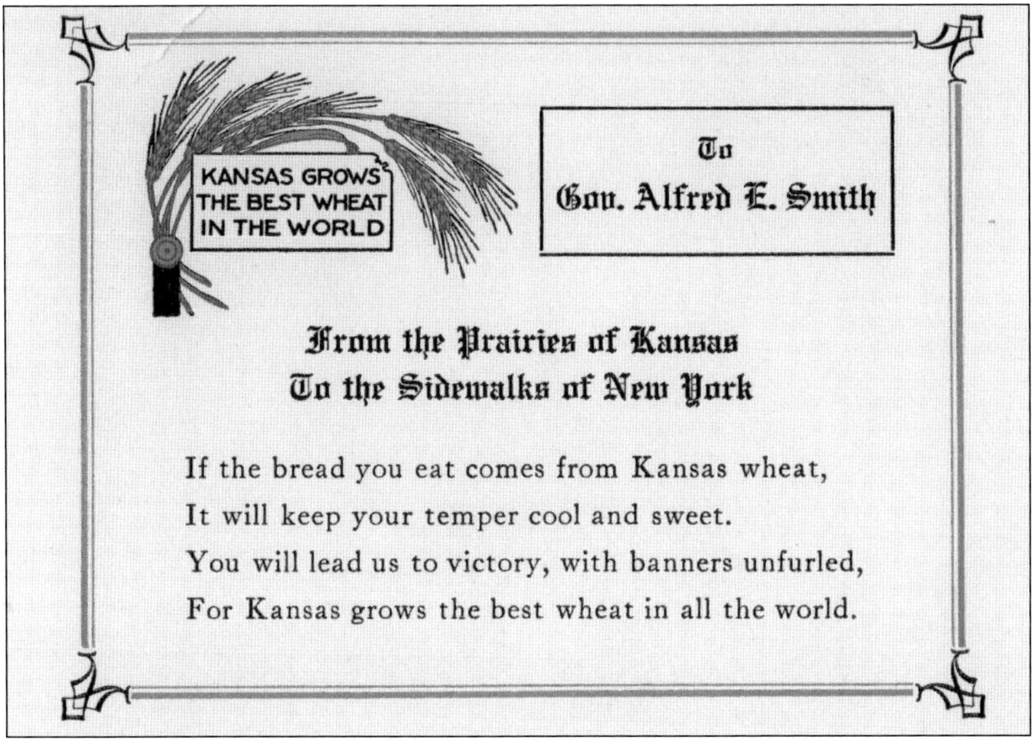
To
Gov. Alfred E. Smith

KANSAS GROWS
THE BEST WHEAT
IN THE WORLD

From the Prairies of Kansas
To the Sidewalks of New York

If the bread you eat comes from Kansas wheat,
It will keep your temper cool and sweet.
You will lead us to victory, with banners unfurled,
For Kansas grows the best wheat in all the world.

Heinie Schmidt was a progressive Democrat when elected to Ford County register and appointed Dodge City postmaster. During the 1928 presidential campaign, Schmidt printed this card as a greeting to give to Al Smith at the Democratic National Convention. Smith, governor of New York, ran against Herbert Hoover and lost. Promoting Kansas wheat and a presidential candidate at the same time, this card reflects the humor and wit of printed promotional items of the 1920s. Schmidt printed many items each year that he was in politics—a kind of early social network. Below, Republican governor Alf Landon of Kansas ran against Franklin D. Roosevelt. Landon lost; his daughter was later elected senator.

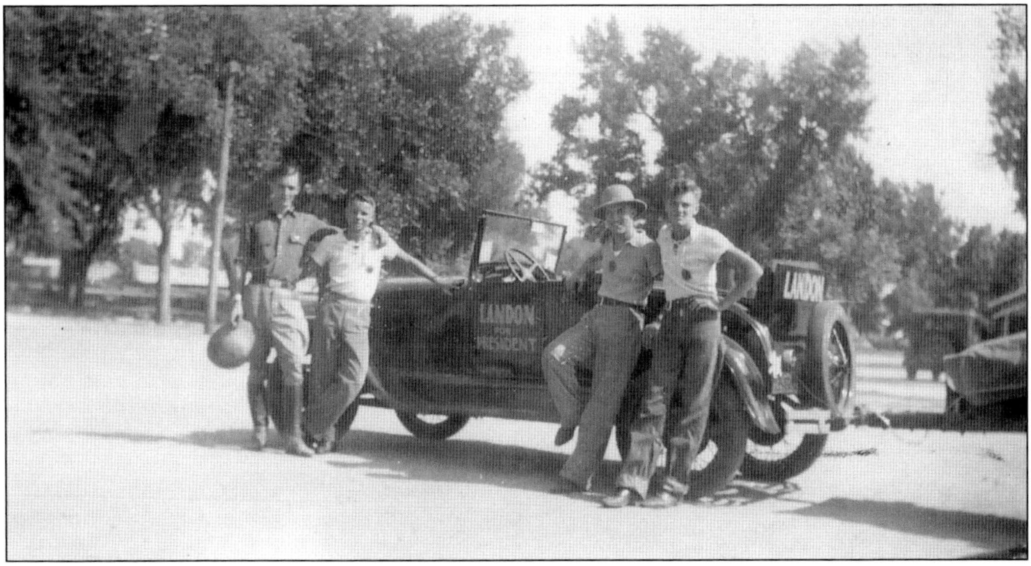

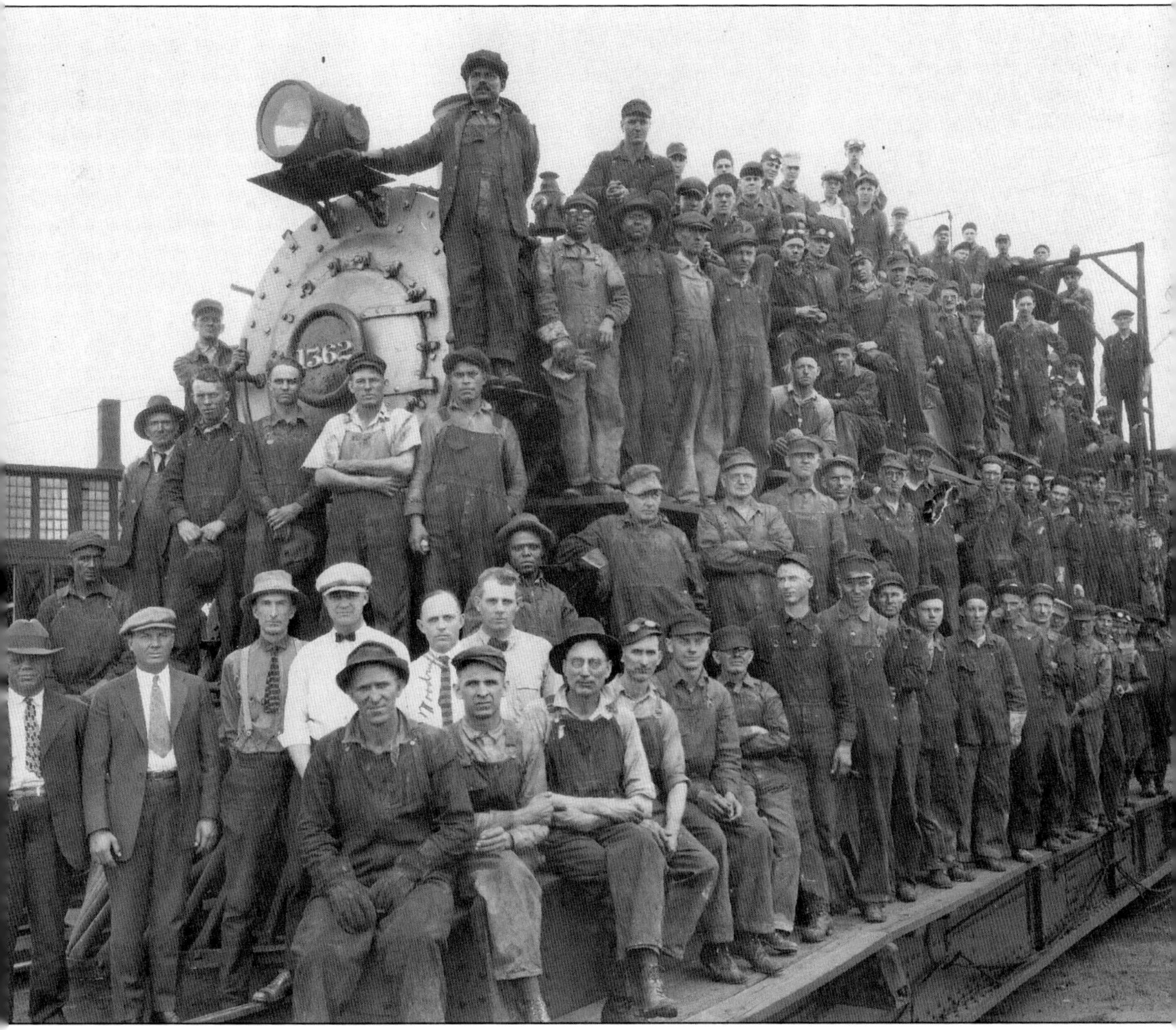

The railroad systems defined the location of towns throughout Kansas, and many small towns disappeared when the railroad tracks passed them by. Dodge City had the terminal of the Atchison, Topeka & Santa Fe Railroad and a huge roundhouse right from the start of the town in 1872. The professionals of that day were the engineers, and others connected with the trains. Here is a full crew of workers from the Dodge City roundhouse, pictured around 1930.

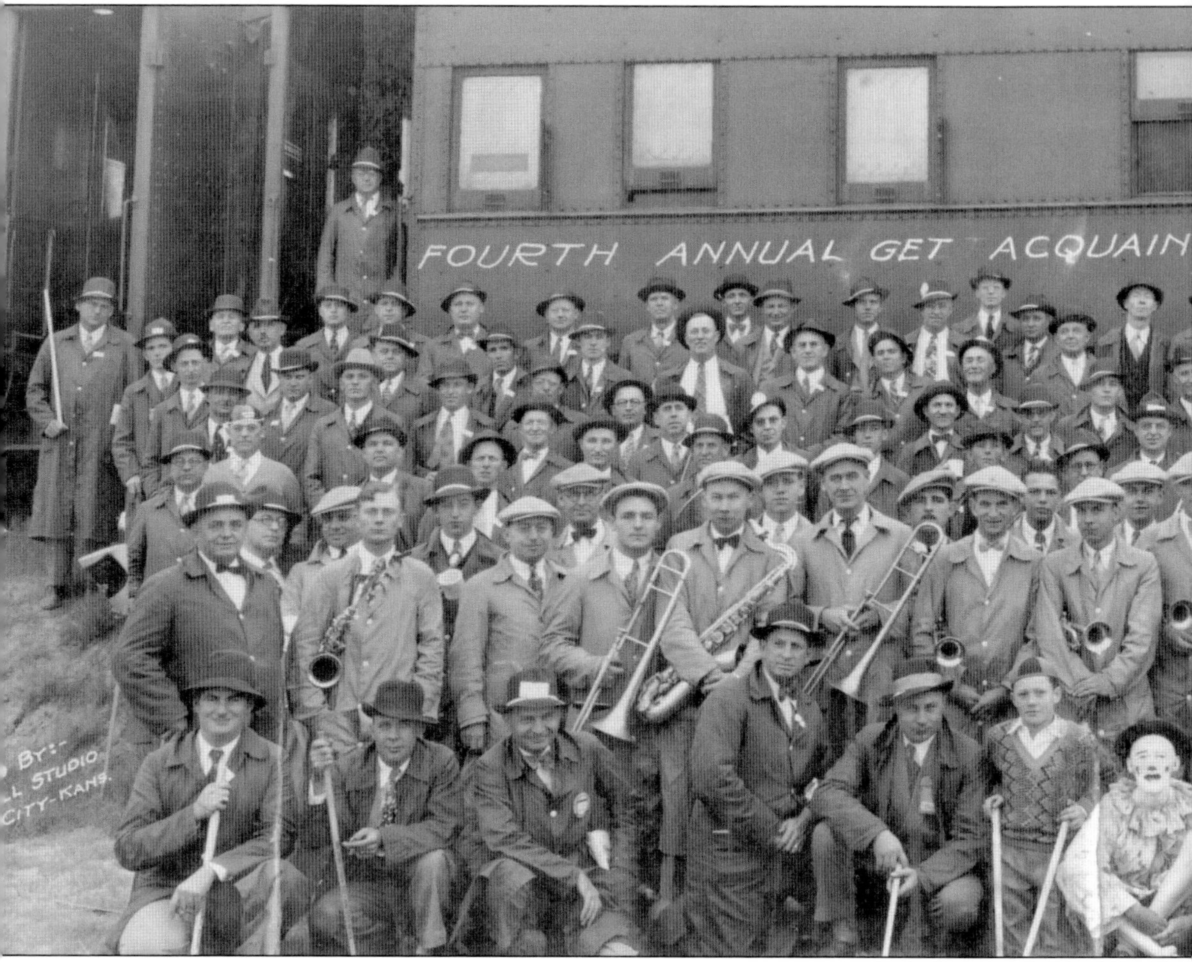

The Fourth Annual Get Acquainted Trip of the Dodge City Chamber of Commerce was held September 5–6, 1929. Ida Ellen Rath writes that this photograph was given to the Ford County Historical Society by Violet Watson, longtime friend of pioneer sheriff and marshal Ham Bell, who

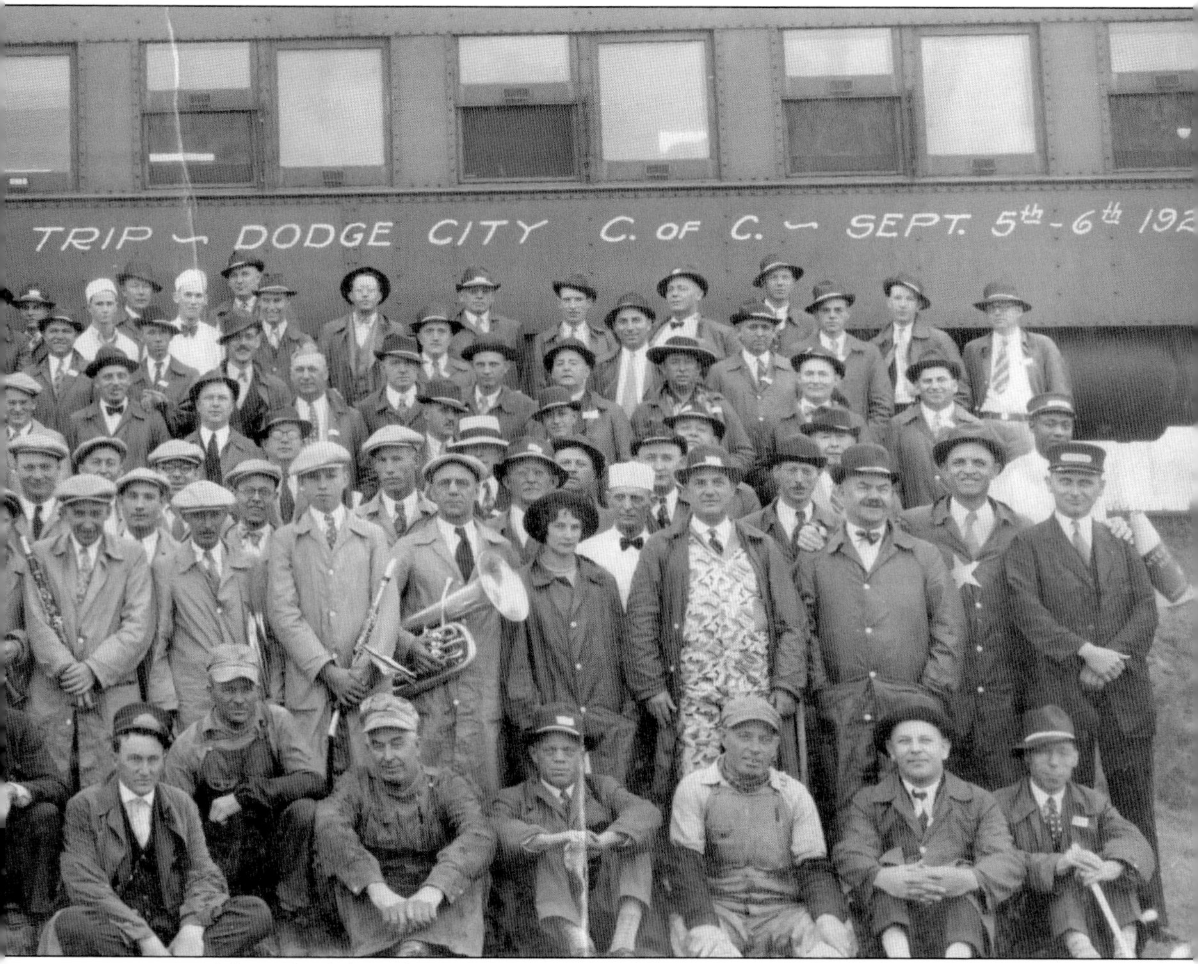

appears second from the left in the top row, looking straight at the camera. The Great Depression would begin a few months after the time of this photograph.

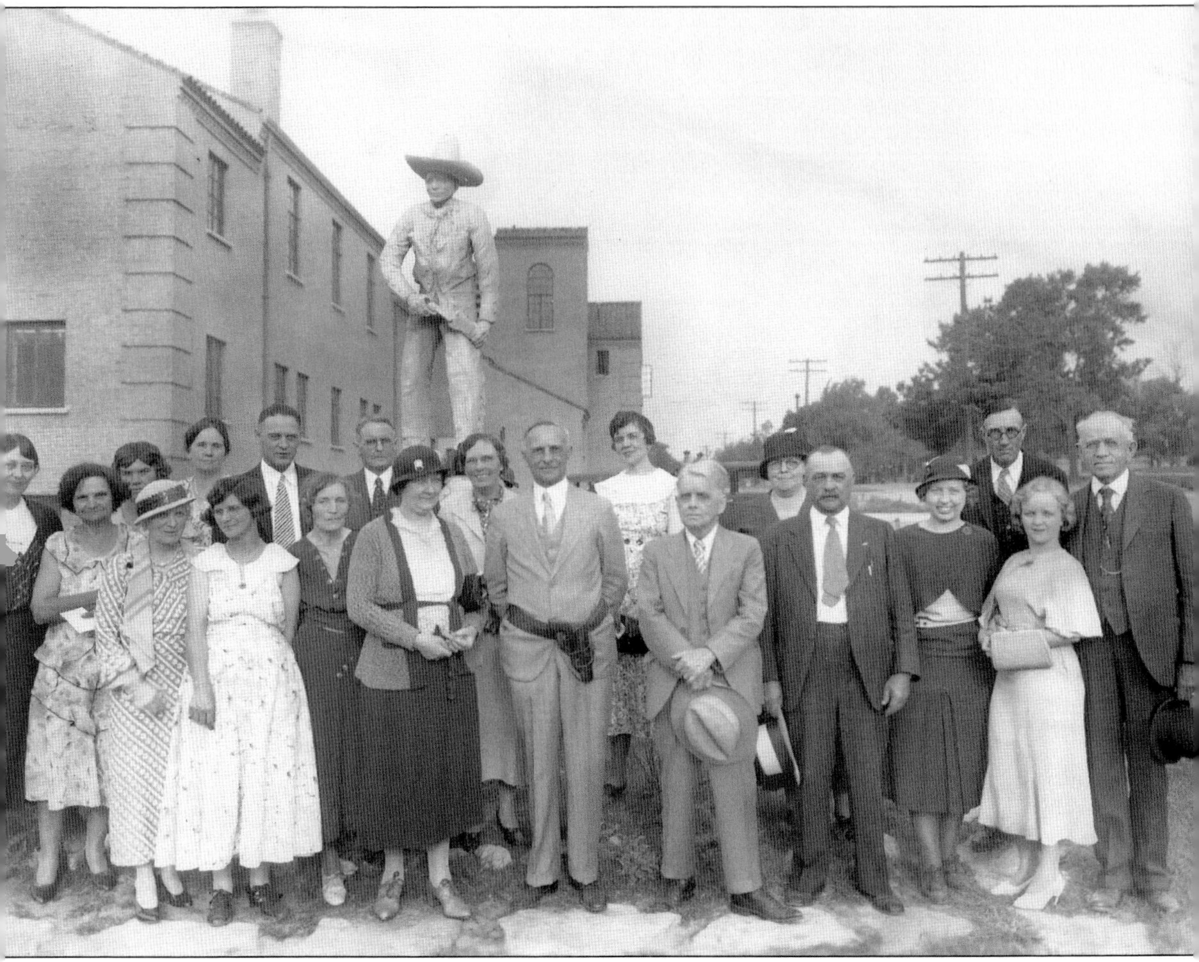

The Kansas Authors Club is pictured in 1933 at the Dodge City Municipal building (1929) on Boot Hill. Ida Ellen Rath appears in the white dress in the first row, fourth from the left; Lola Adams Crum is in the dark dress, second from the right; and Heine Schmidt, tall with dark glasses, is in the back row, second from the right. Lola Adams protected Dodge City history. She had a great love of pioneer farms, the sod houses of her parents, and the plains. This 1930s event was held during Ida Ellen Rath's presidency of the club. The famous, live-cast Cowboy on Boot Hill statue is behind the crowd. Dr. Oscar Simpson, DDS, in the back row to the far right, was a pioneer Dodge City dentist and inventor of gold inlay fillings (patent finally won in 1912). He made the cowboy statue. Simpson had his old pioneer lawman friend Joe Sughrue lay in a box while a mold was made with plaster. He then filled the mold with concrete. The statue has been on Boot Hill since 1929. Dr. Simpson also made the first Boot Hill tombstones for tourists to view.

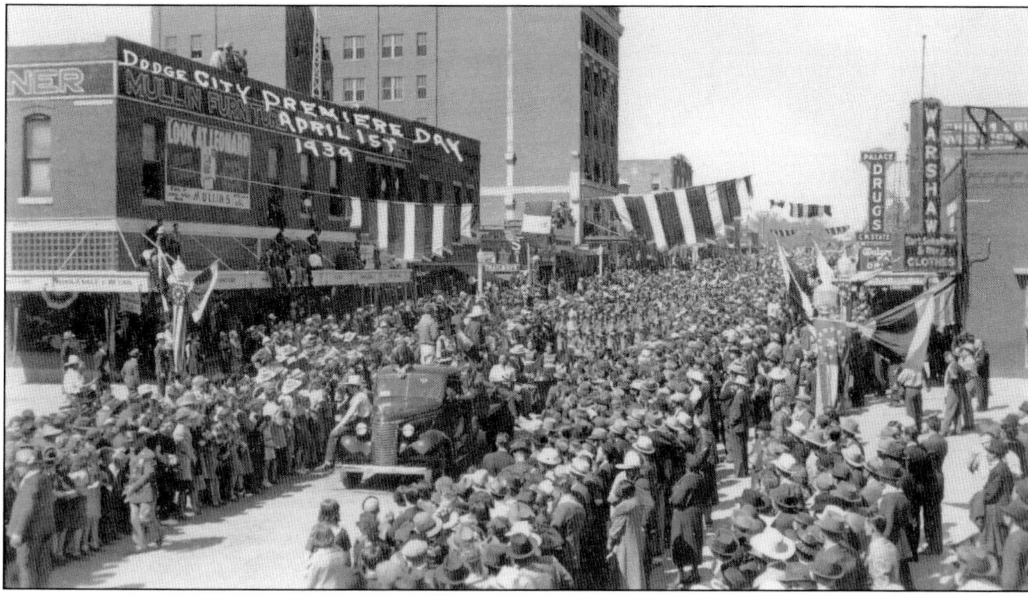

The April 1, 1939, world premiere of the movie *Dodge City*—the first held outside of Hollywood—brought a crowd of 50,000 to Dodge City. Warner Bros. sent the cast on a special train with over 100 people, including Errol Flynn, Ann Sheridan, Jean Parker, Hoot Gibson, Buck Jones, Guinn "Big Boy" Williams, Alan Hale, and Rosemary Lane. According to Susan L. Sutton, "As the Warner Bros. Special was leaving California for Dodge City, a second Santa Fe train left New York for Dodge. Aboard the New York train were members of the east coast press corps, including, among others, Ed Sullivan, *New York Daily News*, Ivan Dimitri, *Saturday Evening Post*, photographer Kay Mulvey, *Ladies Home Journal*, Jean Herrick, *Look*, Paul Peters and Helen Morgan, *Life*, Quentin Reynolds, *Collier's*, Frank Nugent, *New York Times*, Howard Barnes, *New York Herald Tribune*."

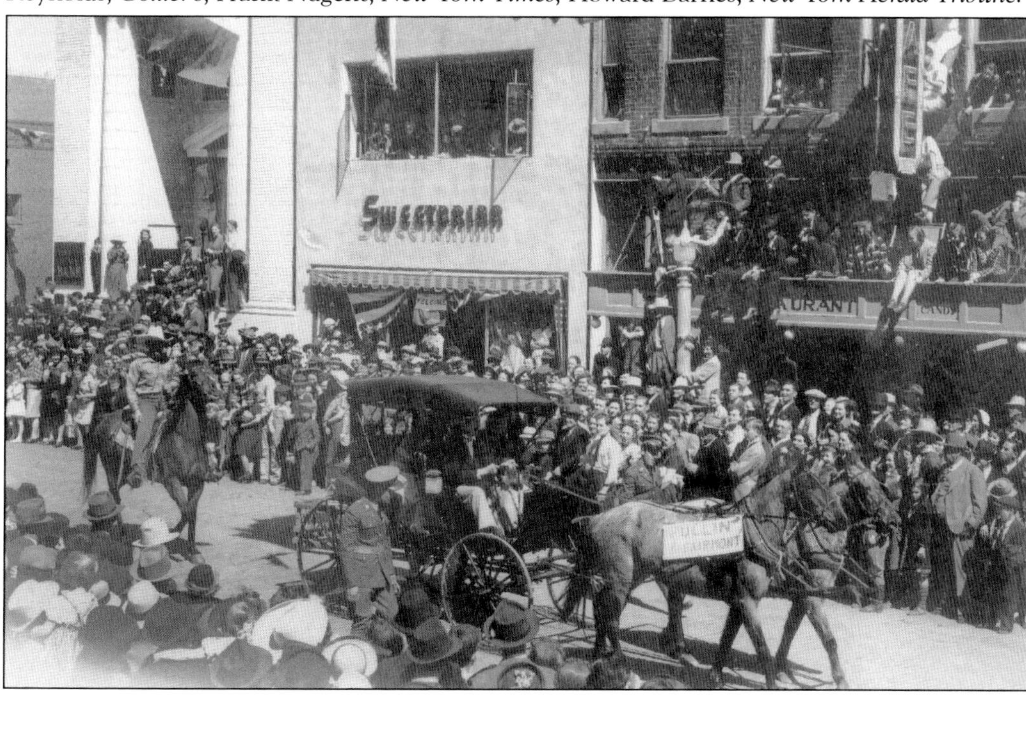

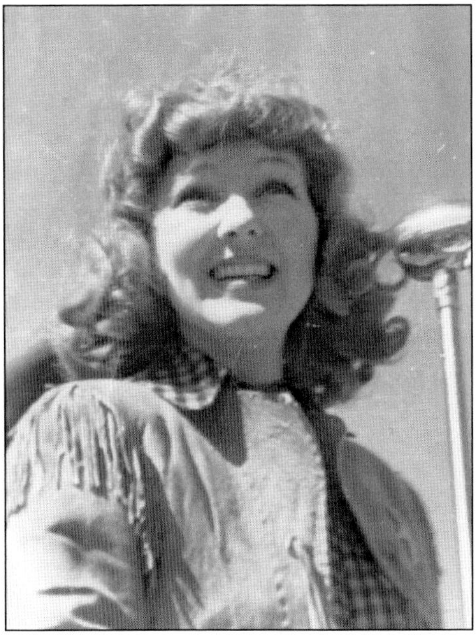

Errol Flynn and Jean Parker, pictured below in the April 1, 1939, Dodge City parade, were some of the big stars of the day. Susan Sutton continued, "In late September 1939, Ann Sheridan [pictured left], traveling on the Santa Fe Chief, briefly stopped in Dodge City. Members of the local press boarded the train to talk momentarily with the actress who they noted 'was much prettier than on her previous visit as she wore natural make-up, rather than panchromatic.' Of the premiere, Sheridan exclaimed, "Let me tell you one thing. Dodge City can be proud of the crowds that were here. All the way home we raved about the grand reception given us. Everyone was so courteous, and no one mobbed us or tried to grab souvenirs, something we don't find when visiting big cities."

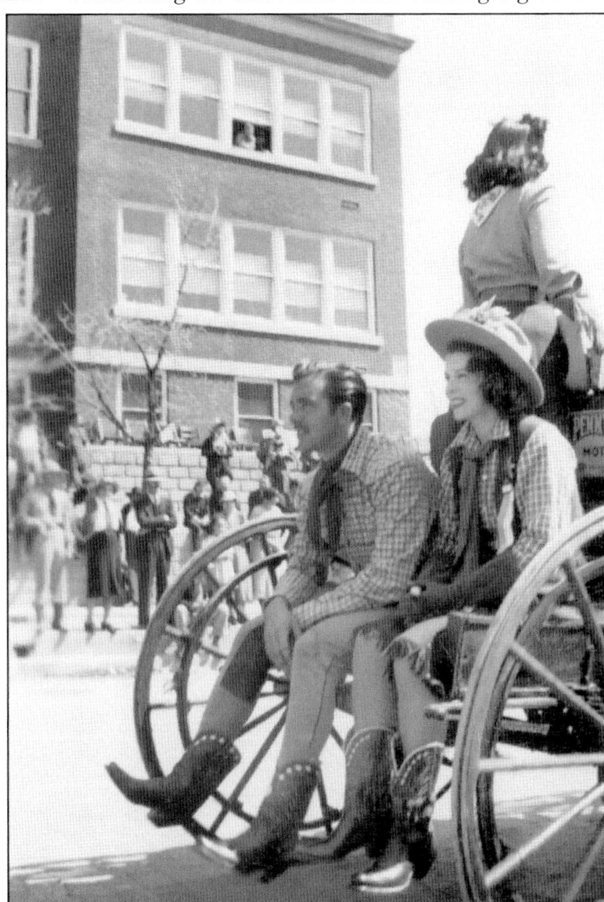

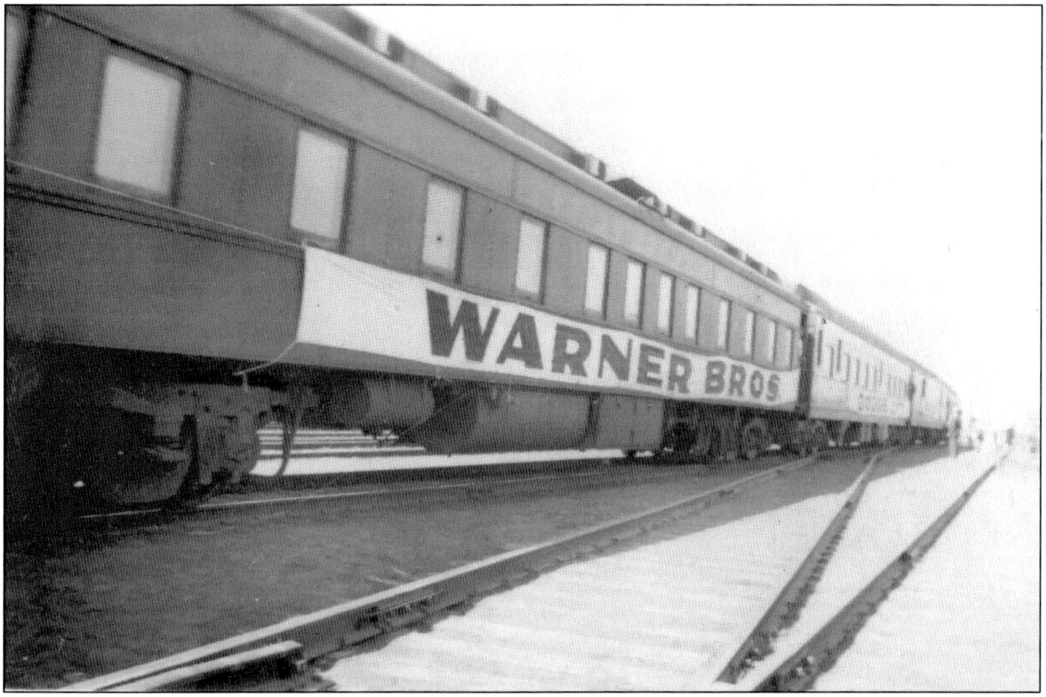

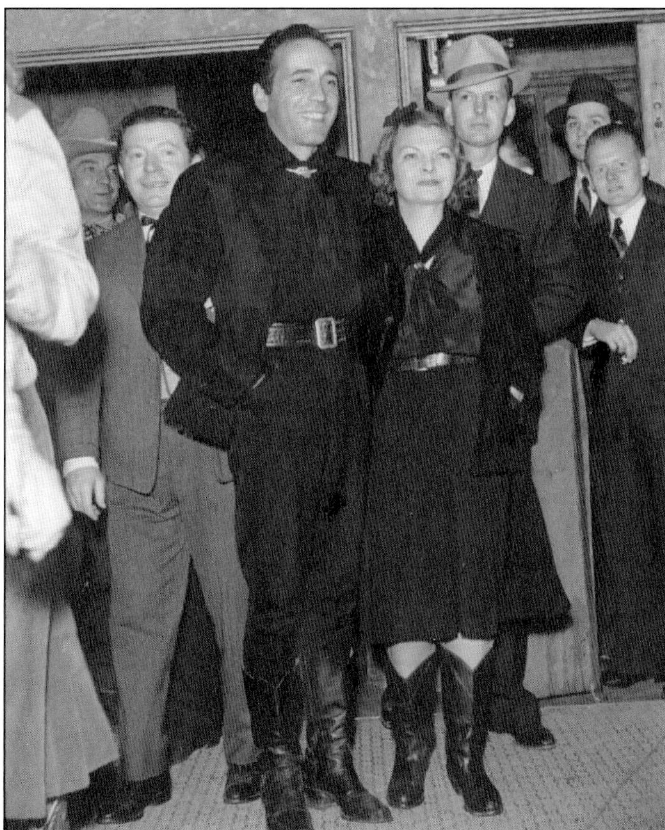

Humphrey Bogart was also sent to be an emcee at the film's showings in the three theaters in Dodge City. His wife at the time, actress Mayo Methot, is with him in front of the Lora-Locke Hotel doors. Bogart would star in *Virginia City* a few years later. "After introductions from the Santa Fe depot concluded, police from Hutchinson, Great Bend, Dodge City, Garden City, the Highway Patrol, and National Guard held back the crowds along a path for stars and fellow travelers to make their way to premiere headquarters at the Lora Locke Hotel. Inside, a limited number of citizens partook of a star-studded luncheon. The menu featured ice cream molds in the shape of horses for dessert." According to Susan L. Sutton, the movie's slogan said, "West of Chicago, there was no law—west of Dodge City, no God!"

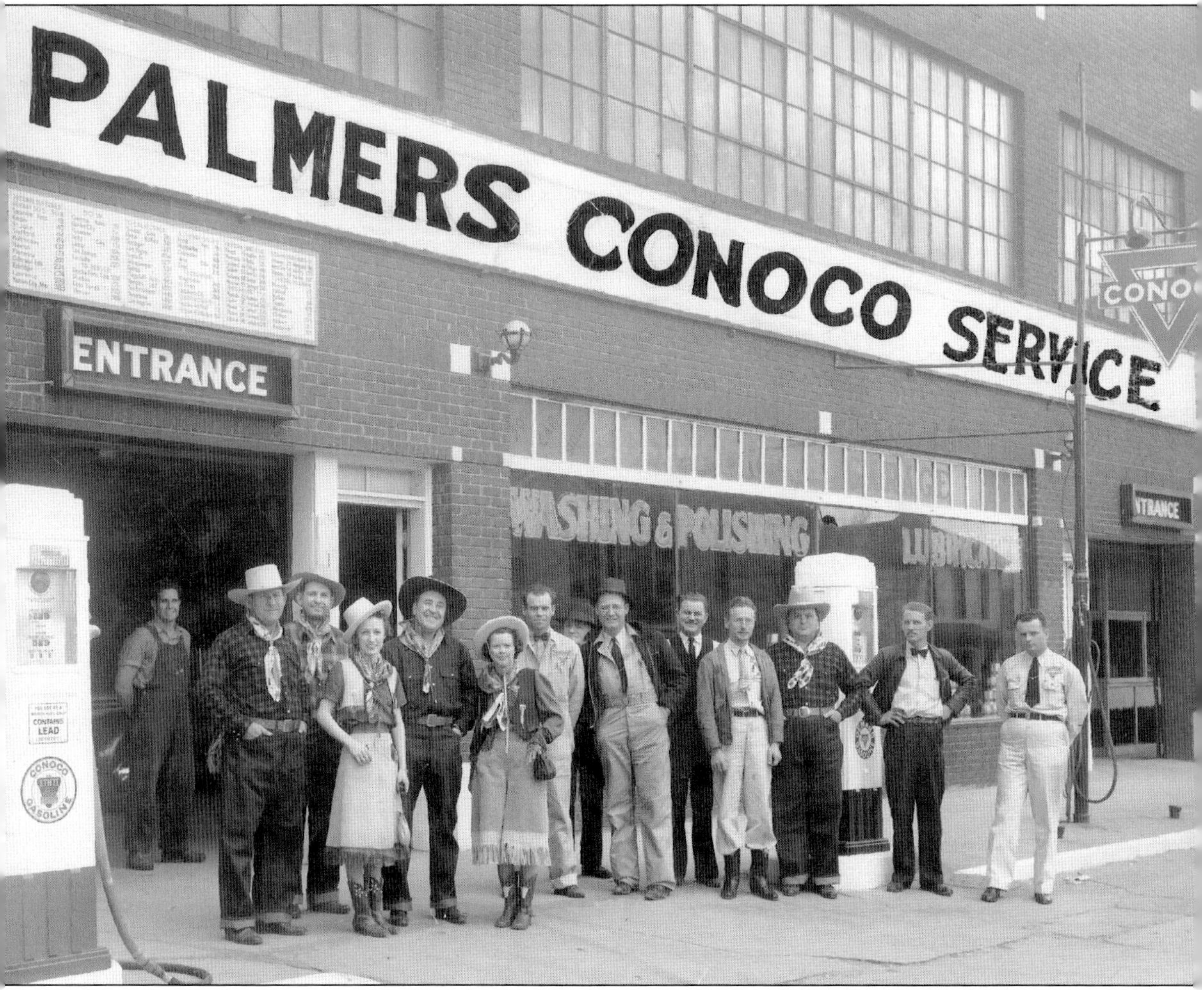

At the new Palmers Conoco gas station at the northwest corner of Military and Central Avenues, the former site of George M. Hoover's house and flower greenhouse, all the employees and owners dressed in Western clothes on April 1, 1939, for the world premiere of *Dodge City*. As many as 50,000 people were at the events that week, with the three local movie theaters showing the movie. Dodge City's population was less than 9,000 at the time.

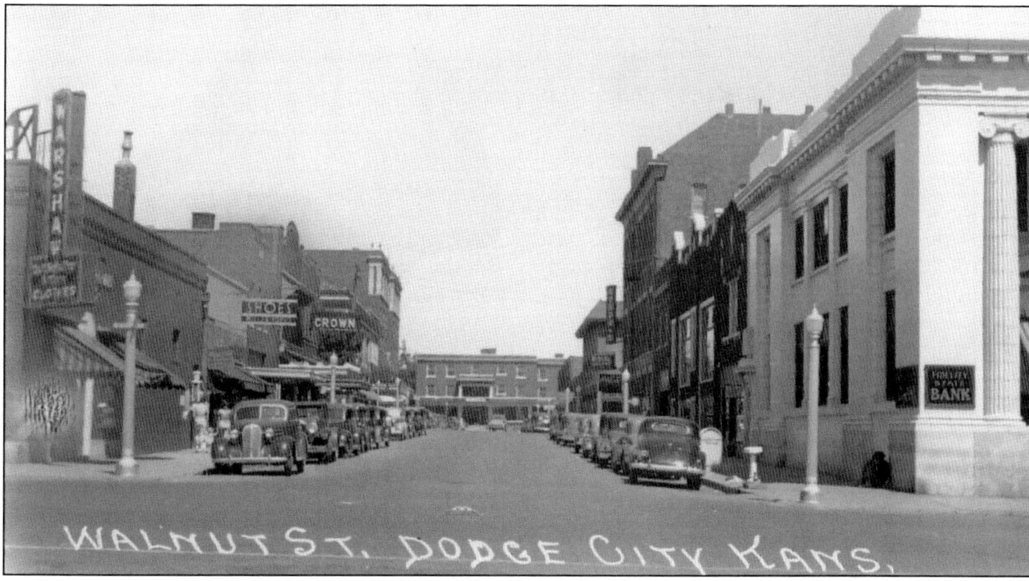

Pictured above is the O'Neal Hotel at the end of Walnut Street, looking east from Second Avenue in Dodge City. On the left is Warshaw's Clothing, and on the right is Fidelity State Bank. Pictured below is the O'Neal Hotel dining room around 1939. Many railroad workers deadheaded in Dodge City, and the O'Neal was across the street from the Atchison, Topeka & Santa Fe Railroad depot. The dining room was the important part of the hotel. Although service clearly was not on the level of the Harvey House across the street, very hardy meals were the norm. Each room in the O'Neal had a sink, if not a bathroom. The hotel was torn down in 1970 during urban renewal in Dodge City and is now a public parking lot.

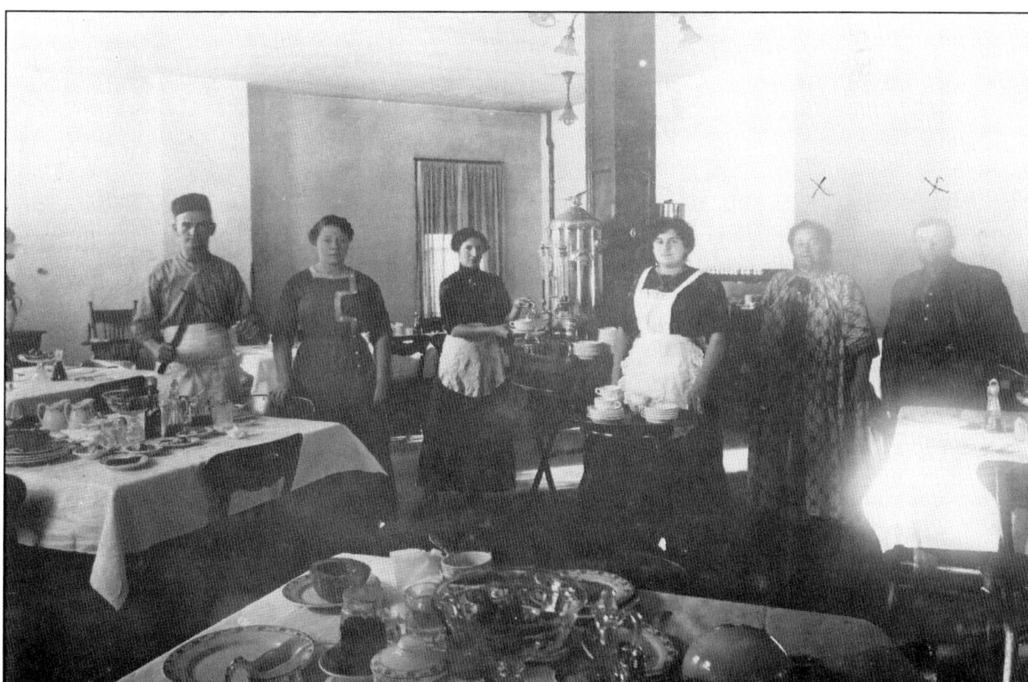

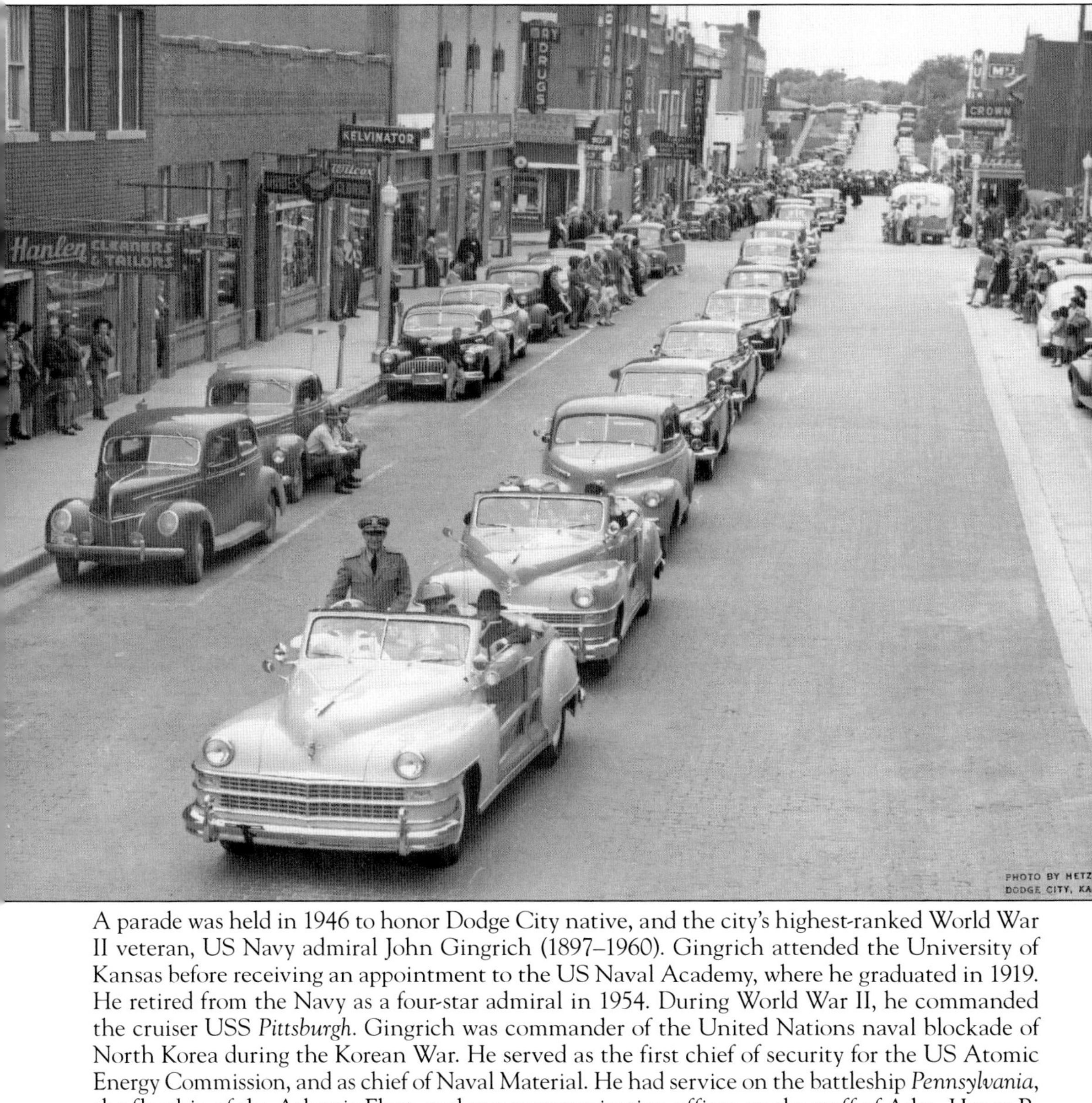

A parade was held in 1946 to honor Dodge City native, and the city's highest-ranked World War II veteran, US Navy admiral John Gingrich (1897–1960). Gingrich attended the University of Kansas before receiving an appointment to the US Naval Academy, where he graduated in 1919. He retired from the Navy as a four-star admiral in 1954. During World War II, he commanded the cruiser USS *Pittsburgh*. Gingrich was commander of the United Nations naval blockade of North Korea during the Korean War. He served as the first chief of security for the US Atomic Energy Commission, and as chief of Naval Material. He had service on the battleship *Pennsylvania*, the flagship of the Atlantic Fleet, and as a communication officer on the staff of Adm. Henry B. Wilson Jr., commander in chief, Atlantic Fleet. This view of the parade faces west down Walnut Street (later named Gunsmoke Street) with Boot Hill in the background.

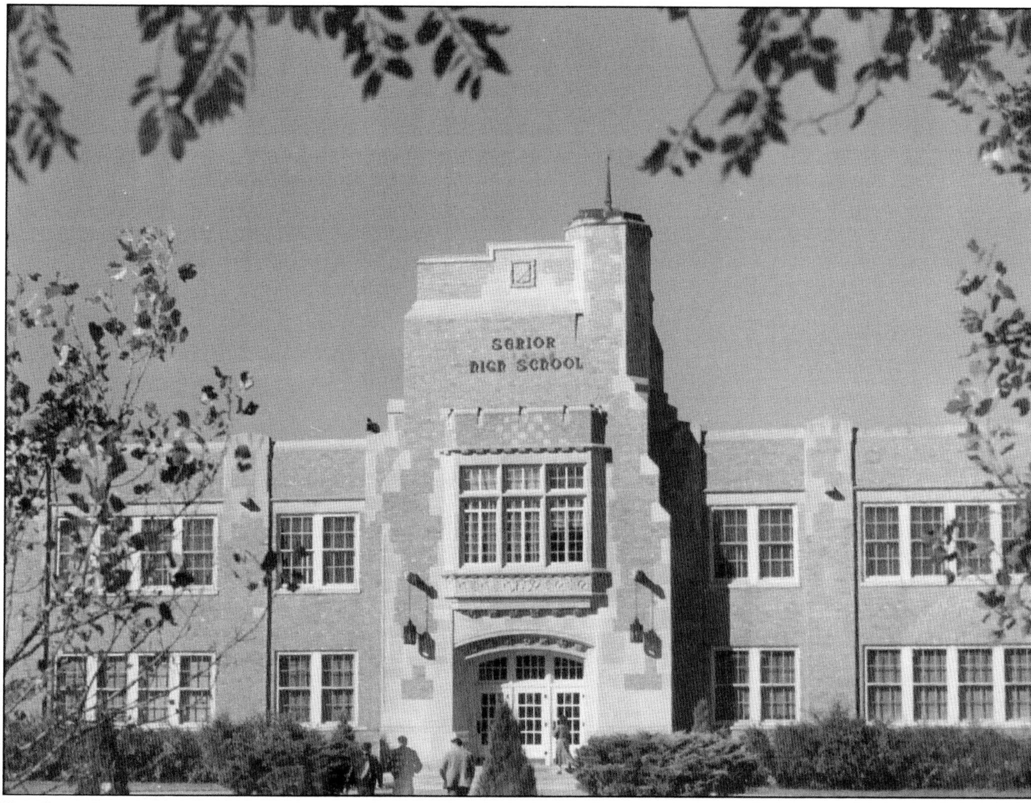

Dodge City Senior High School is pictured above and below. The high school building was constructed in 1928 and initially included the Dodge City Junior College. The classic building is still being used as a middle school, having been expanded and remodeled from the senior high school in 2002.

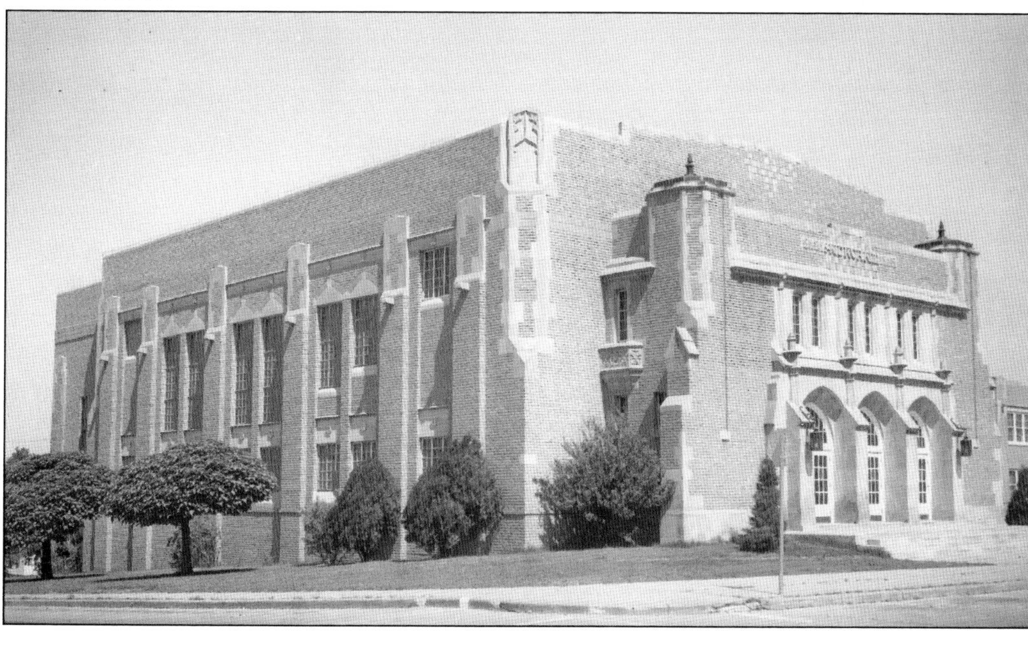

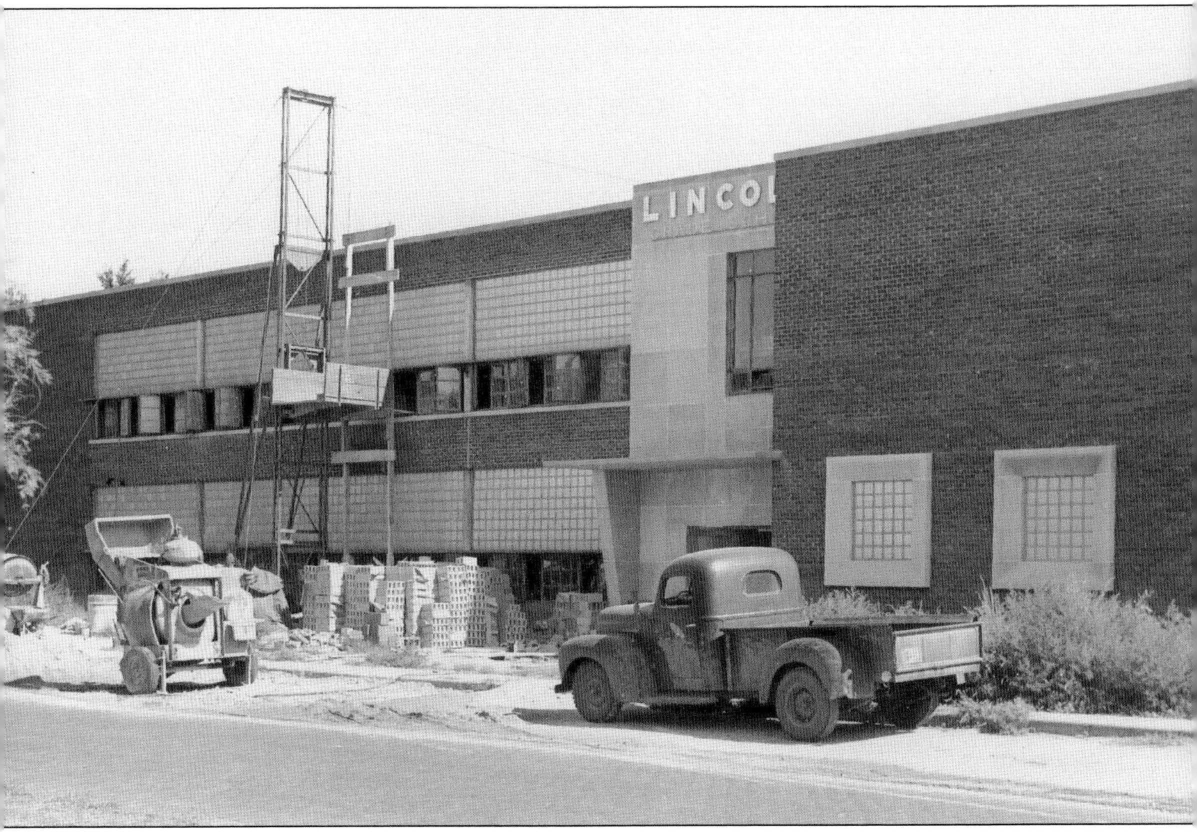

Lincoln School is being expanded in this c. 1955 photograph. Originally built in 1926 to replace the condemned Third Ward School building on Boot Hill, Lincoln School is located at the top of a hill on the corner of Sixth Avenue and Cedar Street. It was the model neighborhood school through the 1990s, when it was closed. The building is still being used for a nonprofit group office and storage. The small houses on the hills east of Lincoln School included one of the largest number of Prairie Classical Revival cottages in existence.

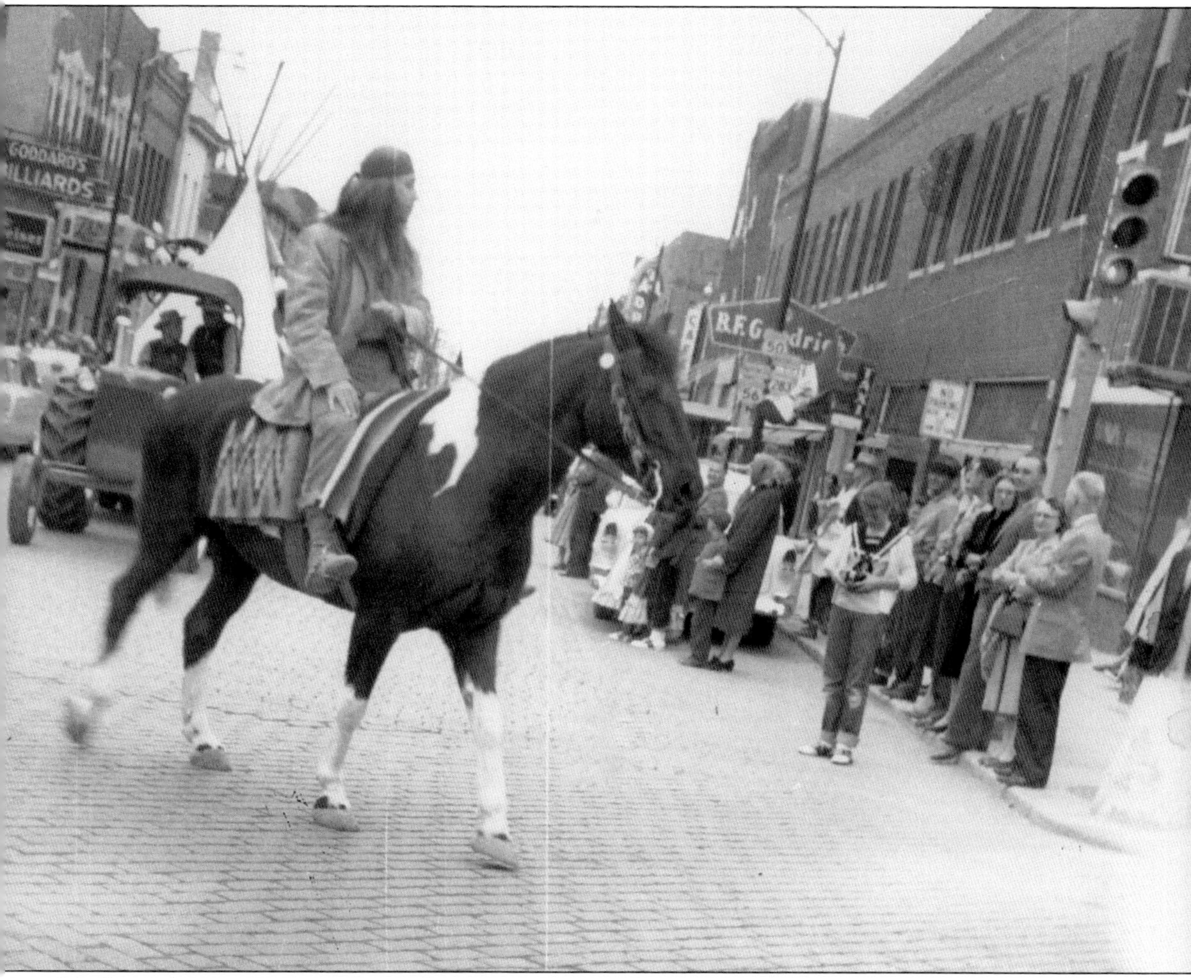

Michael Ansara appears as Cochise in a 1958 Dodge City parade connected with the start of construction of the Front Street Replica at Boot Hill. His television series was the popular *Broken Arrow (1956)*, in which he played the lead Native American role (Ansara is Syrian). The rebirth of interest in the Old West can be related to the television series of the time, especially *Gunsmoke*. Walnut Street in Dodge City was renamed Gunsmoke Street, with James Arness ("Matt"), Amanda Blake ("Kitty"), and Milburn Stone ("Doc") at the event.

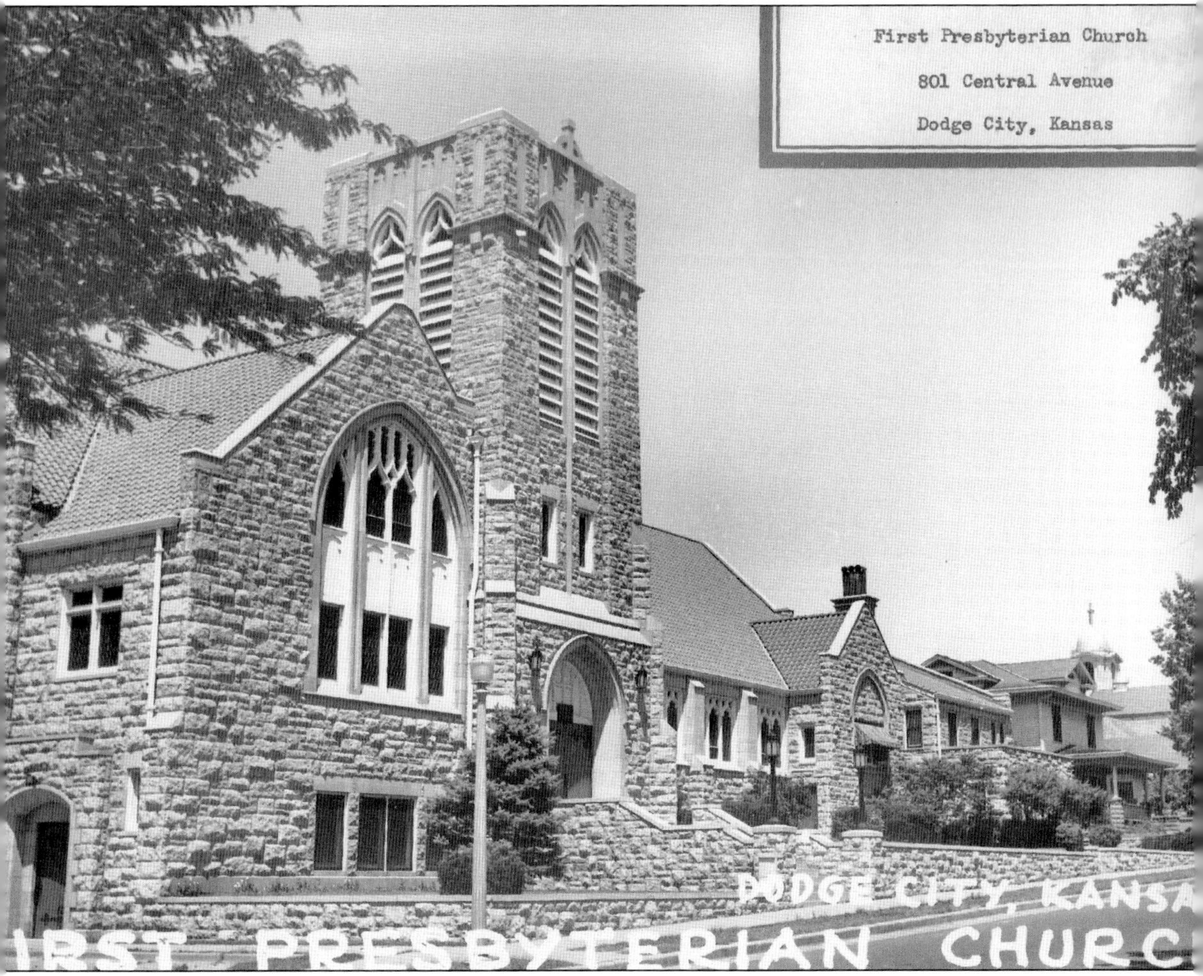

The Rev. Ormond Wright, a young Presbyterian minister, served the Union Church. The church building was used by various denominations from 1875 to 1900. The Presbyterians built a small, frame church with Gothic-style windows in 1880 and remodeled and enlarged the building in 1887 and again in 1900. The present stone Gothic church was built in 1925 at a cost of $155,000. It stands where the first frame building stood, on the northwest corner of Central Avenue and Vine Street.

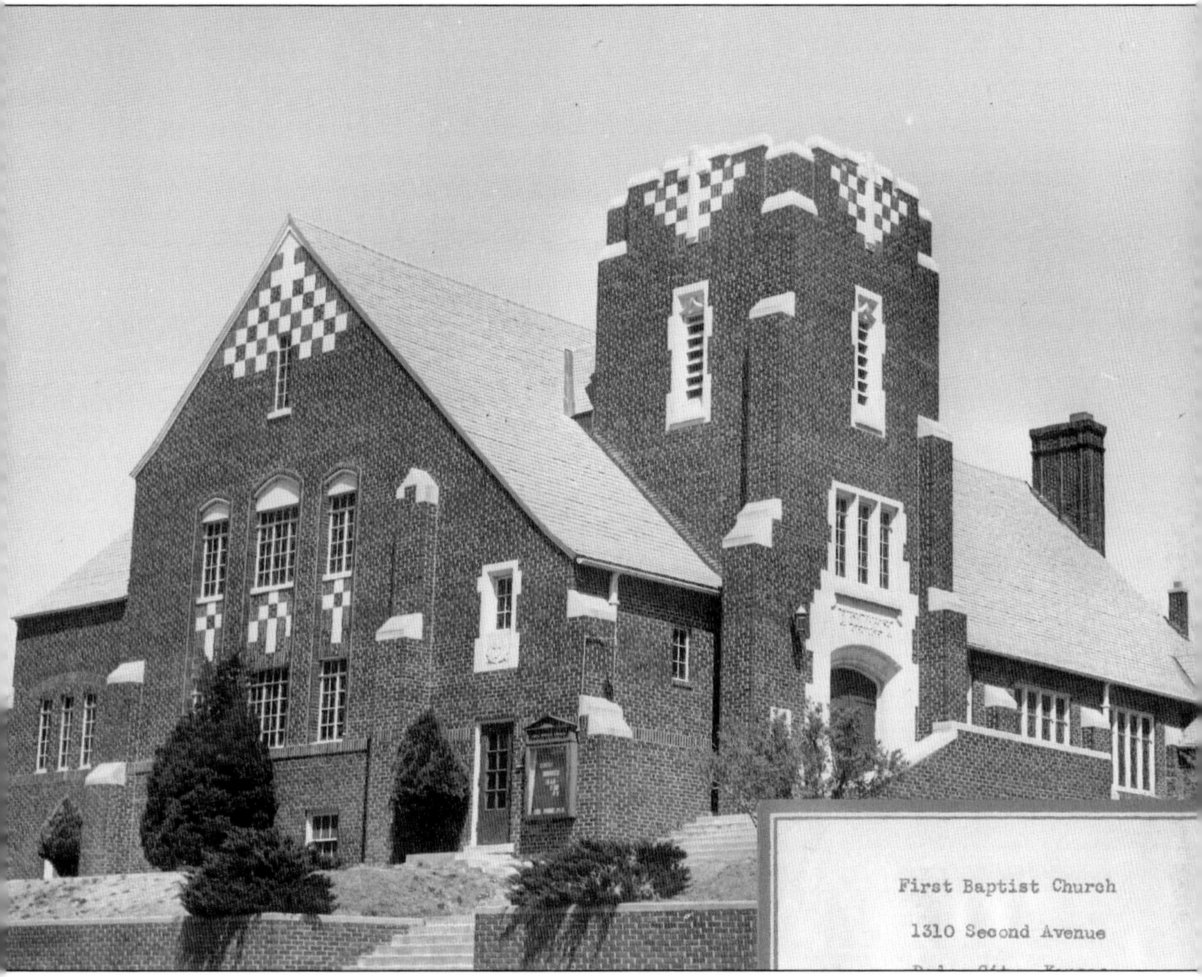

The Baptists organized under Rev. Elder N.G. Collins and built their church in 1885. It was 60 feet by 40 feet and held up to 400 people. It was at the top of the hill on Cedar Street and Sixth Avenue, east of the former Lincoln School. It was later moved to the northeast corner of Second Avenue and Spruce Street. The present redbrick building between Ash and Hickory Streets on Second Avenue was built in 1930.

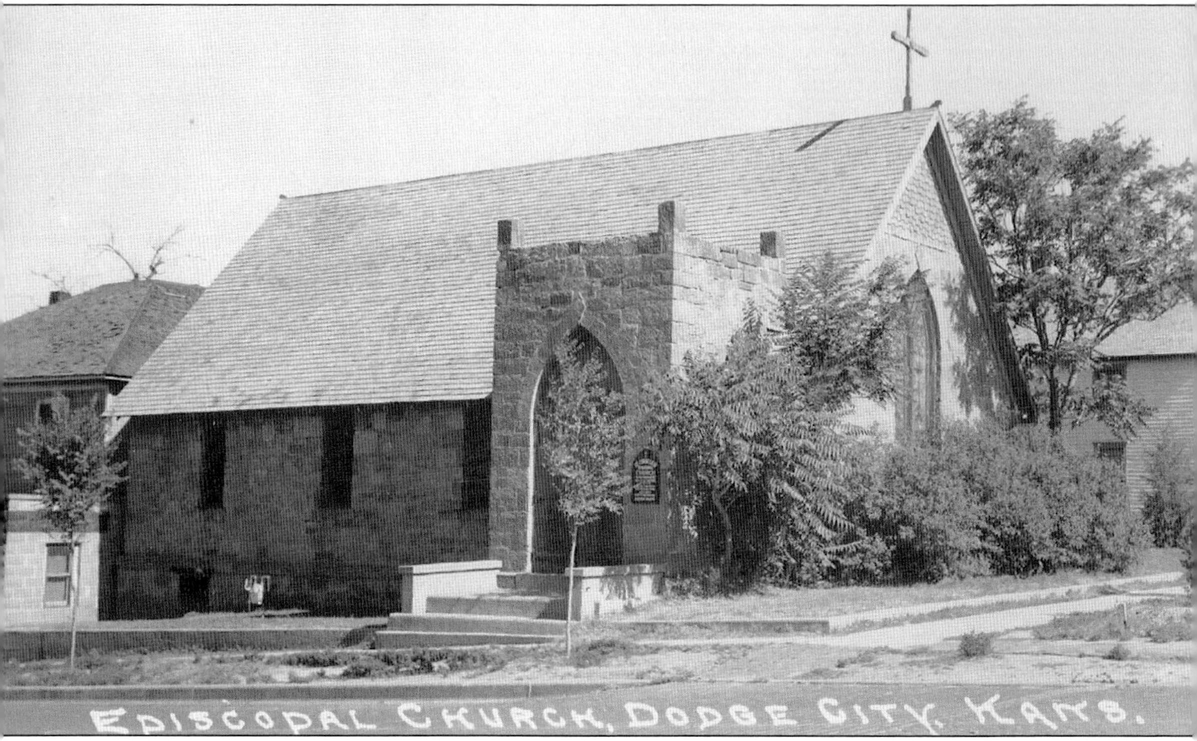

The St. Cornelius Episcopal Church was founded in 1888 as an Episcopal mission, under the supervision of rector Dr. Krum. It is the only one of the first churches that still holds services in the original building, completed in 1898. It was 25 by 50 feet, and seated up to 200 persons. The stone was repurposed from Henry Sturm's icehouse (brother-in-law of Elizabeth Schmidt). Robert M. Wright wrote in *Dodge City, The Cowboy Capital*, "The Episcopal church, though small, is a little gem—the most artistic building in Dodge City. With its brown stone walls, colored glass windows and square bell tower, it is delightfully suggestive of the chapels of rural England."

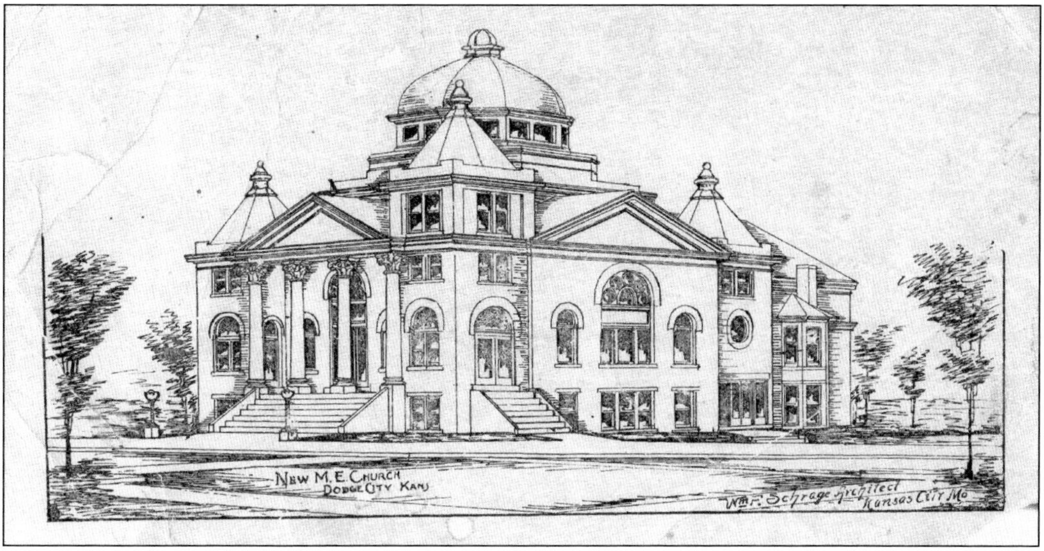

The Methodists organized in August 1878. Under the management of Rev. A.P. George, D.D., they built a church one block west of the Presbyterian church; the project was complete in 1884. Their building was on the southwest corner of Vine Street and First Avenue, and seated 300 people. In 1913, a large redbrick building replaced their little frame church on the same location. In 1964, the property was sold to the city, and the main sanctuary was torn down for city parking (pictured below). The city hall was located in the former education building of the church for about two decades.

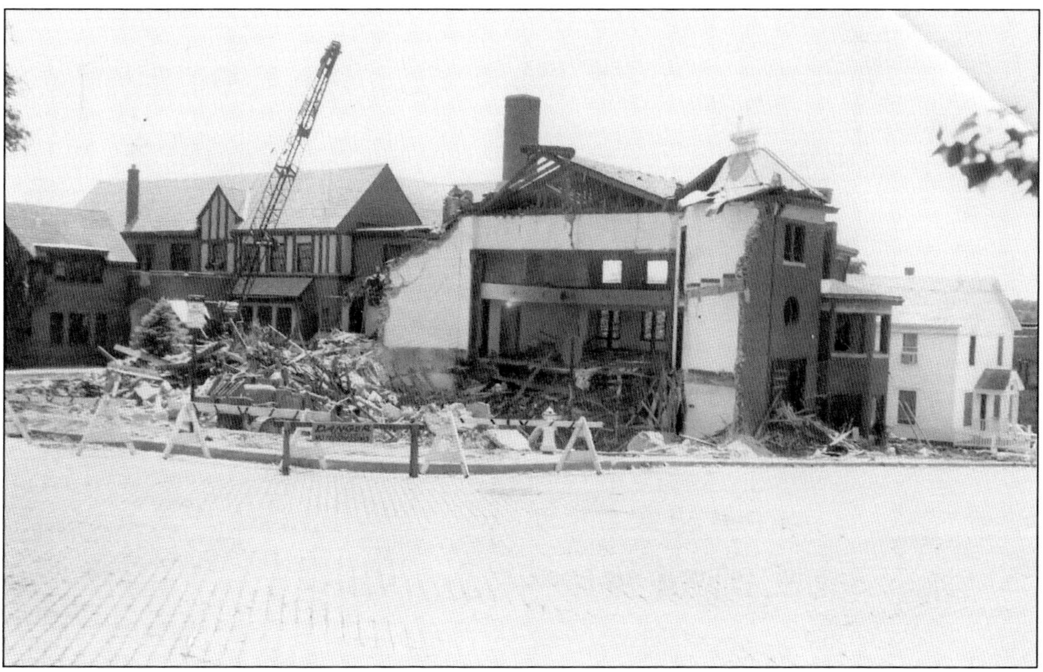

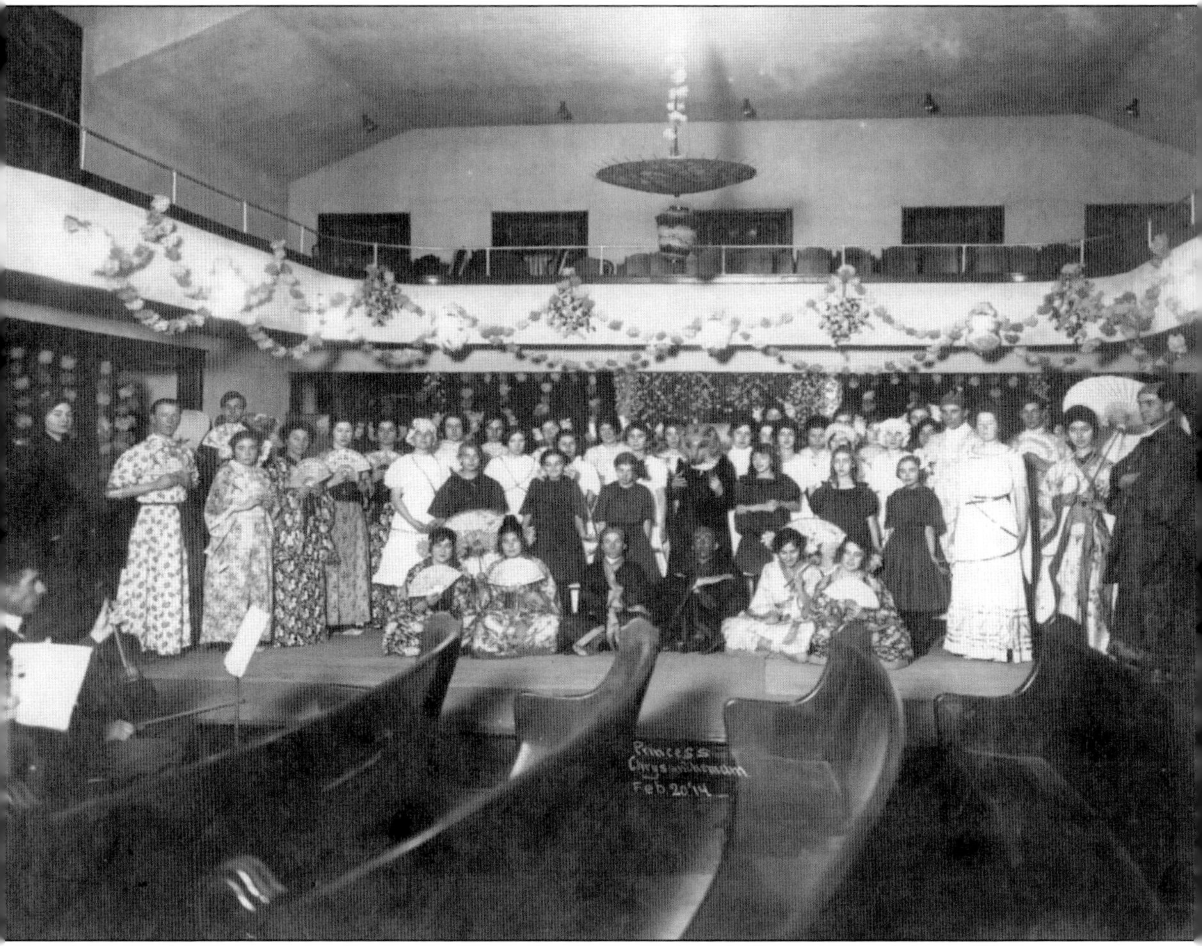

A performance of *Princess Chrysanthemum: A Japanese Operetta in Three Acts,* written in 1907 by C. King Proctor, was held on February 20, 1914, in the Methodist church building.

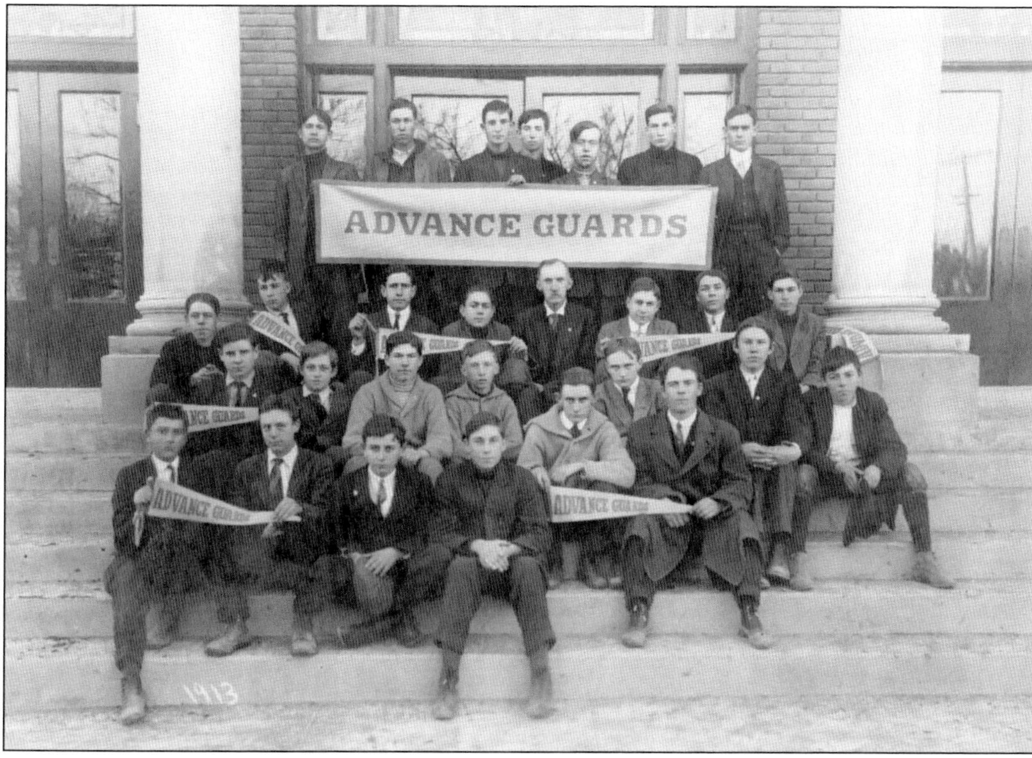

Pictured above, members of the Methodist church youth group Advance Guards gathered on the front steps of the new 1913 church building. The pants, shoes, and other clothes of this group show diverse economic backgrounds among church members. Members of the Methodist women Bible club are pictured below wearing hats on Easter Sunday, April 17, 1926. The economy of the town was still growing during the mid-1920s.

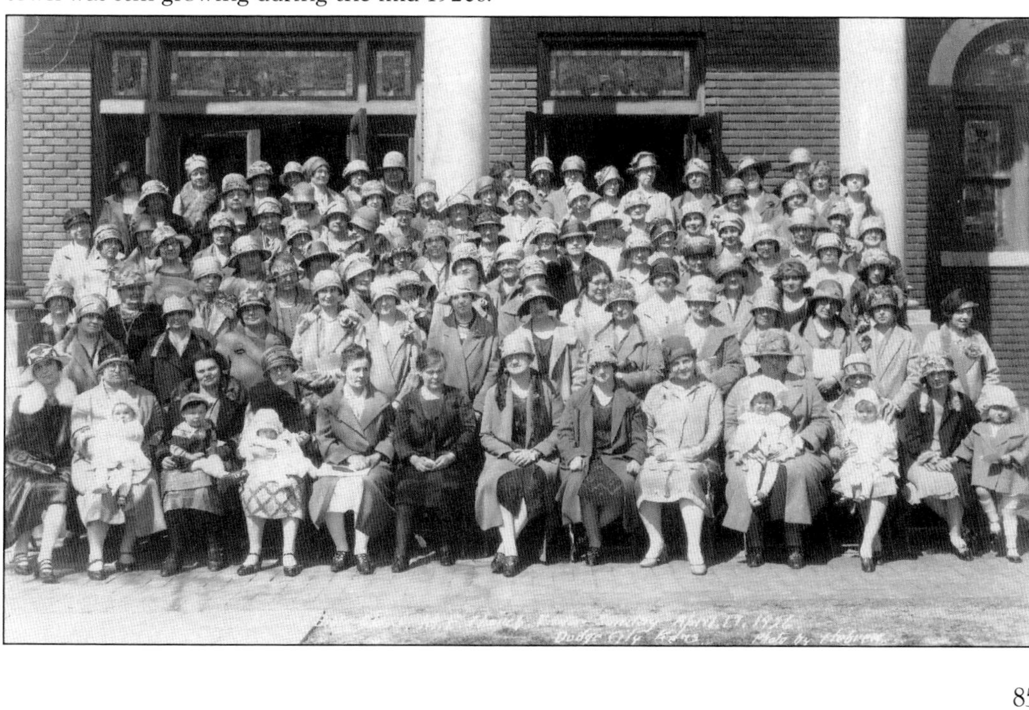

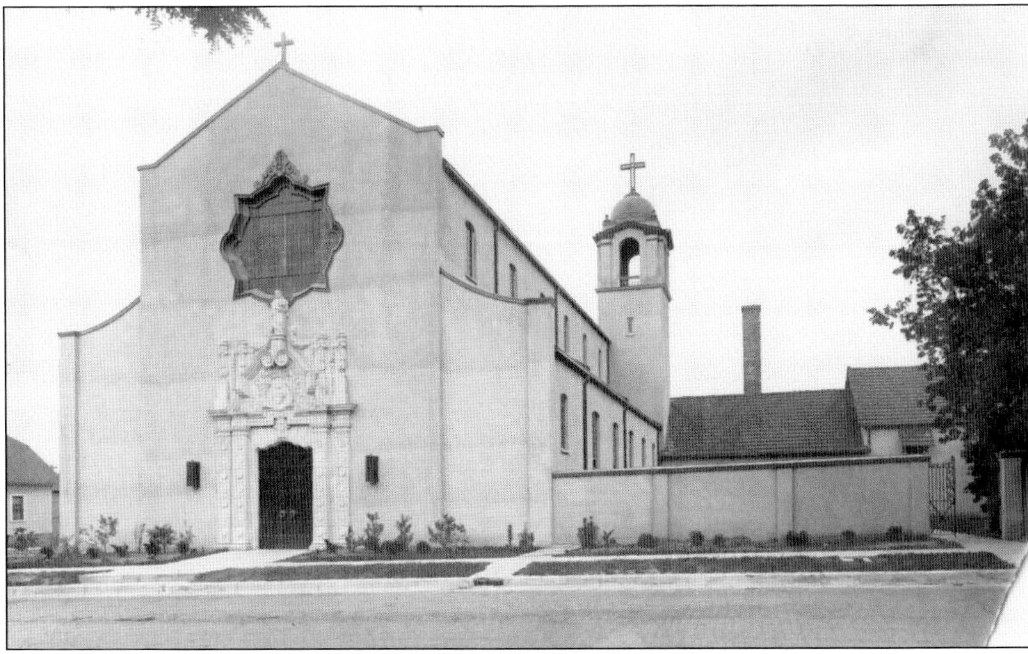

The first Roman Catholic missionary priest in Dodge City held services during early Sunday morning hours at the Union Church. In 1882, the Catholics built a little white frame church on the corner of Railroad (Central) Avenue and Cedar Street. In 1914, it was replaced by the beautiful Sacred Heart Cathedral. Francisco Vasquez de Coronado, a Spanish nobleman, set out from Mexico in 1540 to find the fabled cities of gold. Thirty horsemen, foot soldiers, guides, and a Franciscan Friar, Juan de Padilla, accompanied Coronado. On June 29, 1541, after much hardship, the group crossed the Arkansas River (St. Peter and St. Paul River) near Fort Dodge. Fr. Juan de Padilla held a mass of thanksgiving on the nearby hills, the first Christian service held inside the continent, predating the landing of the pilgrims by almost 100 years. The Holy Cross Lutheran Church is pictured below in 1900. The Schmidts were members.

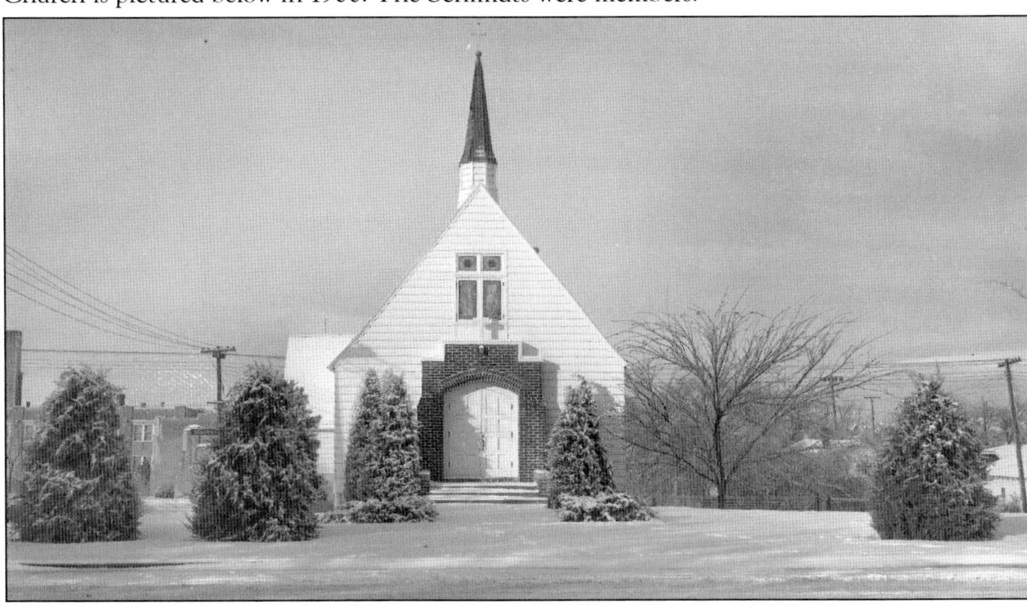

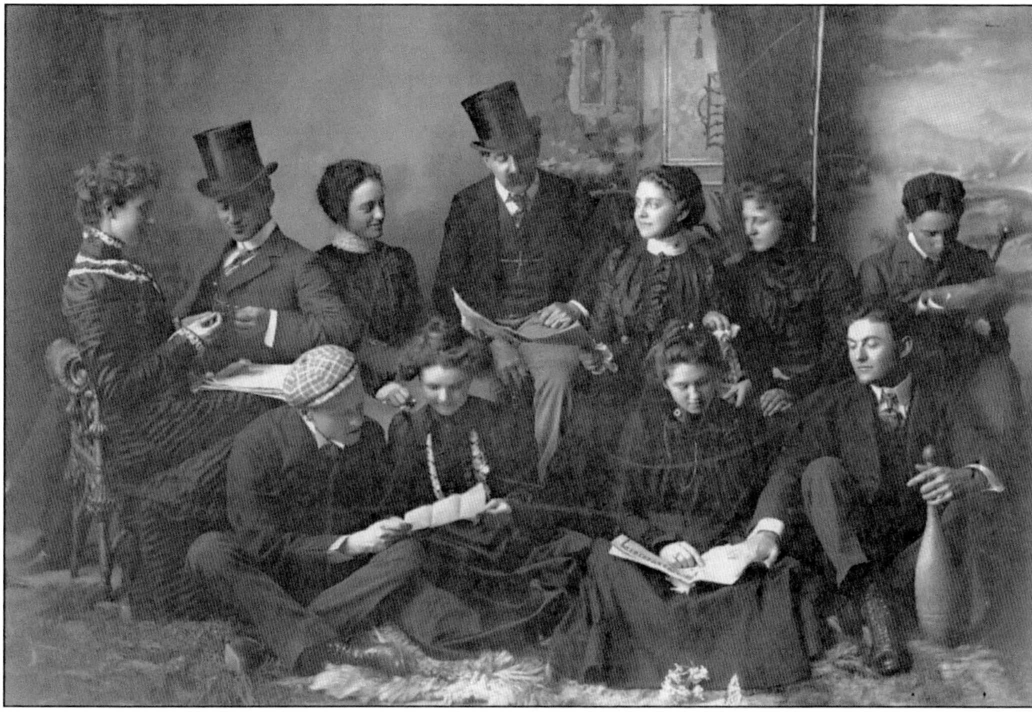

The Christian church organized in 1886. The members were able to build their own church in 1900, where the First National Bank building (now Bank of America) stands. During the summer of 1909, a larger church was built one block north on the southwest corner of Second Avenue and Vine Street. It burned on Christmas Eve of that same year. The congregation moved into a redbrick building on that site the next year, where they worshipped for 45 years. In 1955, they erected a building on top of Boot Hill. Pictured above, an 1895 church class includes Robert Rath (front row, left, with casual cap) and his sister Bertha Rath (top row, third from left), children of buffalo hunter Charles Rath. Pictured below, the "E" stands for Christian Endeavor, the youth group of the Christian church. This display was set up inside the old stone Christian church building, pictured here around 1909.

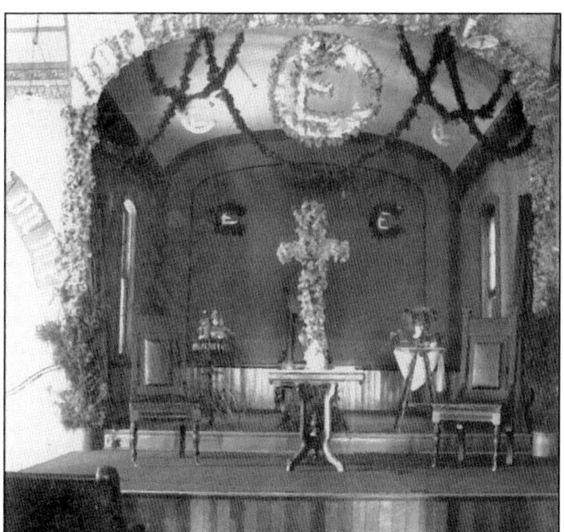

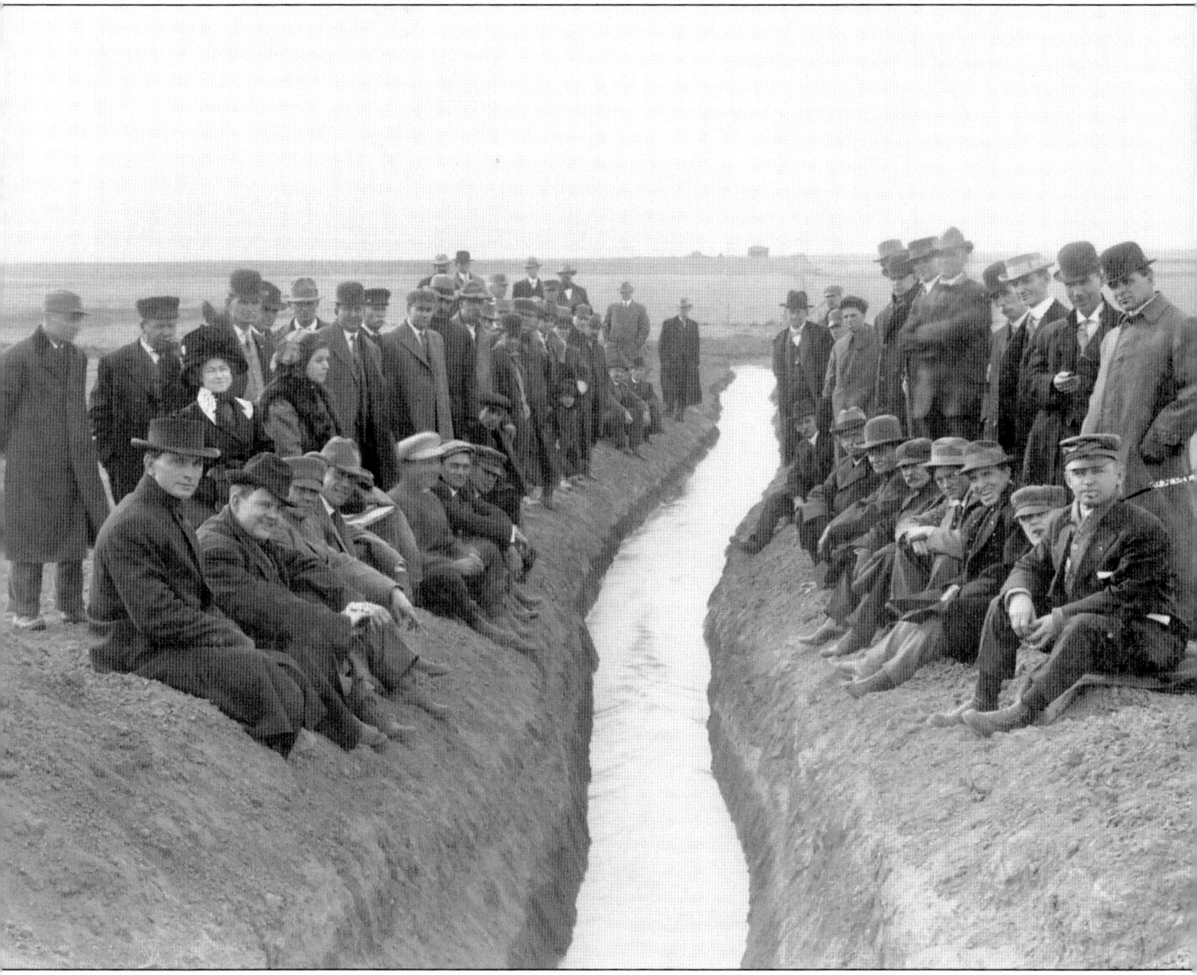

The Soule Canal ("Soule ditch"), six miles west of Dodge City, is pictured here around 1911. The Soule family, for which the canal was named, pronounced it "soul." It is now pronounced more like "you'll" (as in "sou'll"). Water flowed for a very short time in the ditch; the sandy soil absorbed all of the water. The attempt to use the Arkansas River water for crops far from the river was a million-dollar scheme—one that failed each of two times it was completed. Even with modern pumps, it took 30 days for water to reach Dodge City from 20 miles west. More than half the water was lost in the first few miles. Asa T. Soule was a rich upstate New Yorker who had made a huge fortune from medicine. He built the first canal in 1885.

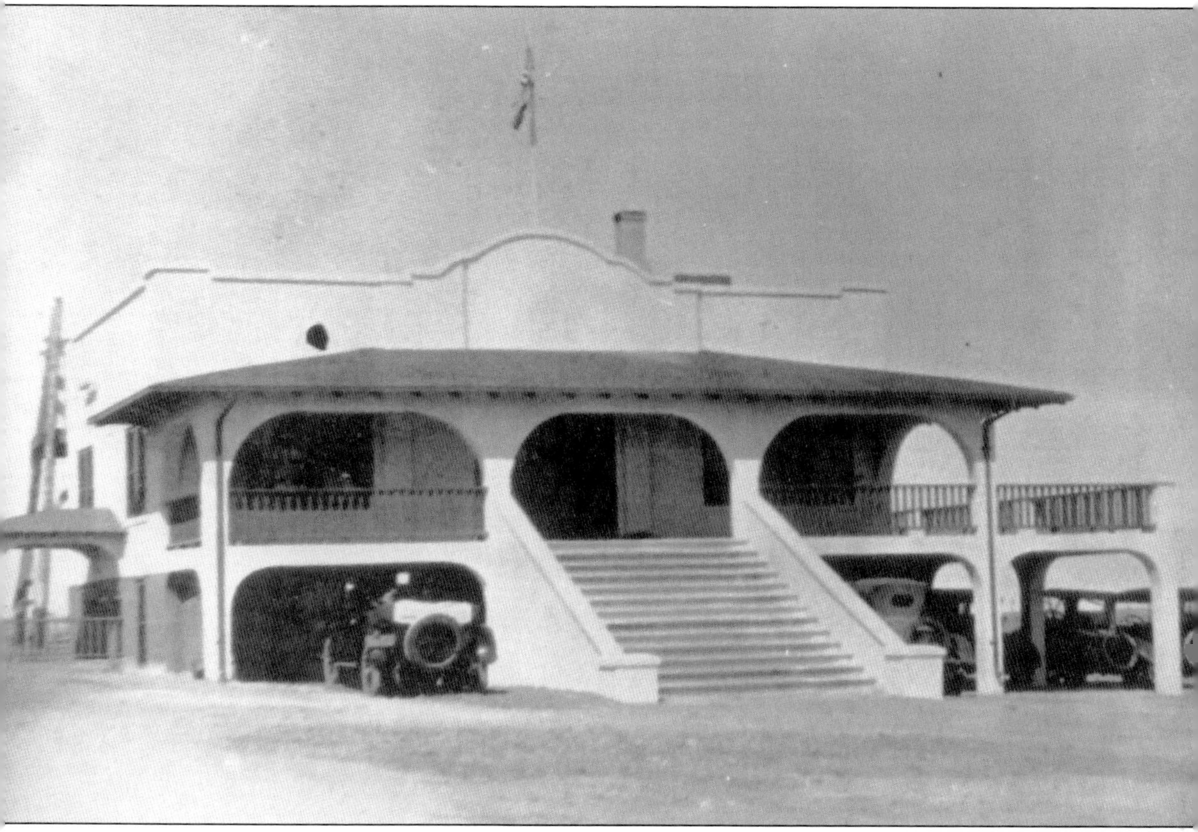

The Dodge City Country Club (DCCC), built in the early 1920s, was set on a prairie with Santa Fe Trail swells, still visible in 2012. There were many snakes on the early golf course. Water was easy to get at the time, and many trees were planted. Early dinners held there were truly family nights—potlucks with liquor bans. Later, members were allowed to bring their own bottles (or label them and leave them at the bar) and pay for setups and sodas. Golf and pool were always a part of the entertainment for DCCC members.

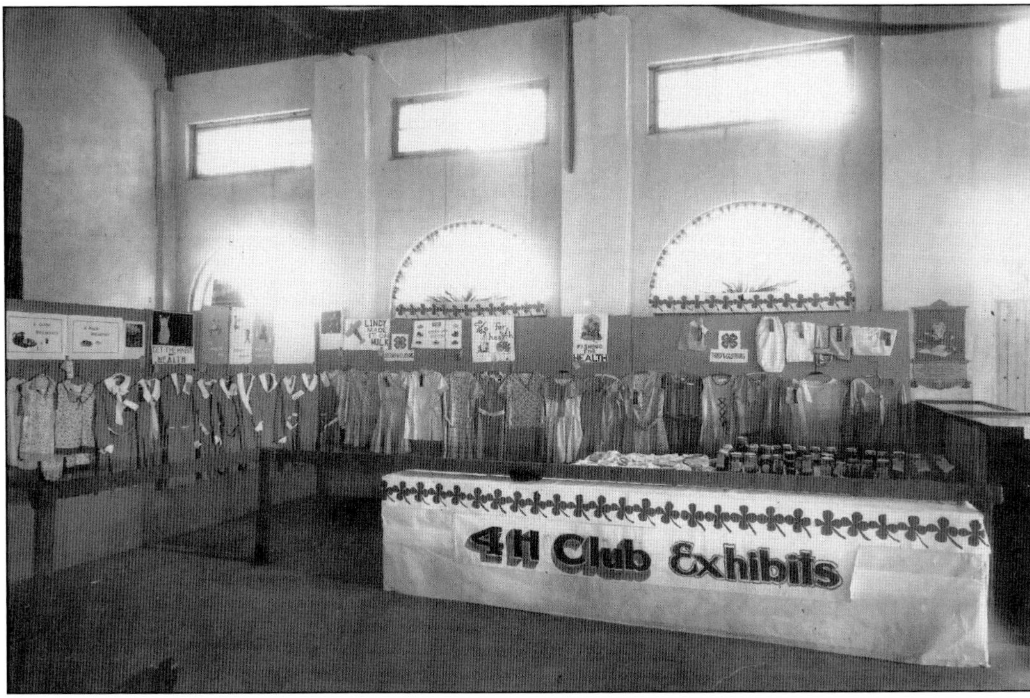

The 4-H Club is a continued activity for children and young adults on the high plains farm and ranch land. Prizes are given for best pies, pigs, lambs, and clothes. Pictured below, dresses are being shown in the Hoover Pavilion at Wright Park, c. 1990.

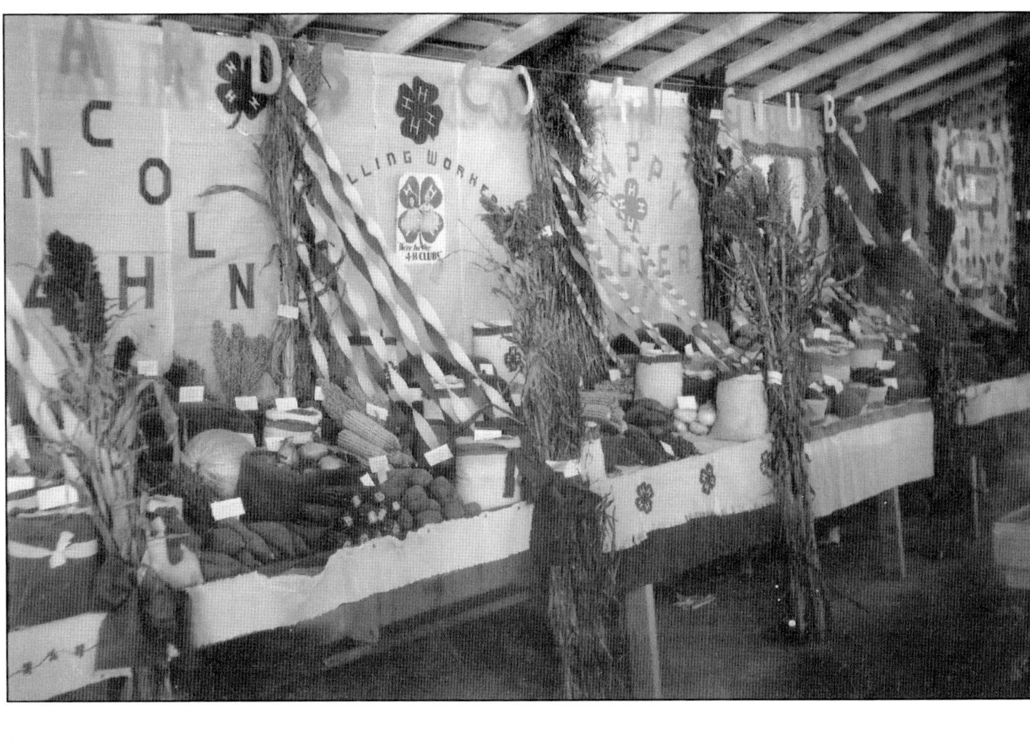

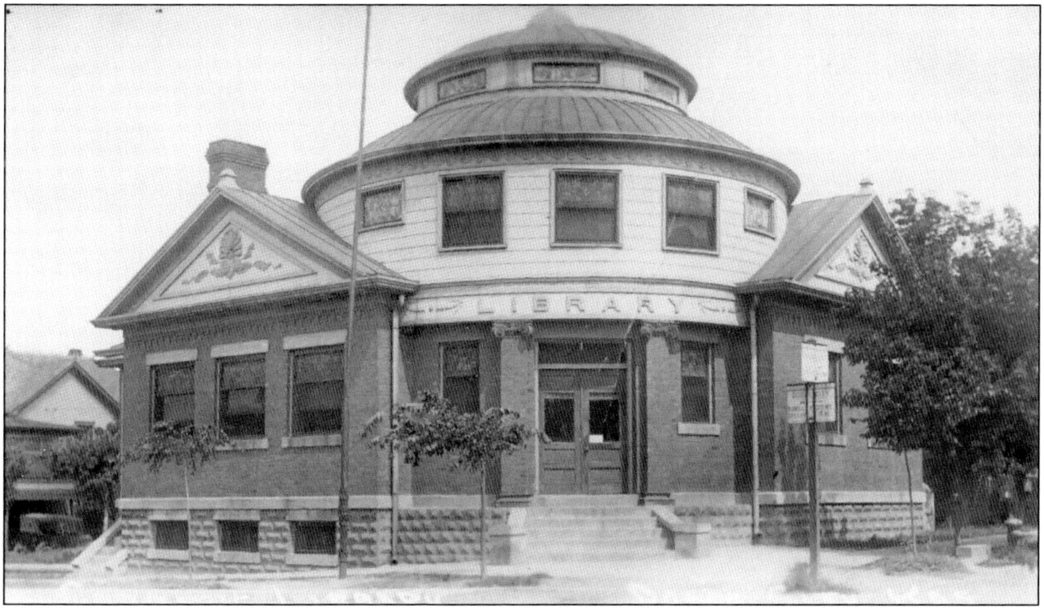

Andrew Carnegie wrote to Judge Madison on February 1, 1905, stating he would give $7,500 for a library building (an amount later increased to $8,500). The funds were matched by Dodge City. C.W. Squires of Emporia was the architect, the contractor was William Foley, W.B. Rhoads performed the cement work, Sturgeon Brothers provided the brick, and Tieffenbach Brothers did the interior decoration. The library opened to the public on February 1, 1907. The 500-square-foot, one-story addition to the west, completed in 1937, used $5,843.55 of Works Progress Administration federal funds. The building is a rare round-type, of which only a few remain in existence, with a Depression-era addition. It is now the Dodge City Area Arts Council Carnegie Center.

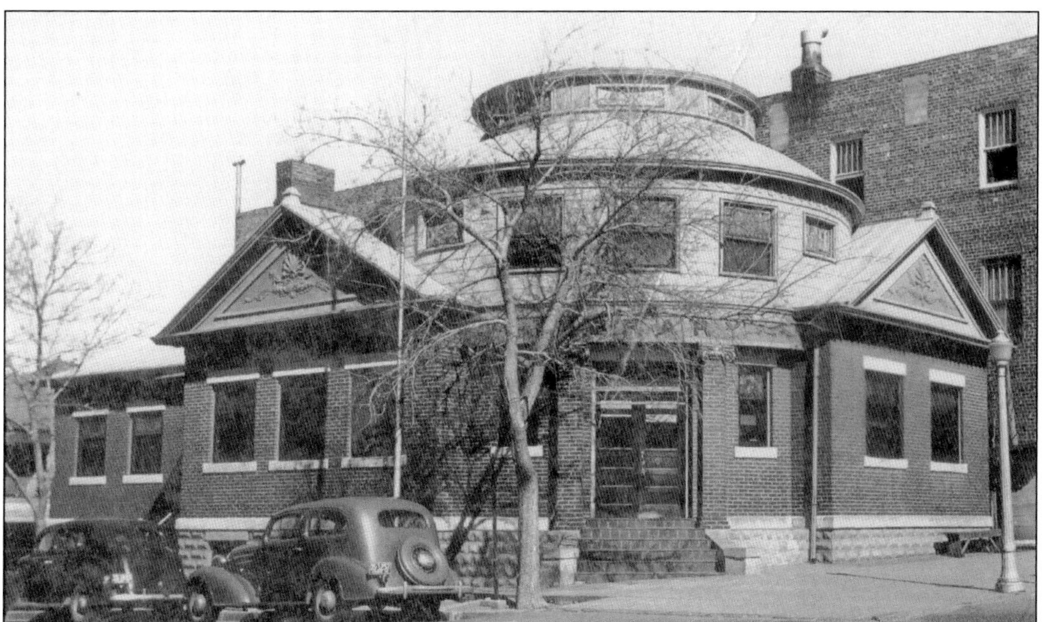

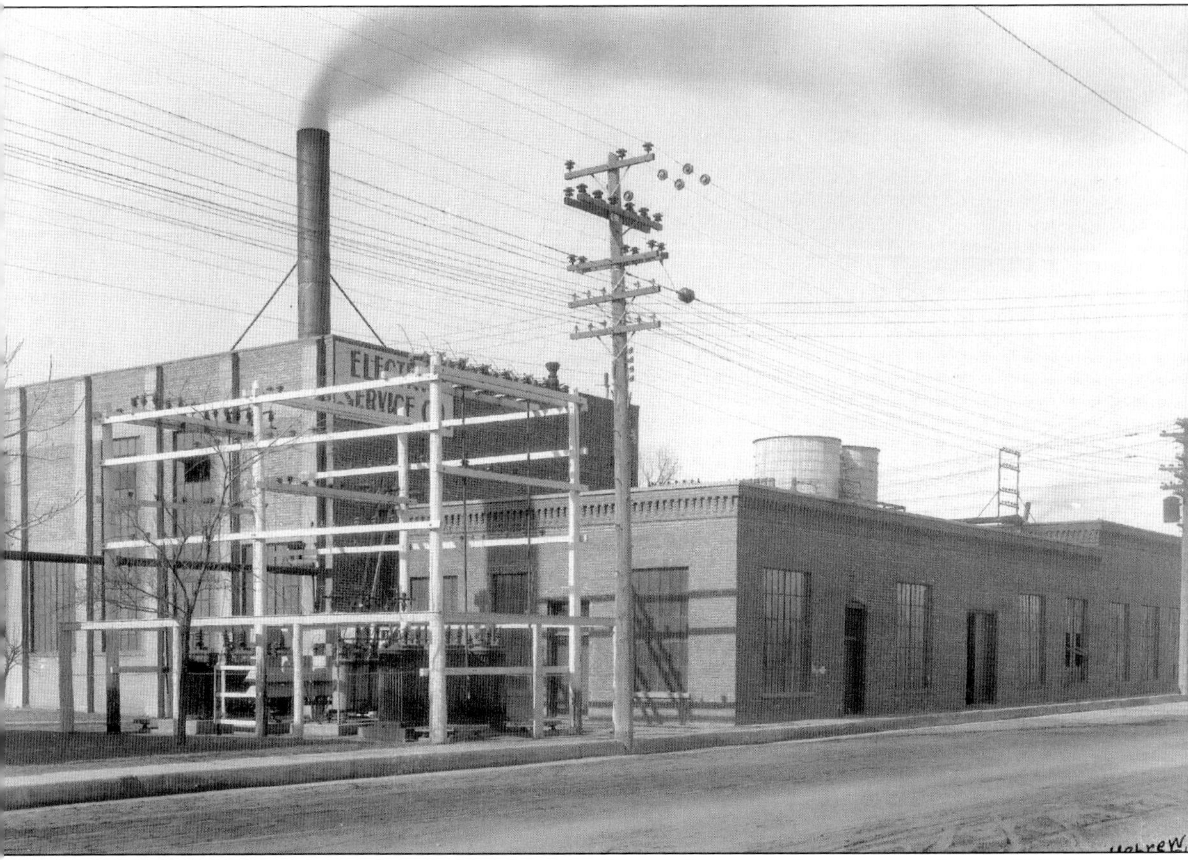

The establishment of a full power plant, complete with an ice plant, came after a 1925 charter between Dodge City and Kansas Power Company (Electric Service Company). The power station is pictured from the northwest, where it was located on Trail Street. The 22,000-volt substation appears in the foreground. This supplied the city with power.

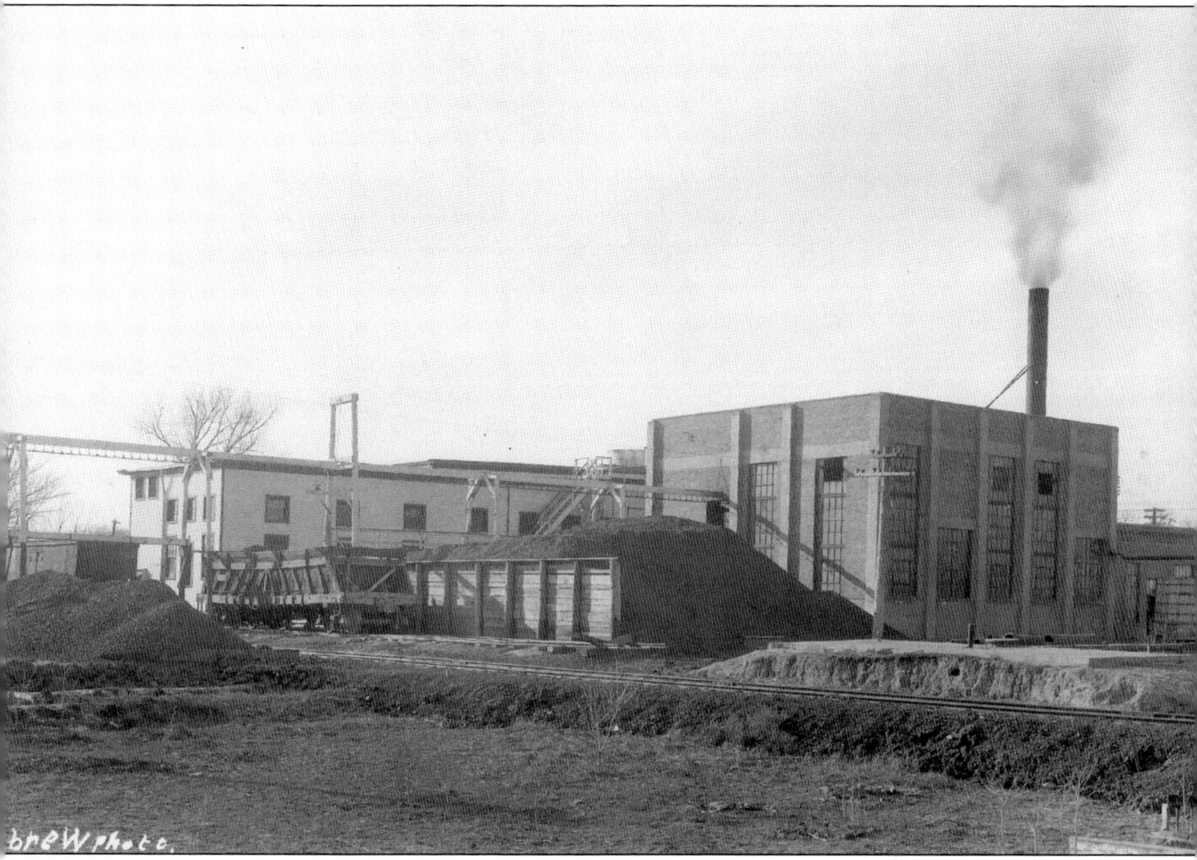

The boiler house and ice plant are shown as viewed from the southeast. During the ice season, 34 tons of pure crystal ice was manufactured daily in the frame building in the left background. A major portion of ice made in Dodge City went to the Santa Fe railroad, both for dining cars and freight storage.

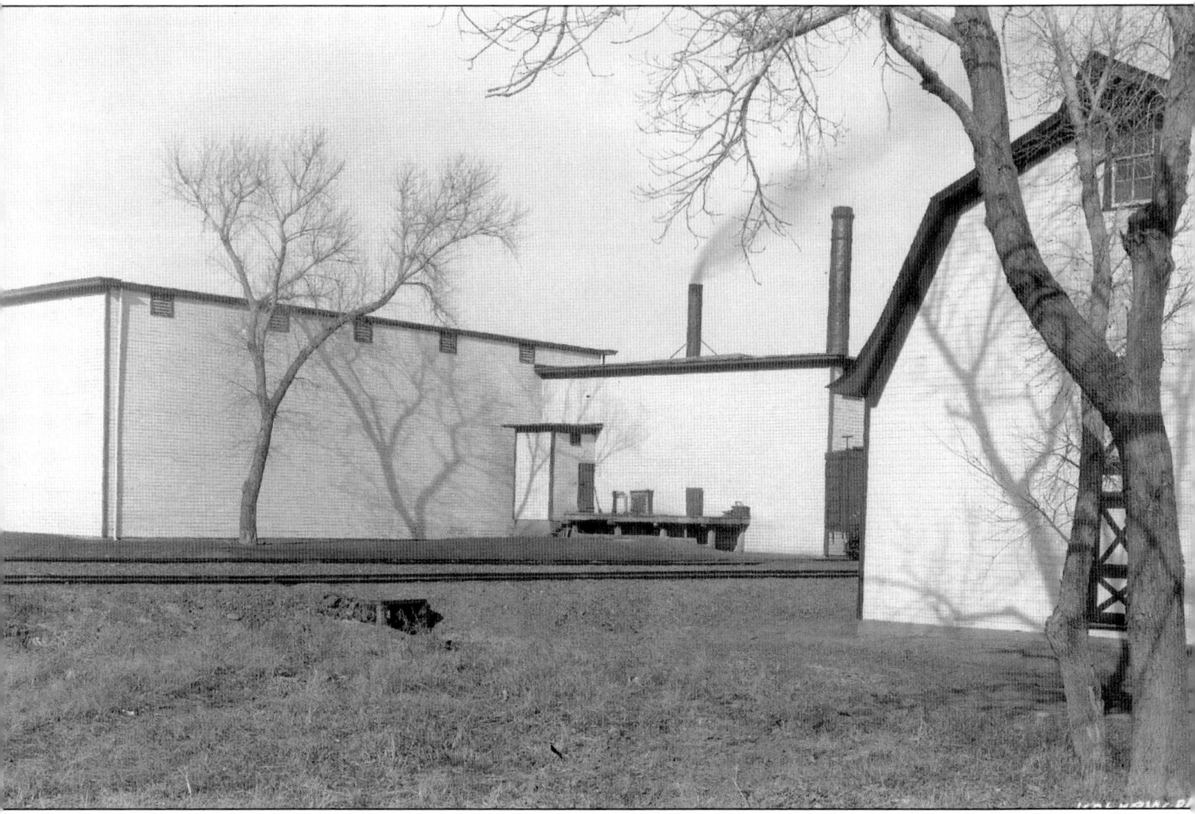

This view of the ice plant is visible from the southwest. On the left is the 1,100-ton ice storage room. Ice was delivered to wagons and trucks from the dock in the center. A portion of the barn that stored ice delivery equipment shown is on the right.

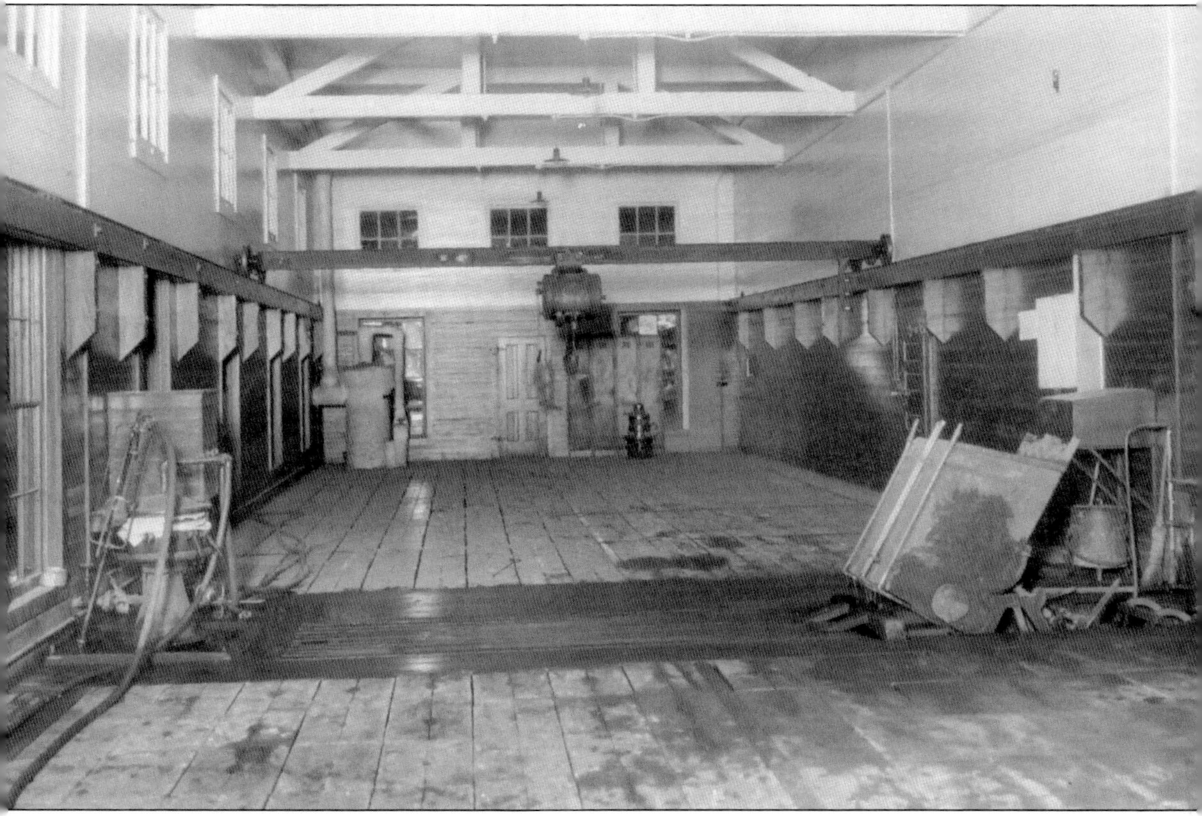

This is the interior of the ice manufacturing plant. Under each cover on the floor was a galvanized iron can in which 300-pound cakes of ice were frozen. The overhead electric crane hoisted two of these cakes at a time and placed them in the can dump at the right, then they discharged into an ice storage room.

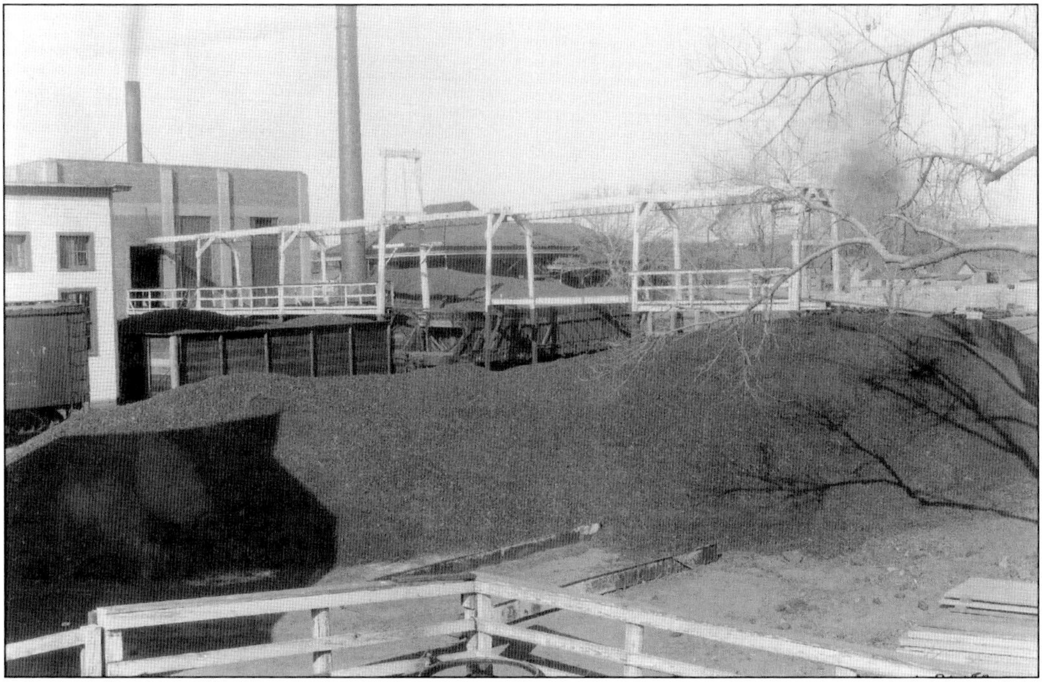

A three months' supply of coal was maintained at the power plant in an 1,800-ton coal storage area. The power company noted, "An effort is made to maintain three month's supply of coal, in order that we may not be shut down on account of railway strikes, coal strikes, floods, etc." Below, a worker unloads cinders from an electric hoist into a cinder car. Approximately four cars were loaded monthly with the cinders from the boiler fire.

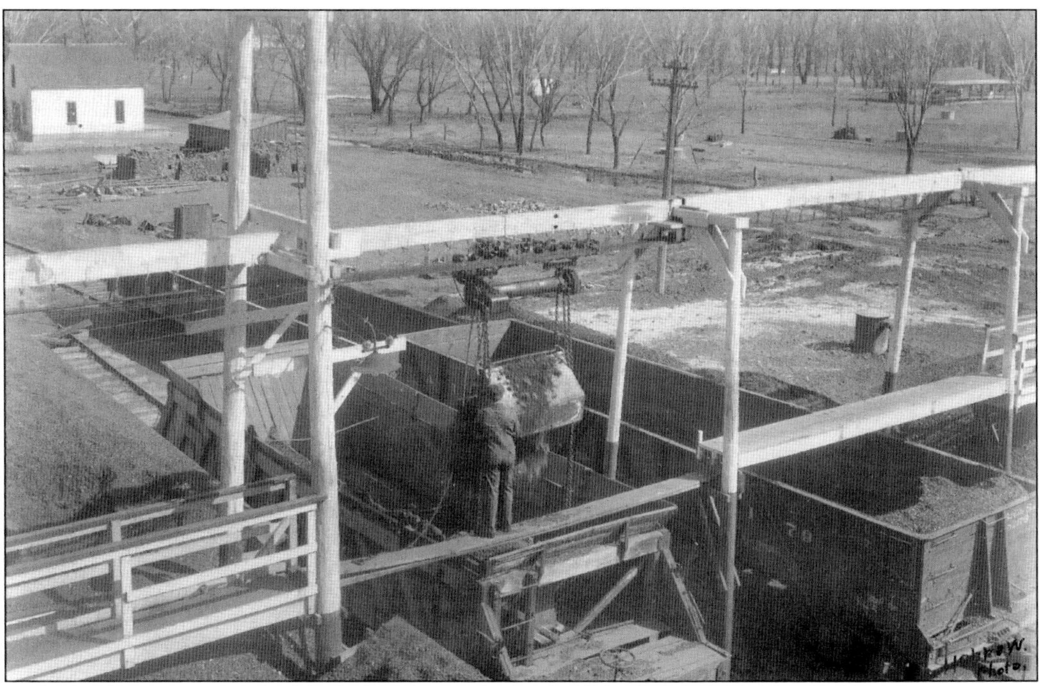

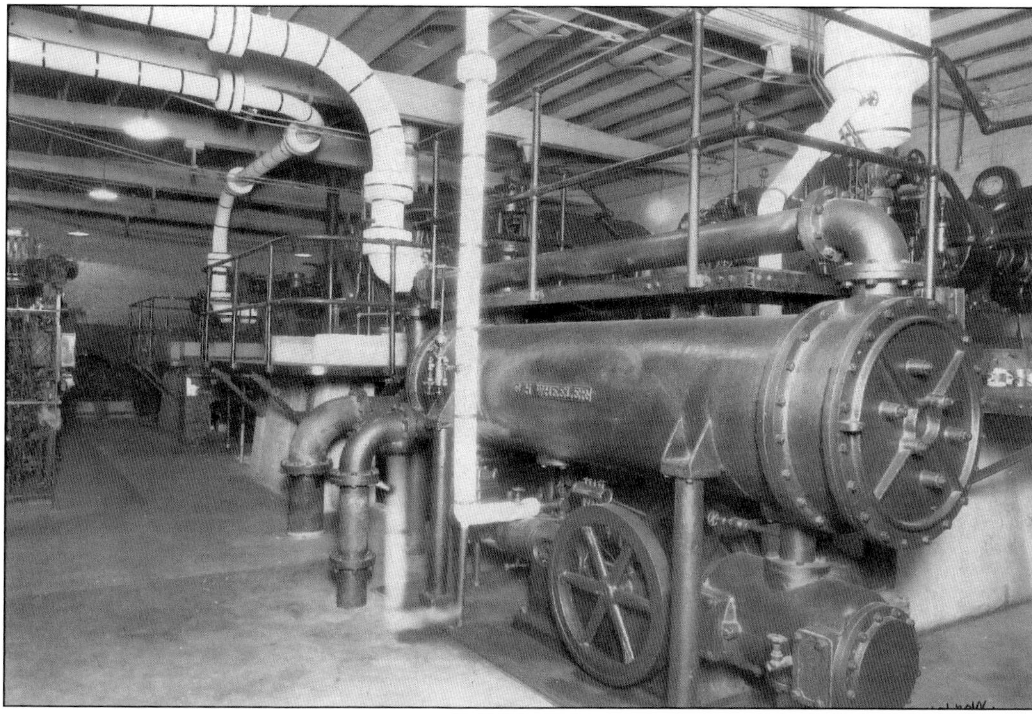

Three turbine generator sets are shown as white pipes bring in steam in the photograph above. In the foreground is a fourth small turbine generator set and condenser. In the photograph below is the switchboard that controlled delivery of all electrical energy produced. All current sent out from the plant was metered by the instruments shown on the board. Automatic switches cut off any line that had trouble; a bell alarm was used to immediately warn the engineer.

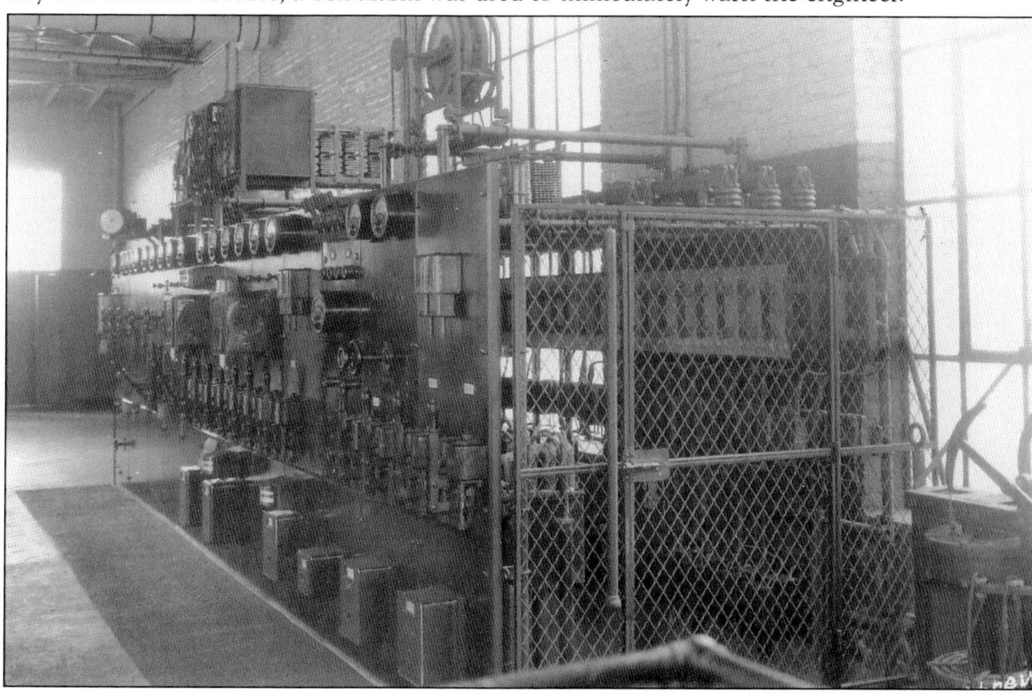

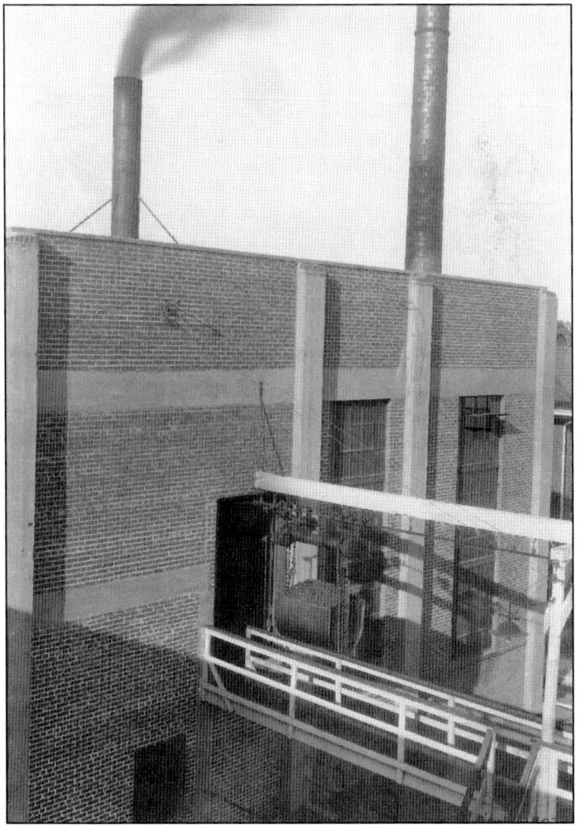

Coal was unloaded out of railway cars into the bucket shown in the photograph at left. It was hoisted and conveyed along the overhead monorail and dumped into hoppers in front of the boilers. The photograph below shows the electric and ice manufacturing plant operating crew. Employees were paid a bonus for efficient and economical operation, as noted by the company.

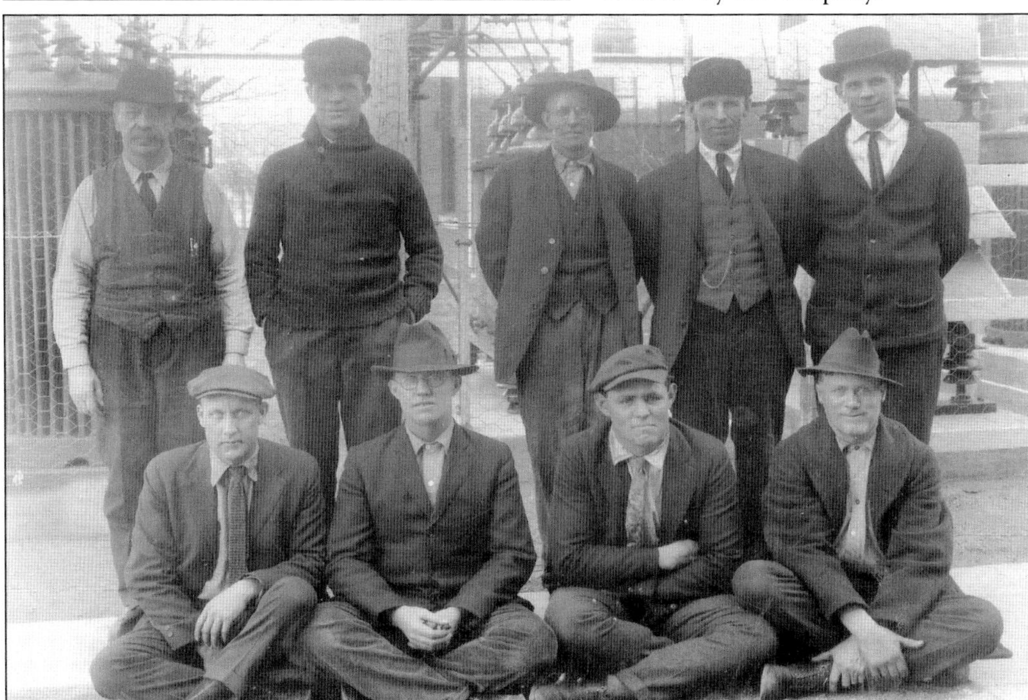

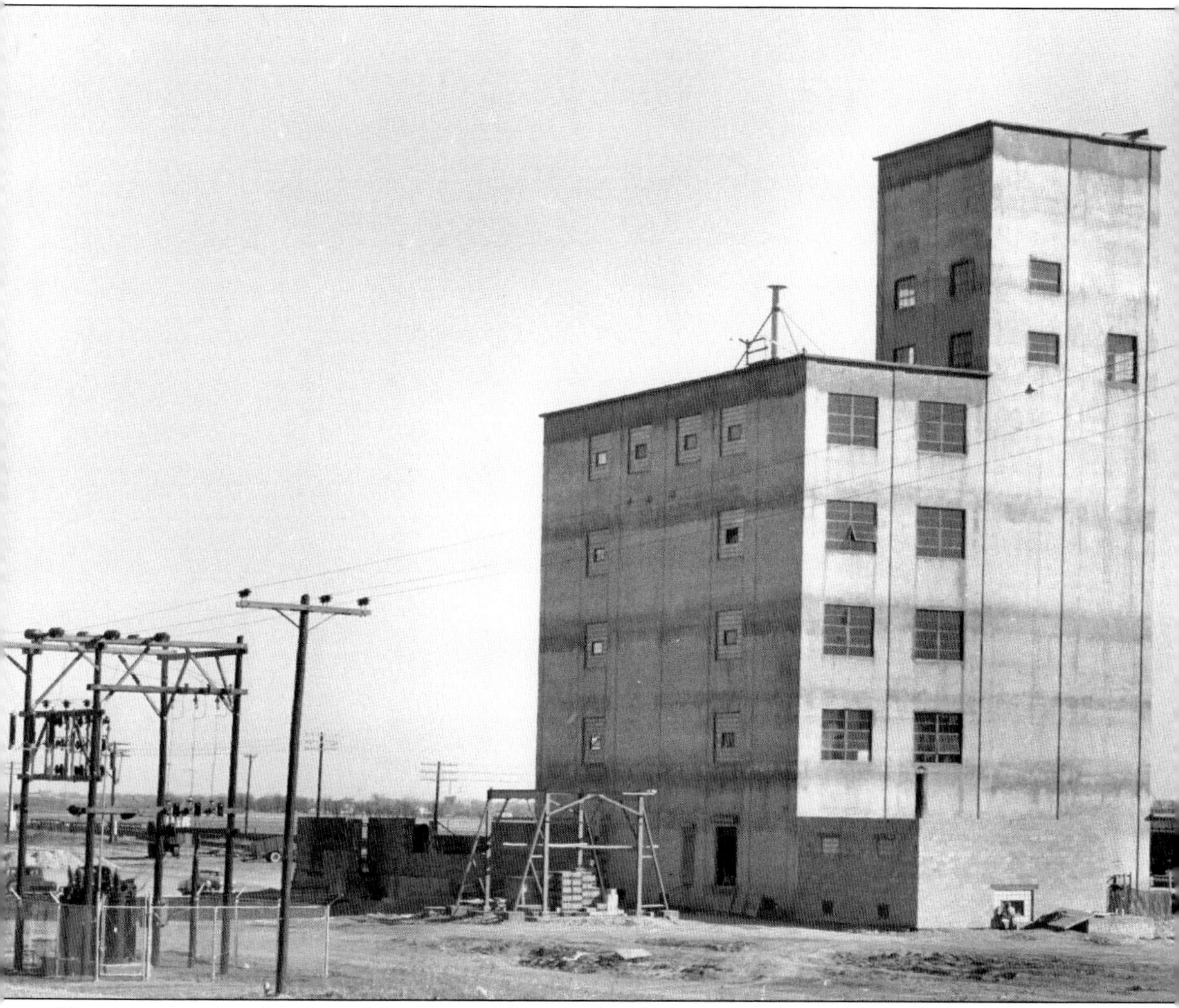

Shown is an outside view of the power plant and icehouse near the Arkansas River. Ice and electricity made modern life possible; Dodge City had both early on. The river was cut up for ice in early days, and it was stored in a stone icehouse under sawdust for the summer.

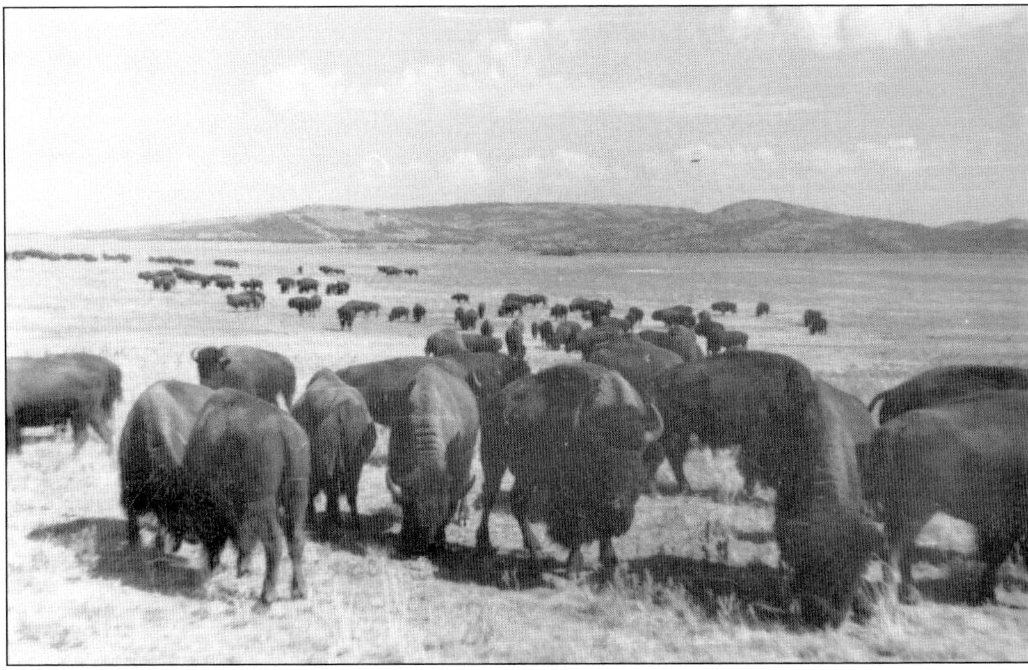

A Bison herd (American buffalo) is pictured near Dodge City in 1929. In *The Destruction of the Bison,* historian Andrew Isenberg wrote, "A spasm of industrial expansion was the primary cause of the bison's near-extinction in the 1870s and early 1880s. During this period, Euroamericans hunted bison to satisfy an increasing demand for hides in industrializing America. Leather belts were the sinews of nineteenth-century industrial production: mills relied on heavy leather belting to animate their machinery." Charles Rath at Rath City, Texas, (near Hamlin) killed off the southern herd. The Rath Trail was the only one established for buffalo hunters, going from Dodge City to Rath City.

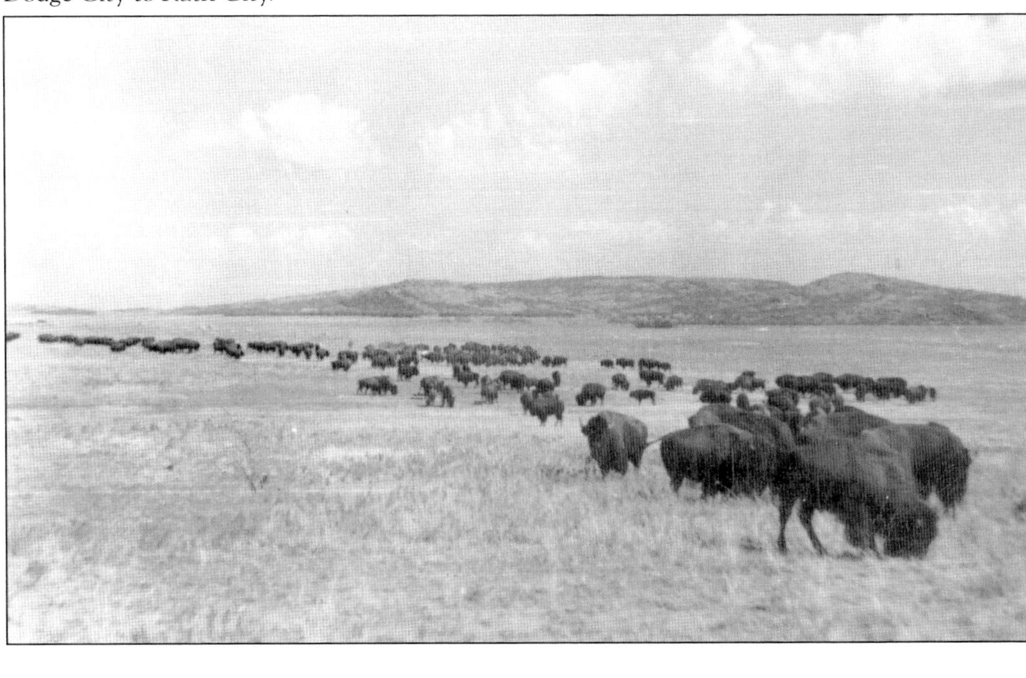

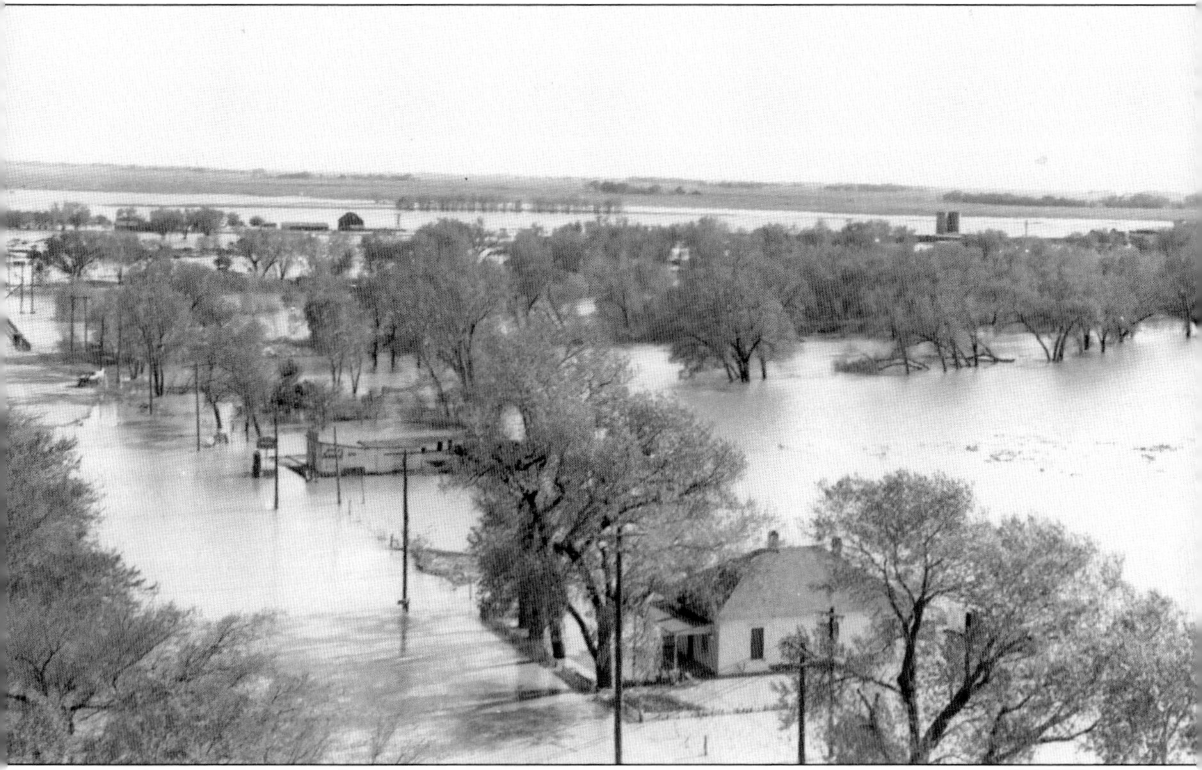

An Arkansas River flood is visible in this c. 1930 photograph, looking south with the Second Street bridge in the center. Written on the back of this photograph is the following: "Fire, Floods, Tornadoes and hell in general is what we have been getting here in Dodge City. If the government wants my car, they can have it—busted glass, ragged tires, back seat driver and all. Here it shows south Dodge all under water. Francis's house was so full of water that it came up to the mattresses in the beds. Well what can you expect?" The Arkansas River flooded every decade or so, until a huge and final flood occurred in 1965. After that, the river was dammed in Colorado at the John Martin Reservoir, and massive increases in irrigation all along the river in Kansas caused the water to disappear. The Arkansas River in Dodge City has been a sand bed for years. It comes back into view before Great Bend, Kansas.

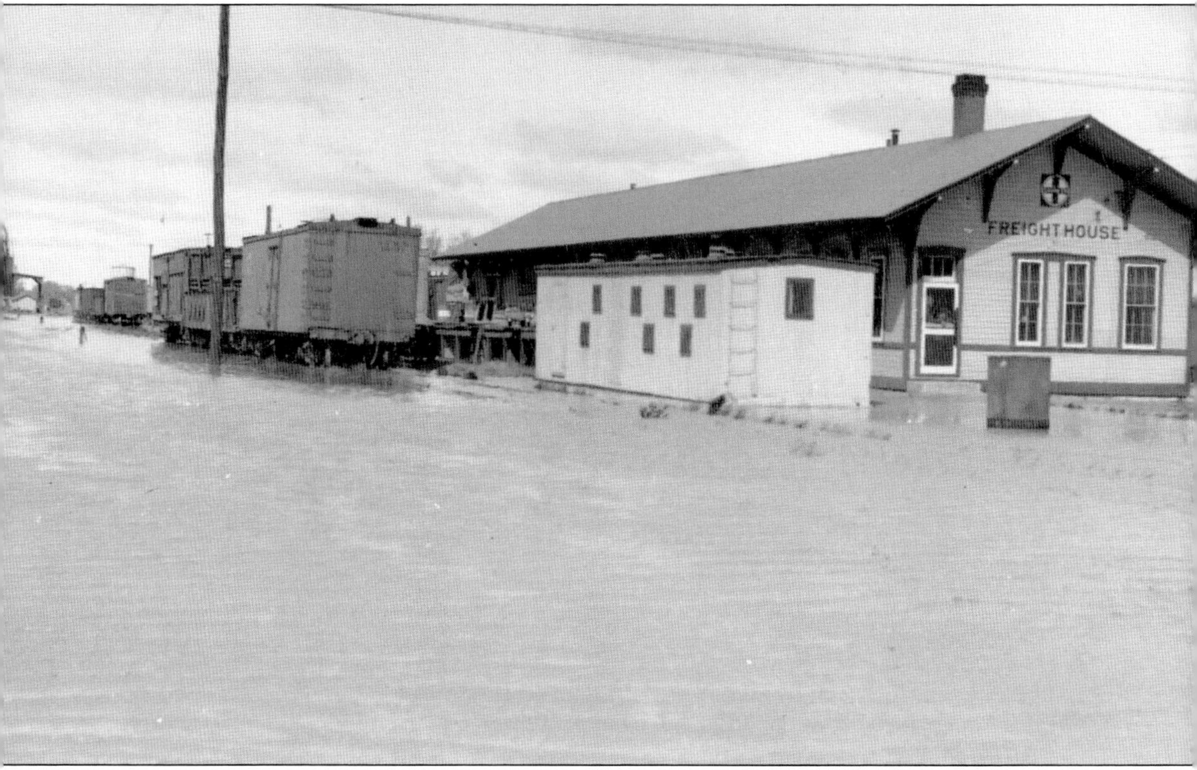

The Atchison, Topeka & Santa Fe Railroad freight house is pictured here around 1930. Restored, it is now home to a restaurant. Looking north, the flooded Arkansas River has covered the tracks. Front Street is the next street to the north. The location of Dodge City was based on the Fort Dodge reservation western edge and the train tracks at the 100th meridian border of the Louisiana Purchase. Dodge City was truly at the edge of the US territory. Written on the photograph is a version of an old song: "Look over yonder, sure as you're born / Cows on the rampage, pigs in the corn / Start across the meadows, run a mile or two / Heaving like I'm wind broken, wet clean through / Work all summer till winter is nigh / Then figure at the bank, then have a big sigh / Worked all year and didn't make a thing / Less money now then I had last spring / Some folks say there haint no hell / Never lived in Dodge, so how can they tell?"

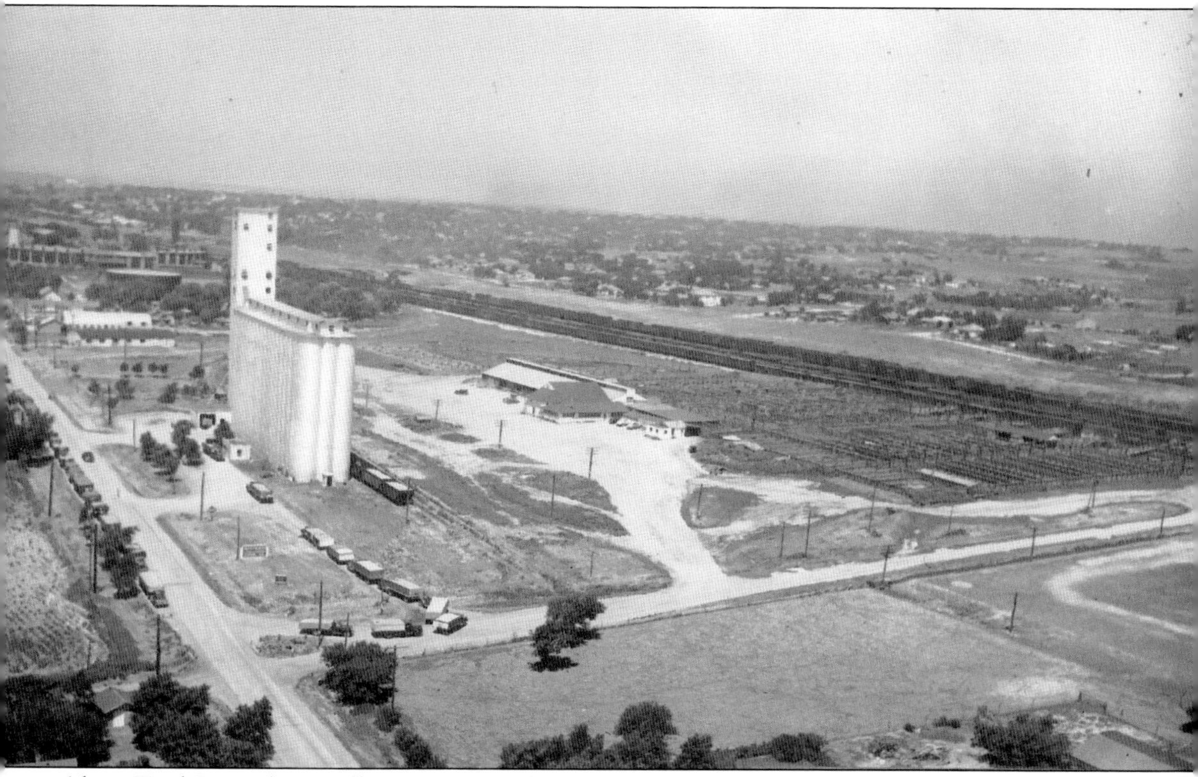

Along Trail Street (originally Santa Fe Trail Street), grain trucks line up at the terminal elevator to unload wheat during harvest season around 1950. The old railroad roundhouse, now gone, can be seen in the upper left. The photograph faces west-northwest, with the McKinley-Winter cattle sales pavilion and stockyards in the center. The railroad tracks are to the northwest, and the east side of Dodge City is in the upper right. Cattle were shipped to Kansas City or Chicago for slaughter until the 1970s, when the first of the huge meat factories and slaughterhouses opened in Dodge City. Now, more than 10,000 cattle a day are killed in Ford County.

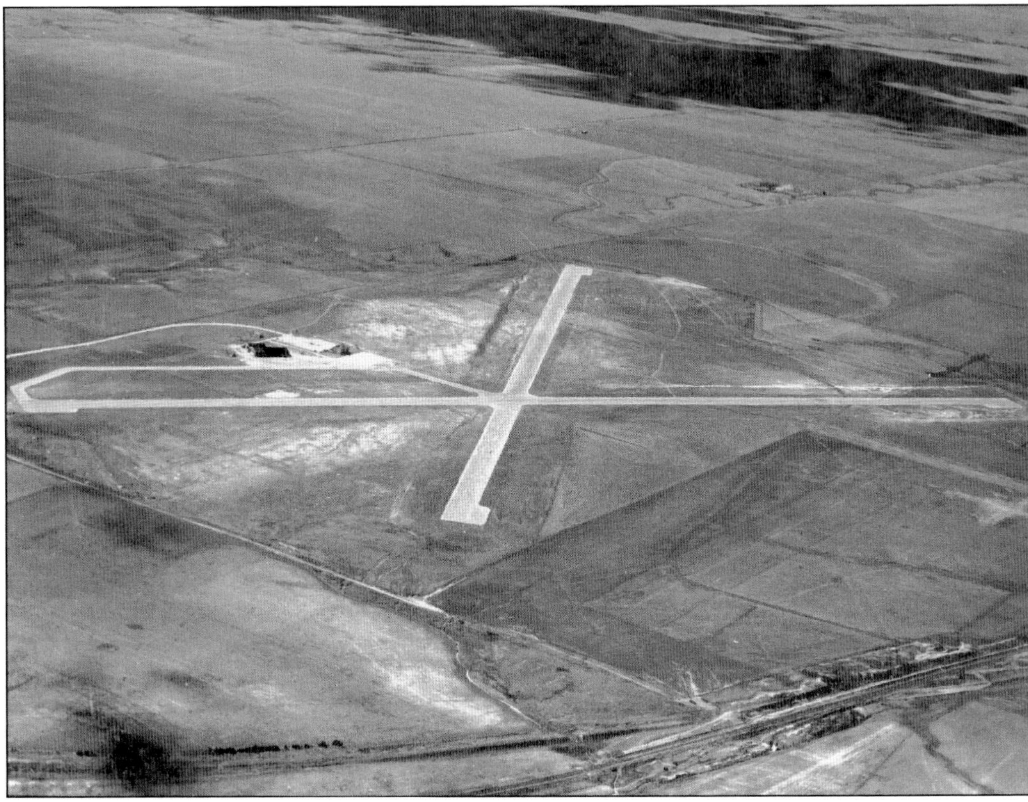

The Dodge City airport was built in the 1930s on land purchased with money left by Dodge City's first merchant, George M. Hoover. The Works Progress Administration (WPA) built a terminal out of river rocks. There was a restaurant for many years in the second floor of the terminal.

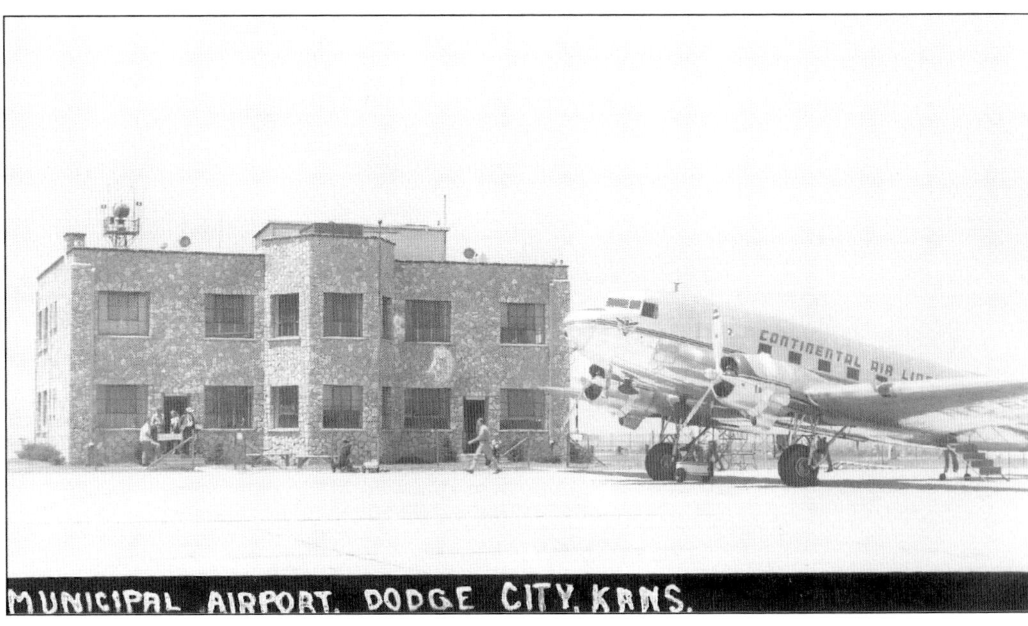

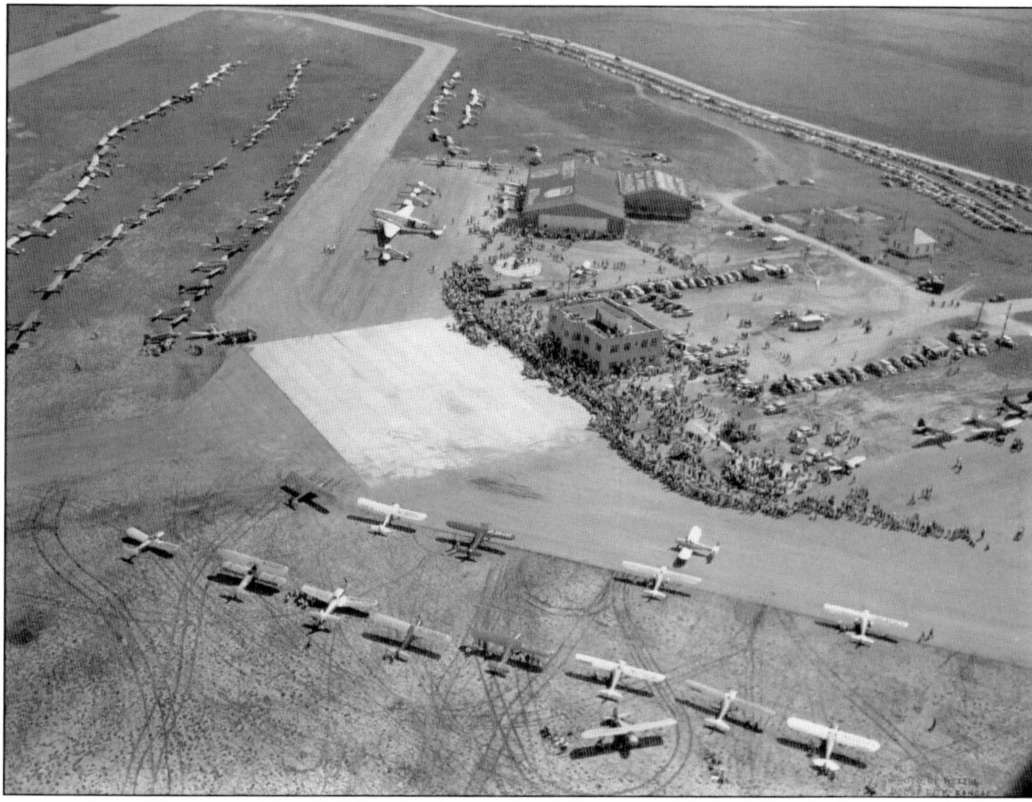

Pictured is a fly-in after World War II, when a large Army air base was built west of Dodge City. Many bombers were trained at the base, and the Dodge City airport was involved. This event was after the war, but note the Army Nissen Quonset huts being used.

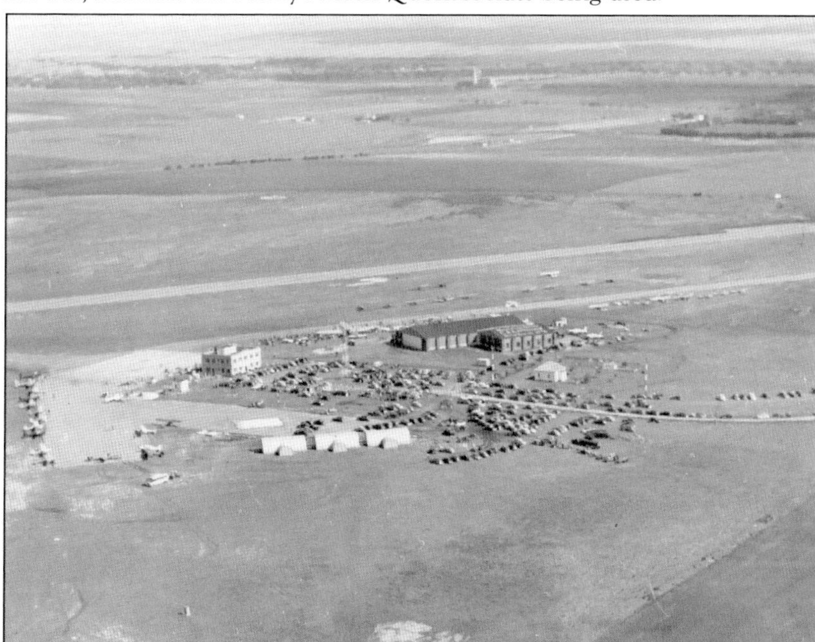

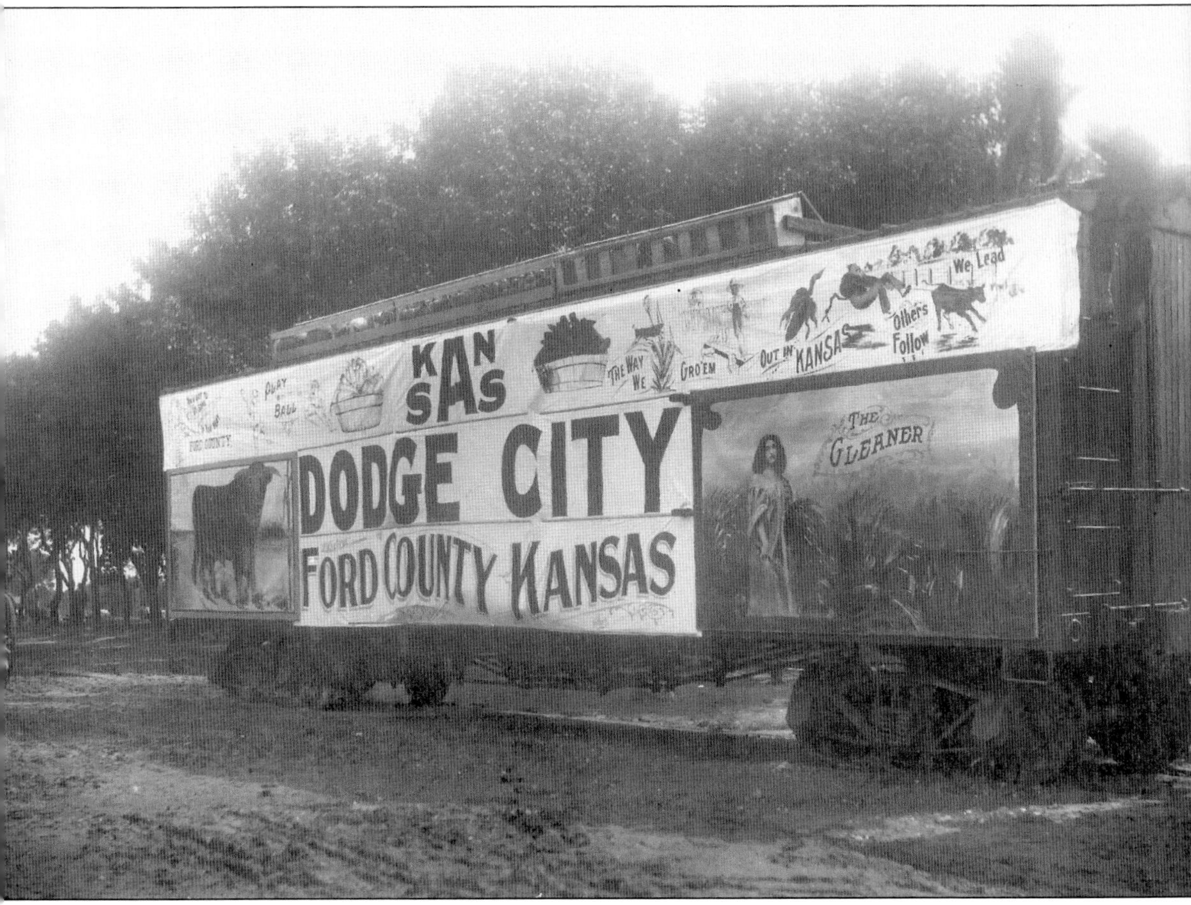

Southwest Kansas and Dodge City have long promoted area advantages, including crops, the black dirt, and even baseball. Here, a train car is pictured with a huge advertisement for Dodge City on the side.

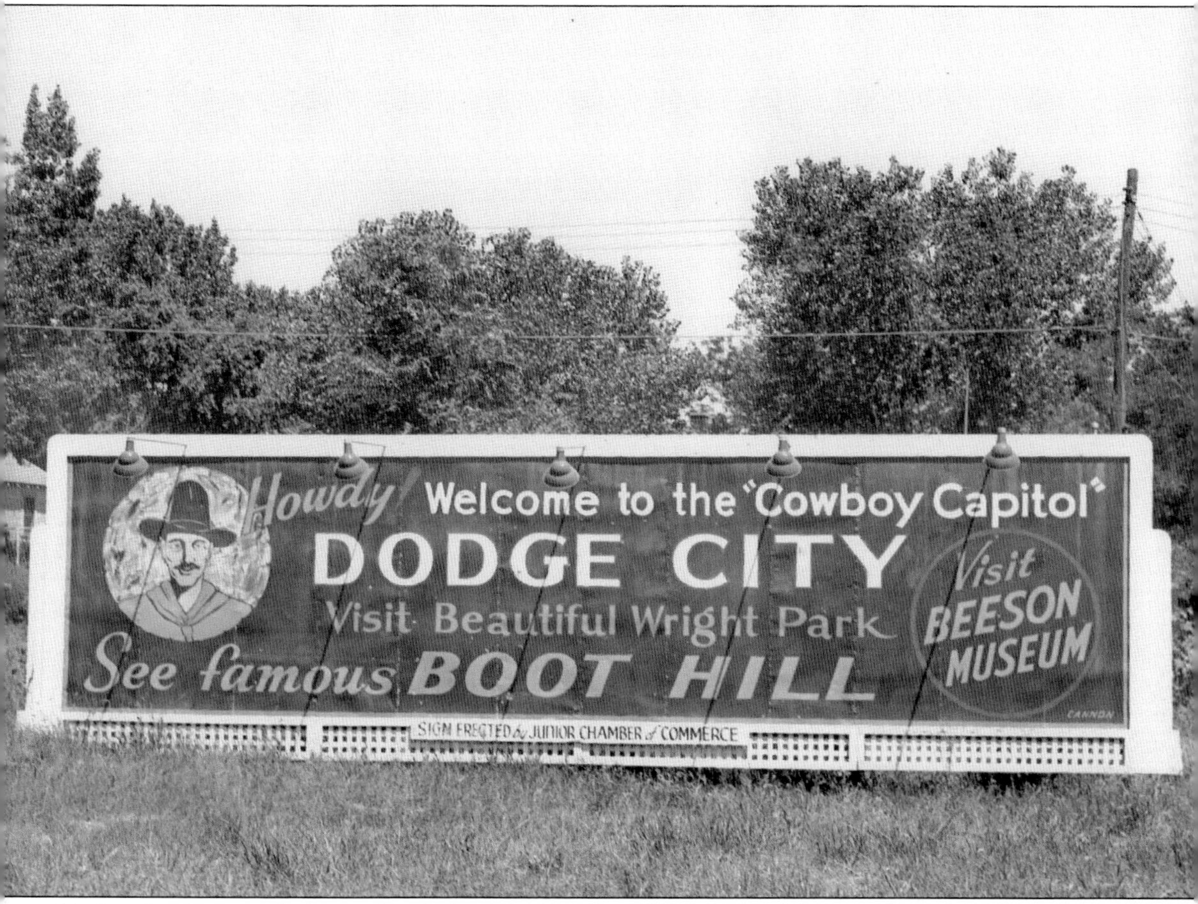

Dodge City became lost in a cloud of myth as early as the 1890s and became famous in the 1930s after the publication of Stuart Lake's book in 1931, *Wyatt Earp, Frontier Marshal*. Lake's true belief in the Wyatt Earp he knew started an Old West revival that created decades of Western books, movies, and television.

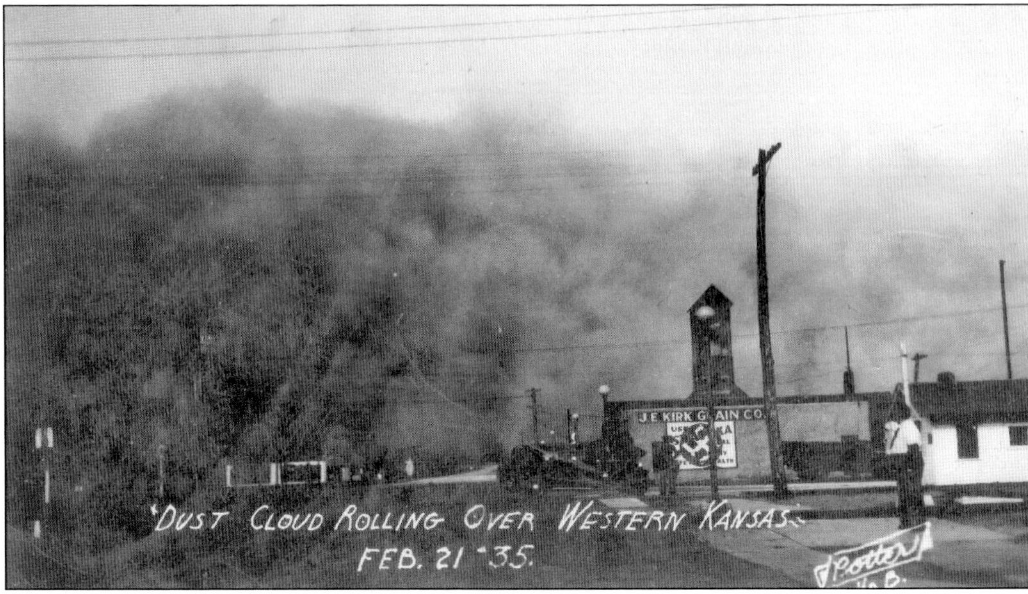

The Dust Bowl started over a period of several years, but by 1935, it grew each month. This photograph, taken in February, does not reveal the total damages. Twenty-five percent of Ford County residents moved in the next year, and a third of the deaths in southwest Kansas hospitals were dust related.

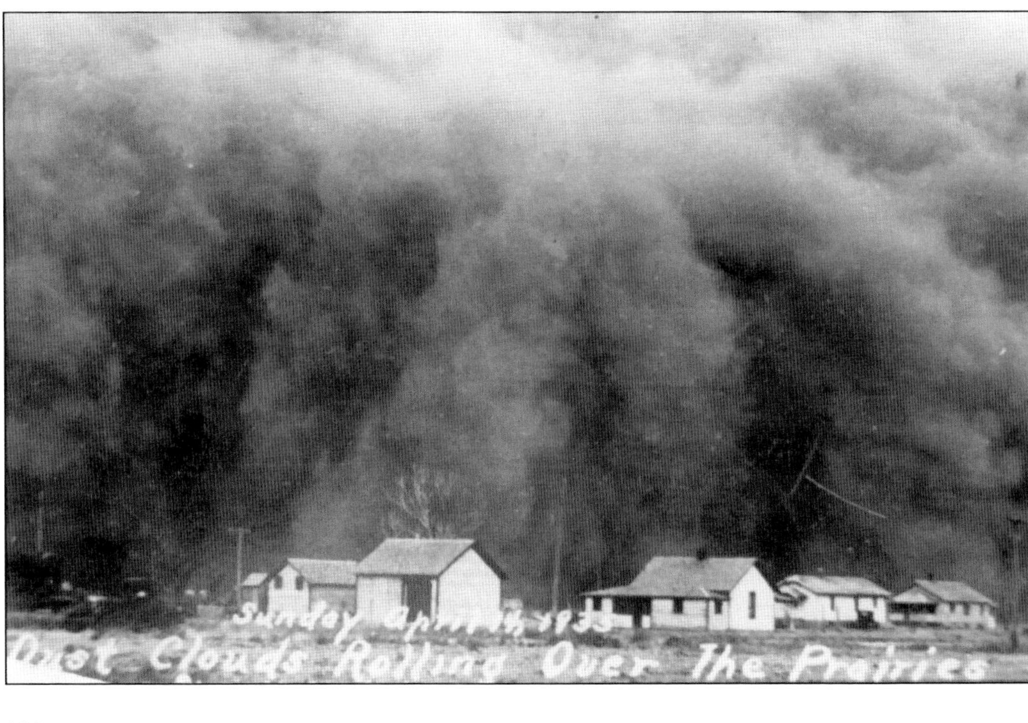

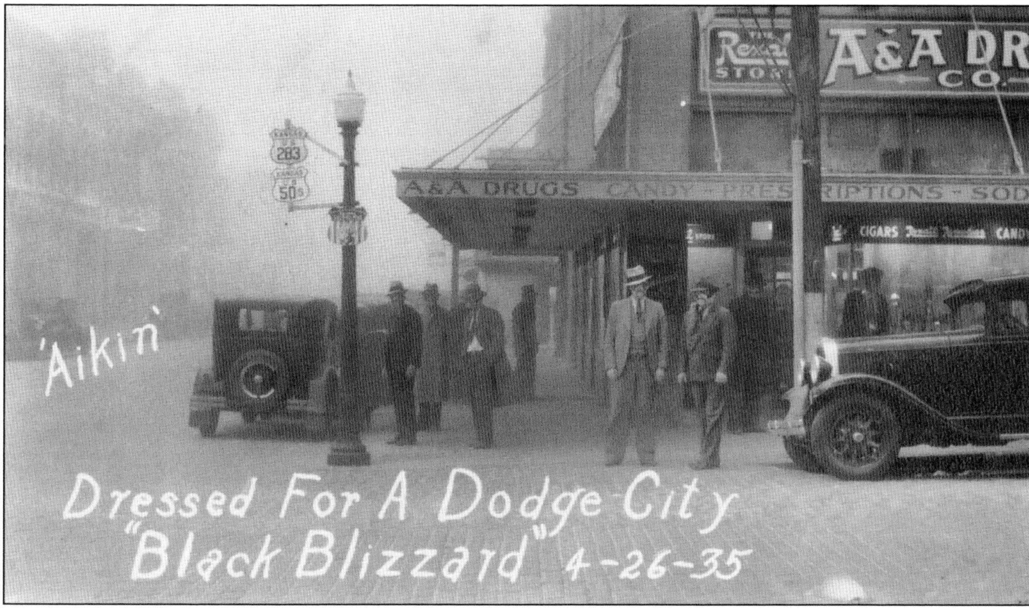

April brought Black Sunday, April 14, 1935, which holds the dust record. A few days later, the businessmen of Dodge City were using gas masks during their work day. Any opening in a house, whether window or keyhole, allowed piles of dust to gather each day. The man-made dust bowl started a drive for better management of farmland during the late 1930s.

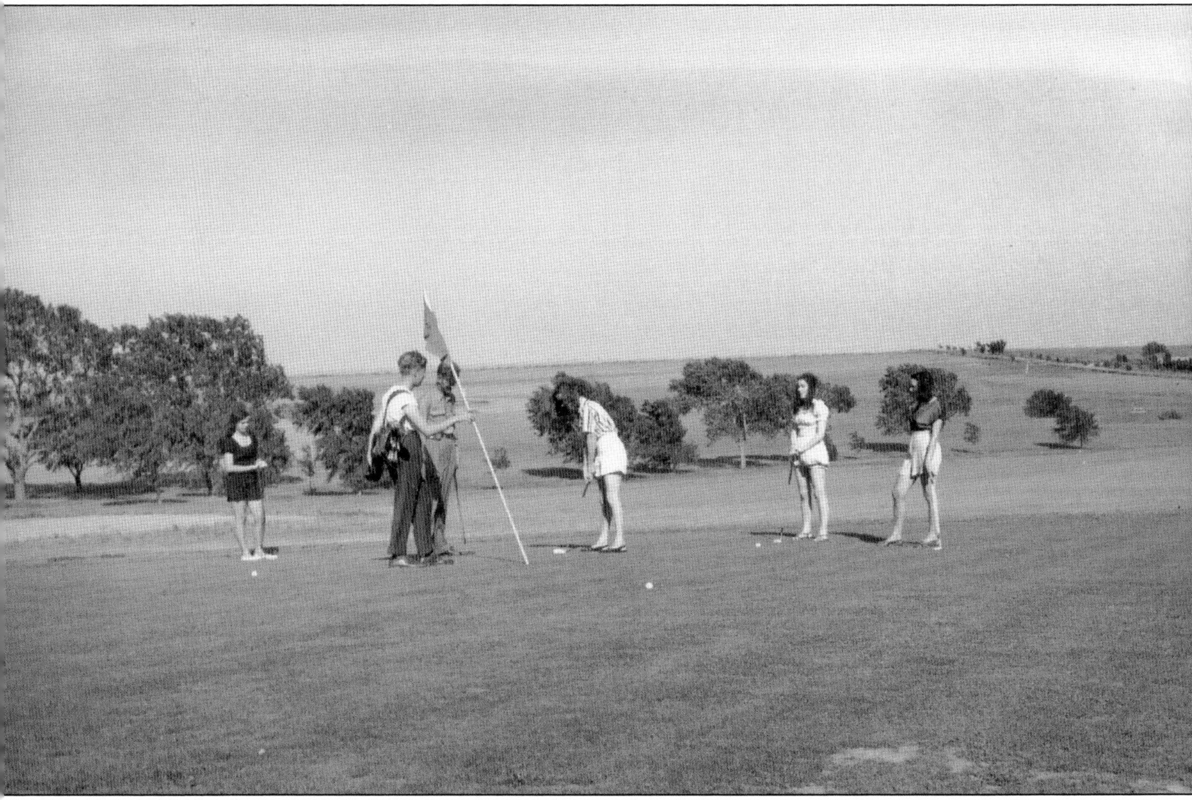

The sports of southwest Kansas include golf, allowed through massive use of water, and originally sand greens. A woman's golf class is shown here around 1950.

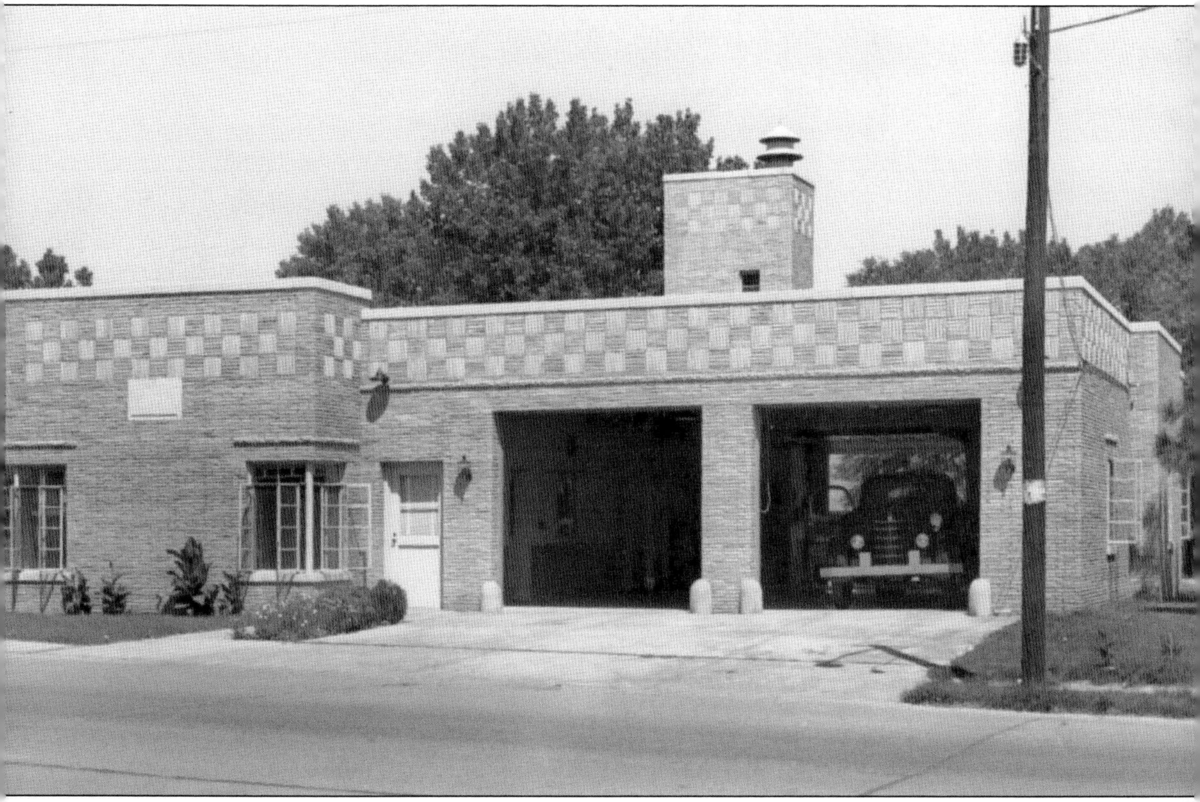

The growth of Dodge City included this fire station, built south of the Arkansas River by the bridge. The building still stands, having been used as a church and a car repair shop among other businesses.

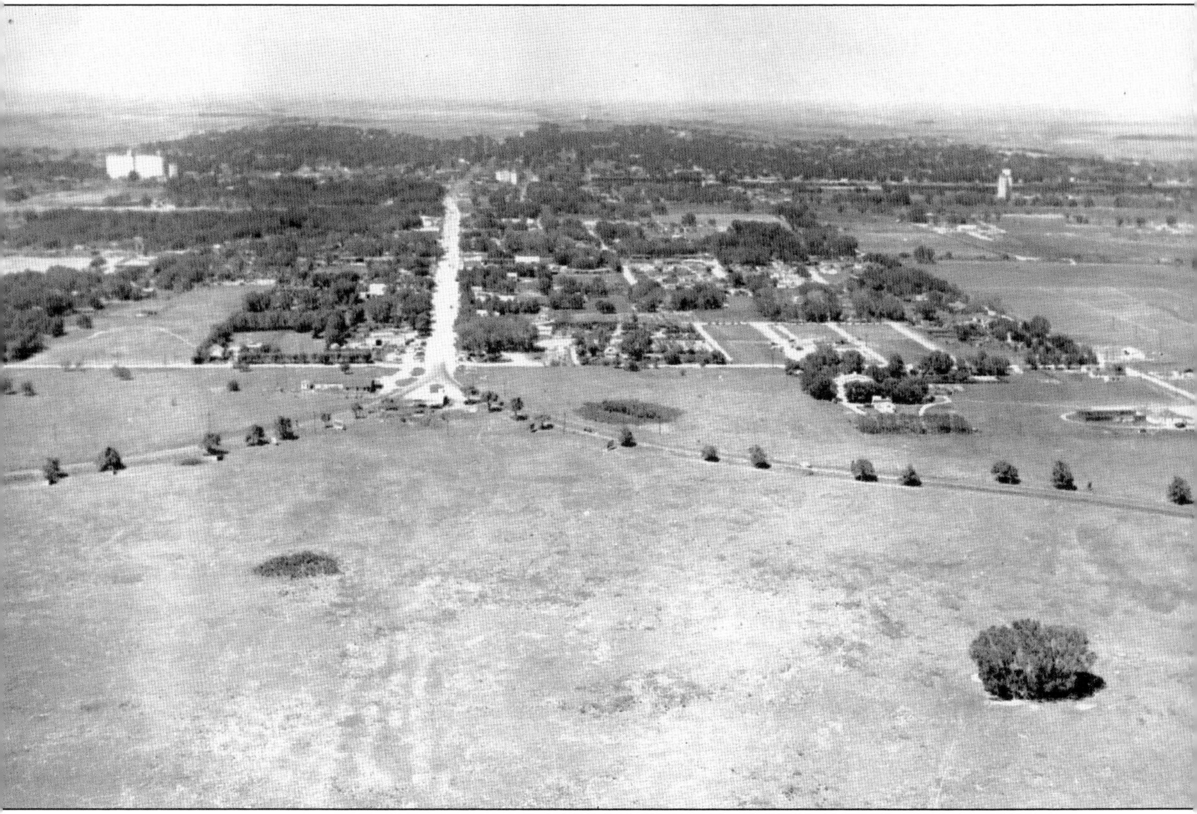

The south end of Dodge City is visible up Second Street to the north around 1950. Note that the town ended where the highways divided.

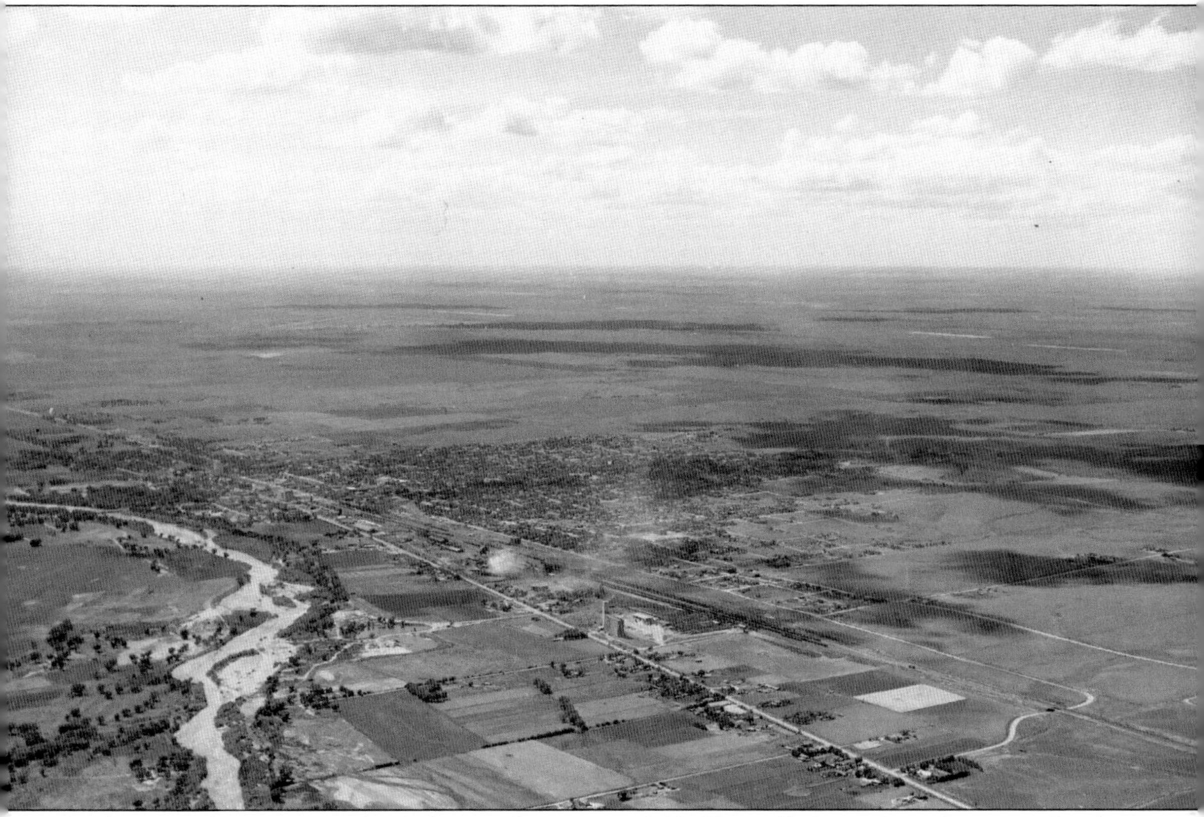

Looking northwest across the Arkansas (pronounced "Ar-Kansas") River from the east side of Dodge City around 1950, the Hoover Grain Mill and other grain elevators are the large white objects. Most of the town is towards the top right of the photograph.

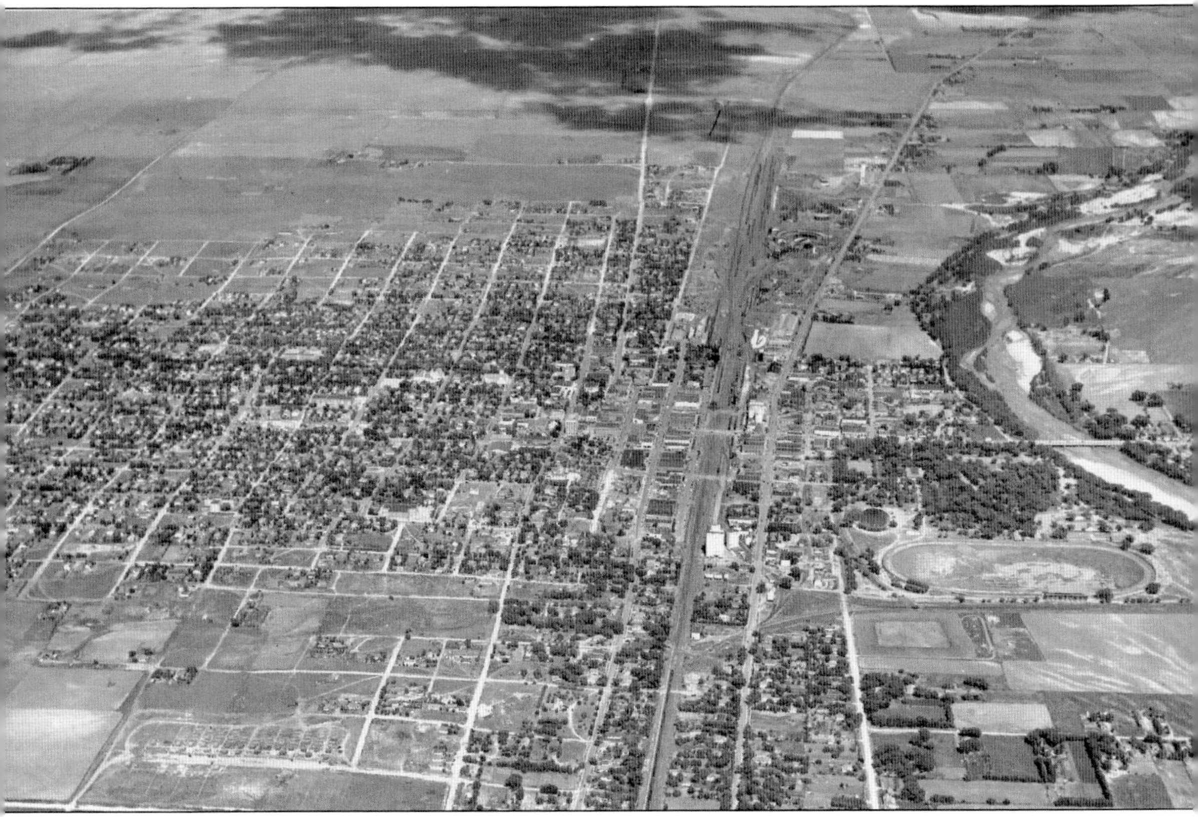

Dodge City appears in this c. 1946 photograph facing east with the Arkansas River on the right side. The world-famous McCarty racetrack is on the lower right, part of Wright Park. The flood of 1965 forced the national motorcycle races to move out of Dodge City. No deaths were recorded at races on McCarty Speedway, which featured two dirt tracks—a half-mile track for motorcycles and horses and a quarter-mile track for cars.

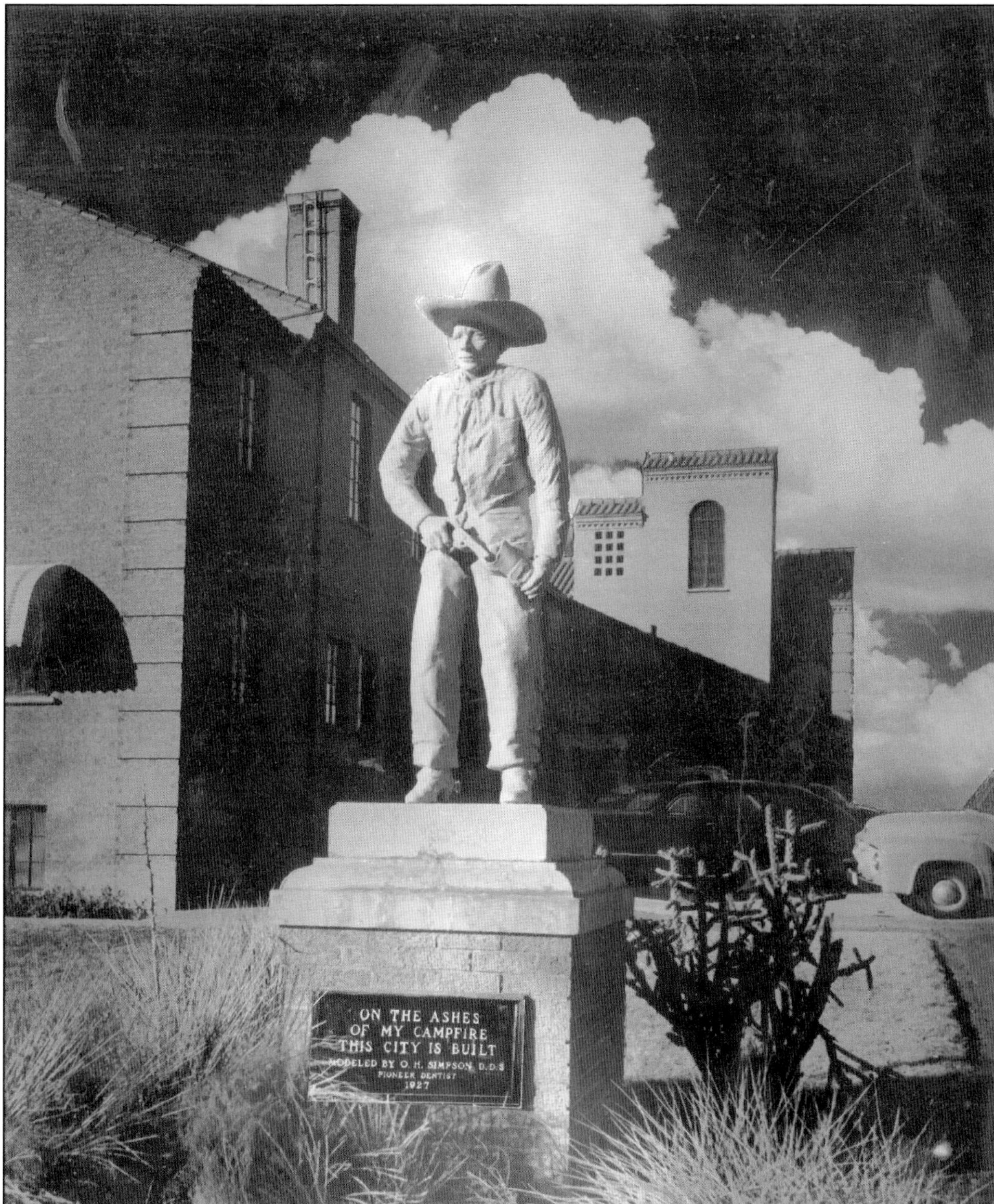

Dr. Oscar Simpson, DDS, pioneer Dodge City dentist and inventor of the gold inlay process for filling teeth (patent finally won in 1912), had his old pioneer lawman friend, Joe Sughrue, lay in a box while a mold was made with plaster. Dr. Simpson filled the mold with concrete. The statue has been on Boot Hill since 1929. Dr. Simpson also made the first Boot Hill tombstones for tourists to view. When Simpson arrived in Dodge City by train, his tall silk hat was the target of a bucket of water from a Front Street bartender. Story goes that Simpson picked up a rock, threw it back and broke the cut glass from the bar back. Dr. John Henry Holliday is the most famous Dodge City dentist, although "Doc" Holliday was in the city only a summer.

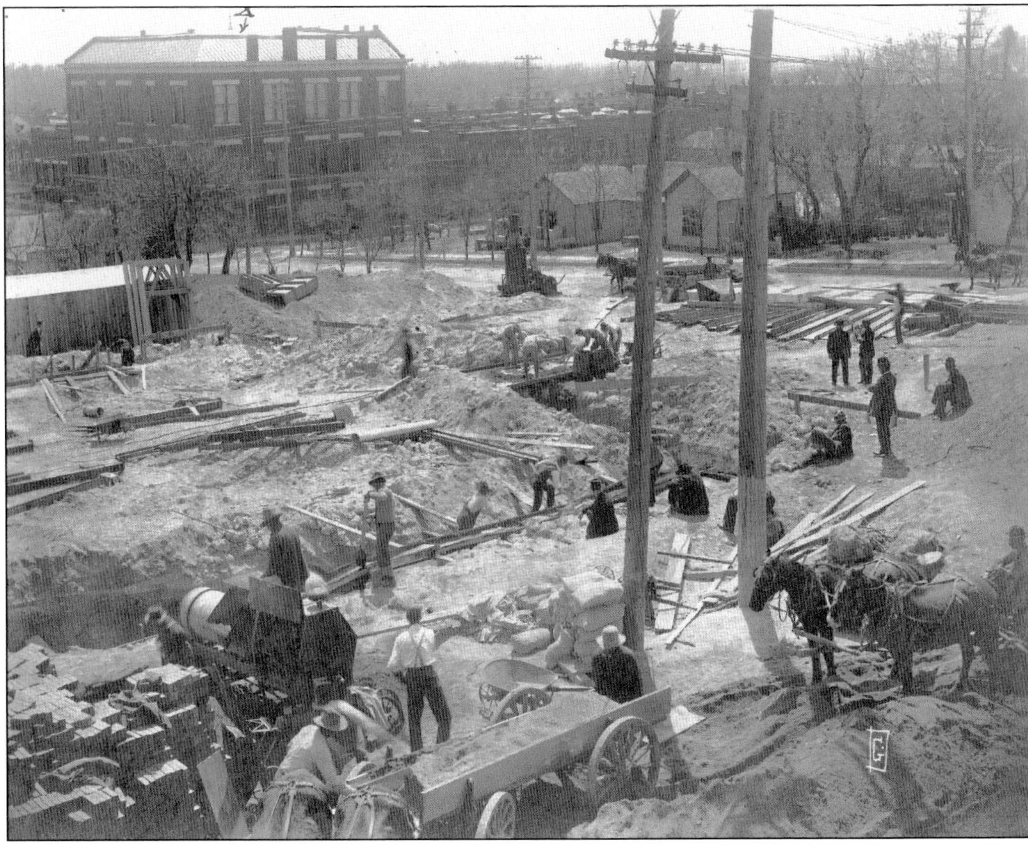

The current Ford County Court House was built in 1913 at a cost of $100,000, replacing an 1880s building on the same location. McCarty Hospital can be seen in the background. The cornerstone was laid in a 1912 ceremony.

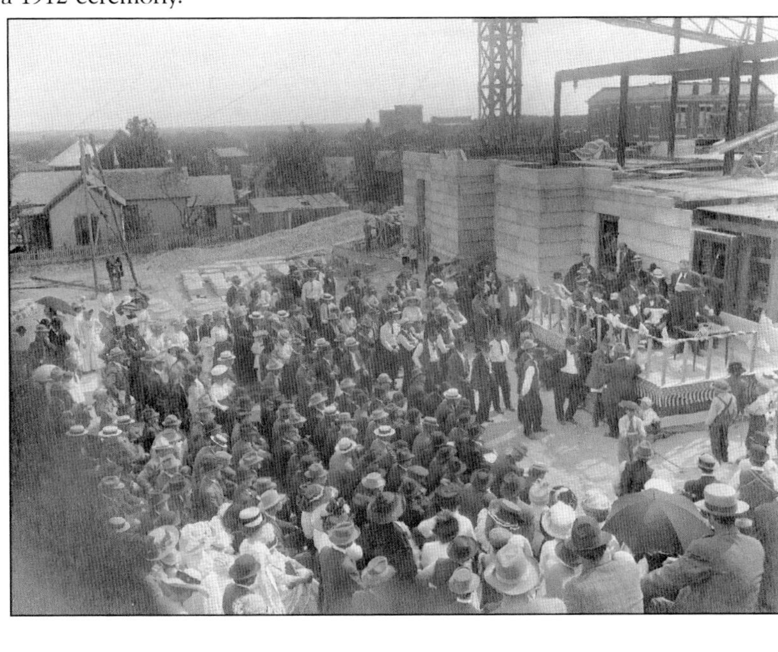

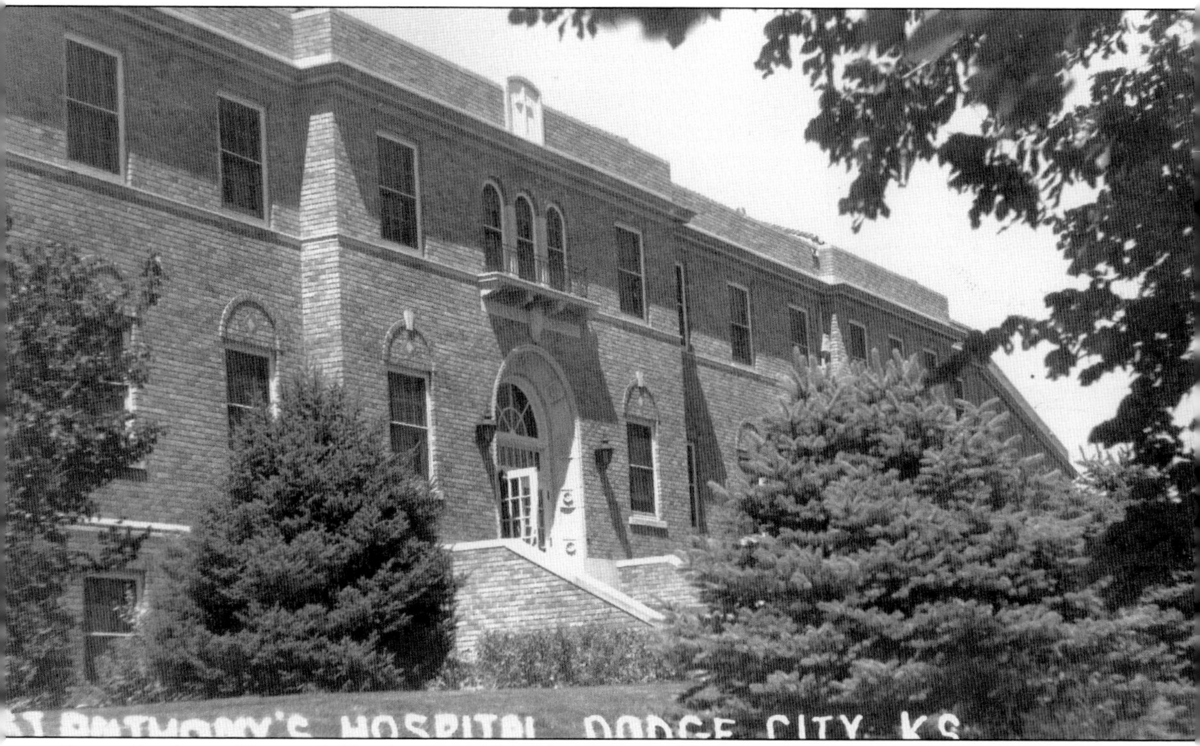

Saint Anthony Hospital (St. Anthony's) of the Sisters of St. Joseph was one of two hospitals in Dodge City up to 1970. Dennis Hopper was born in this hospital. Roy Rogers also visited the hospital in the mid-1950s. It was torn down and replaced with a grocery store.

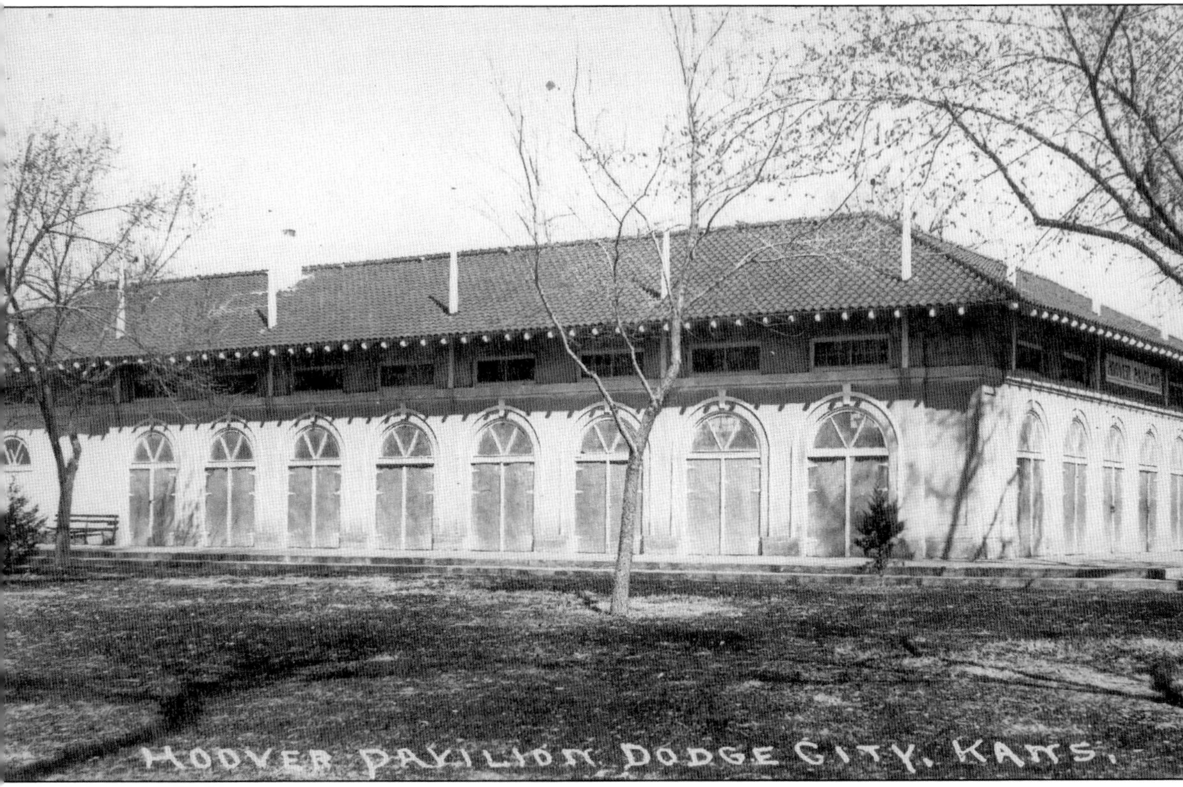

By the time George M. Hoover died in July 1914, he had amassed an estate of at least $500,000 (current value $5 million), leaving $100,000 of it to Dodge City, in addition to thousands of dollars more for churches and $10,000 to build Hoover Pavilion. The building was open initially; doors were added in the 1930s, pictured here. The pavilion was renovated in the 2000s. Hoover also started the State Bank of Dodge, later Fidelity State Bank. It was the first bank in Dodge City.

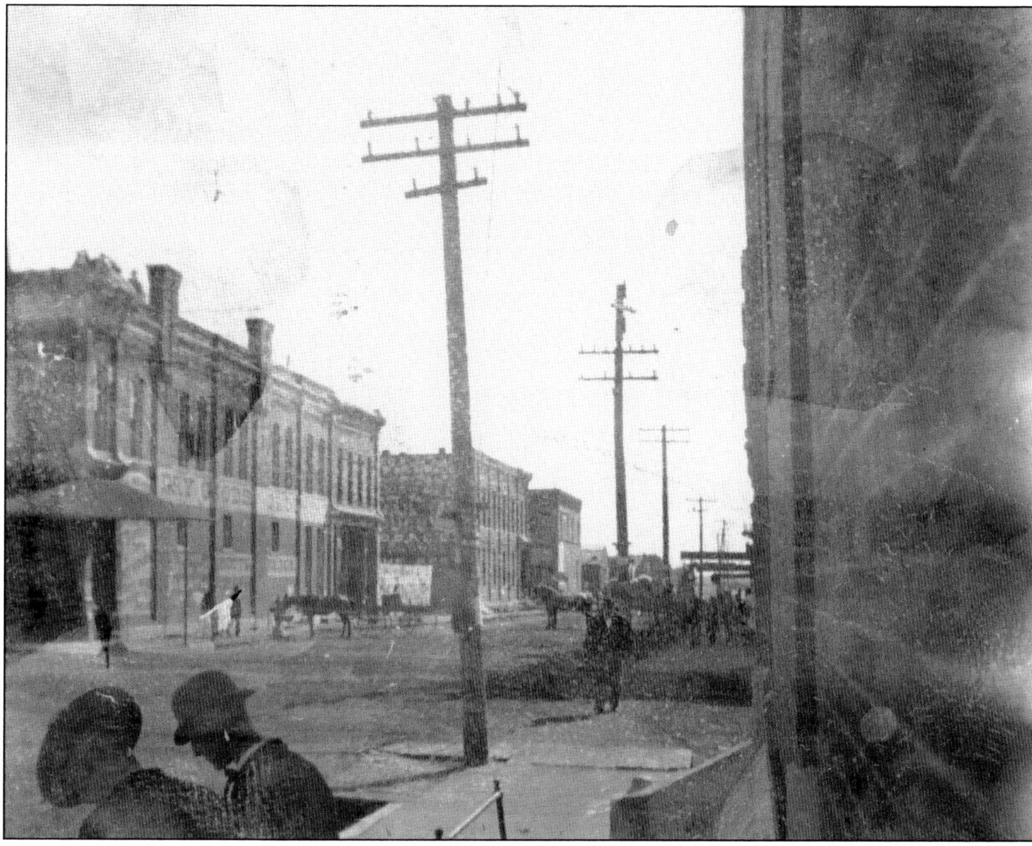

The Dodge City of the late 1890s was bustling with activity. These photographs show rare street scenes.

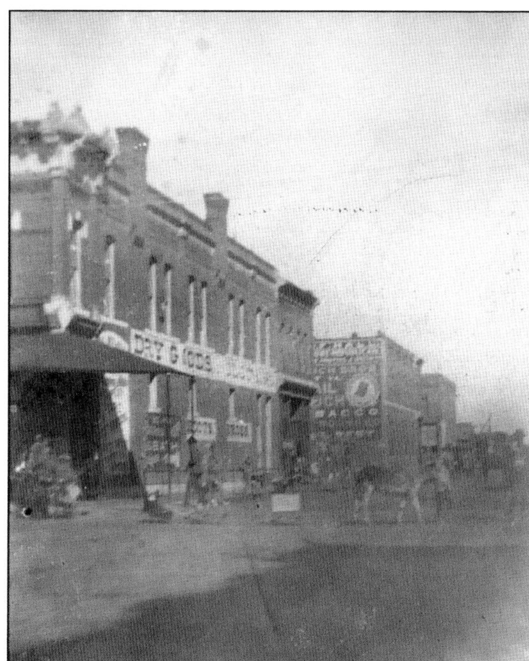

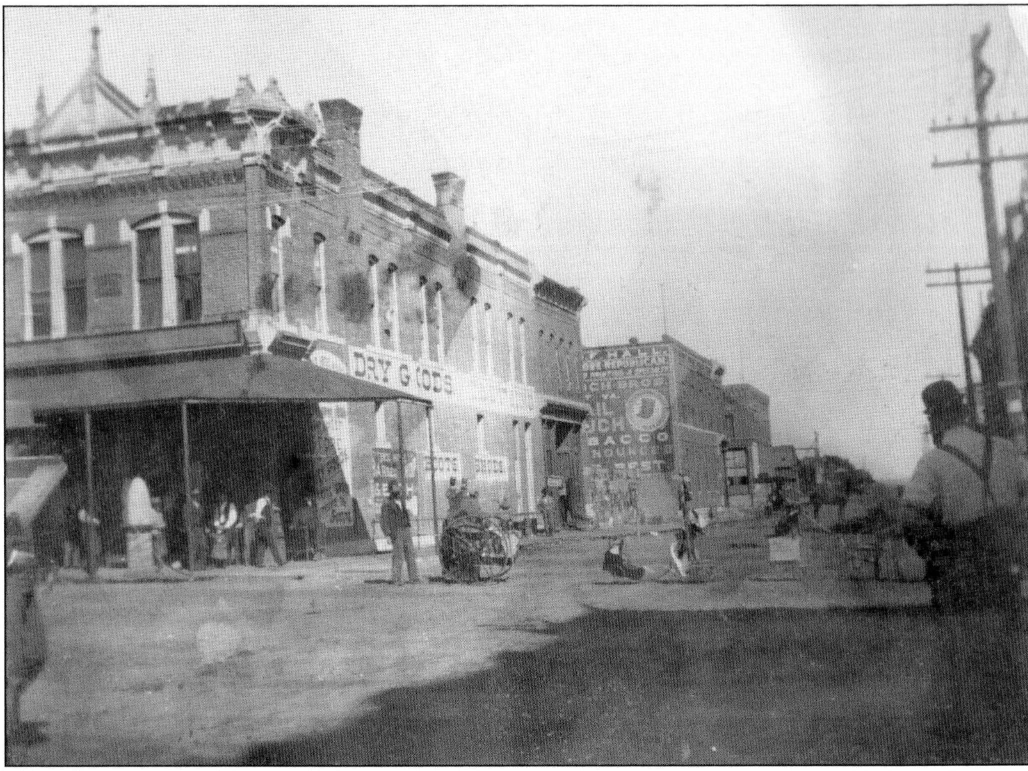

In the photograph above, small animals parade across the dirt streets of Dodge City. Note the signs promoting every type of commercial product.

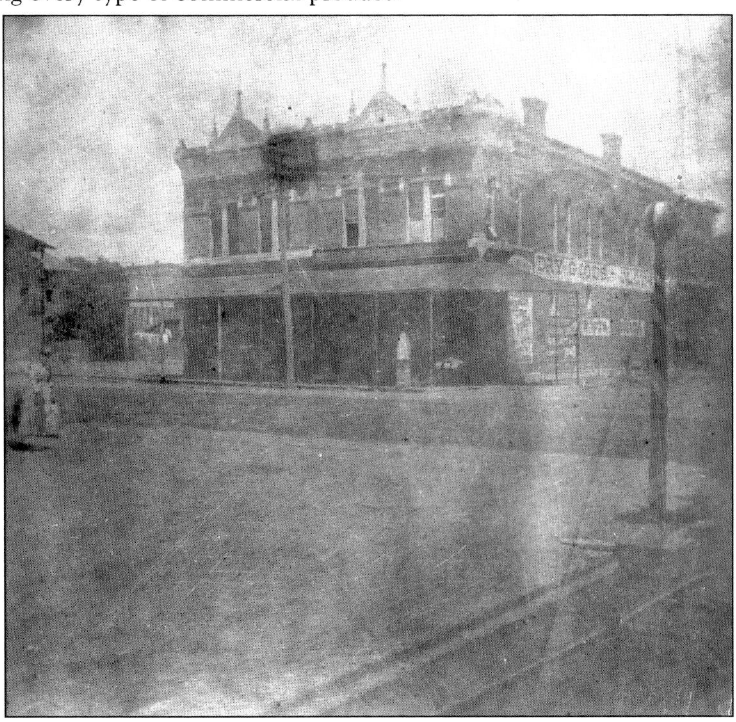

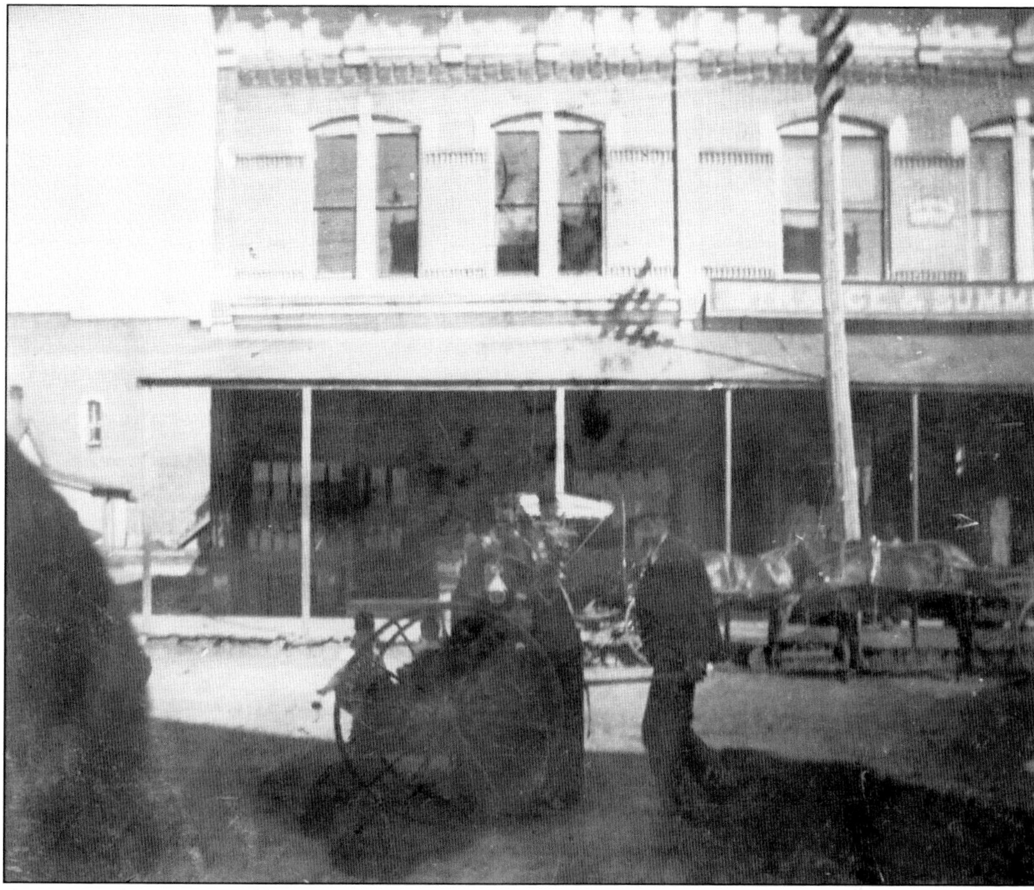

A man pushes a cart, selling items. The commercial aspects of Dodge City are always the element most seen by visitors, and getting visitors' money quickly is the business model, right up until the 2010s, when a new casino opened. The photograph below faces south, towards the Arkansas River. In 1878, Ham Bell introduced the can-can to Dodge City. His dance hall, the Varieties, was south of the railroad tracks or "dead line," where guns and prostitution were permitted. North of the tracks, stricter laws reigned.

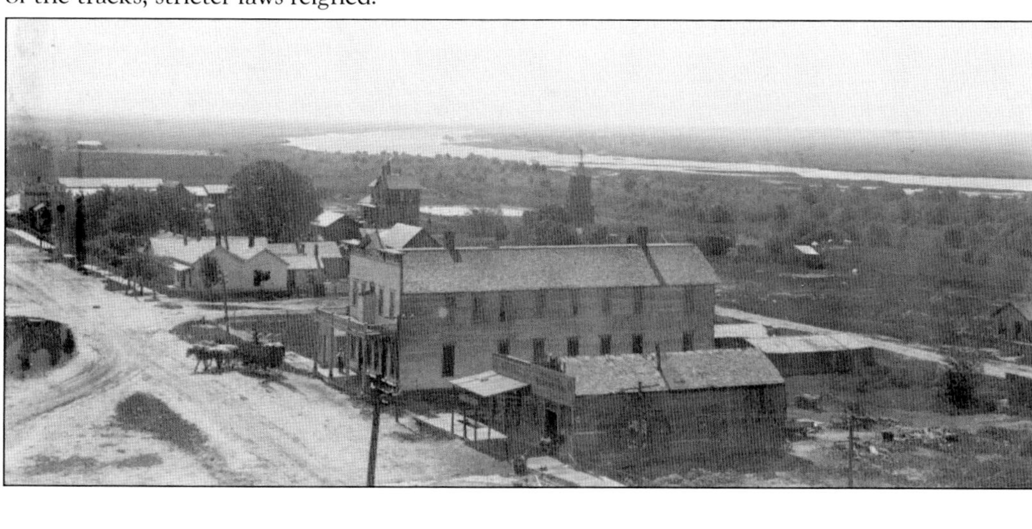

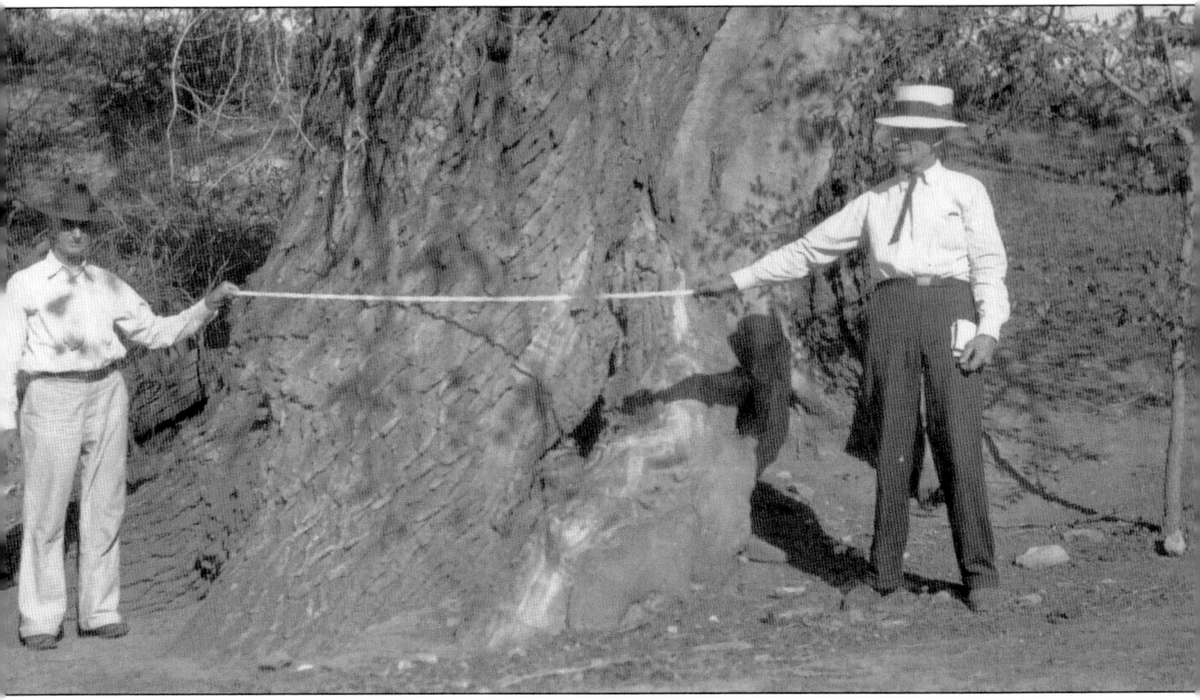

Ham Bell and friends gather at the largest cottonwood tree in the area around Dodge City.

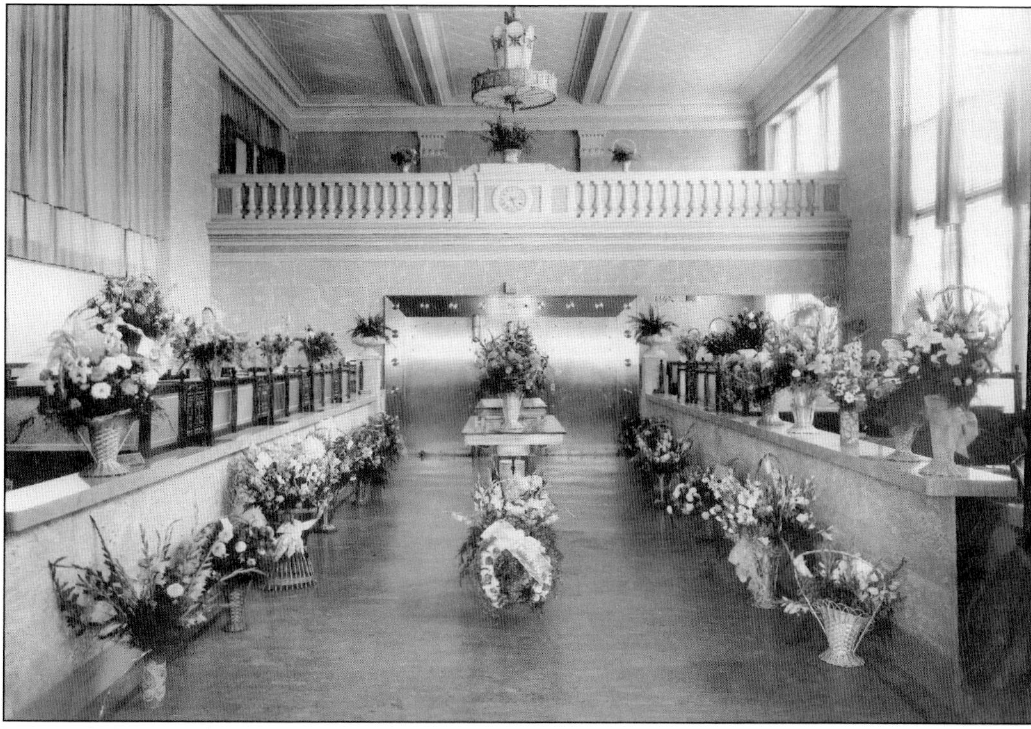

Pictured above is the opening day of Fidelity State Bank, the bank that grew out of George M. Hoover's First State Bank, the first bank in Dodge City. The bank still uses this area.

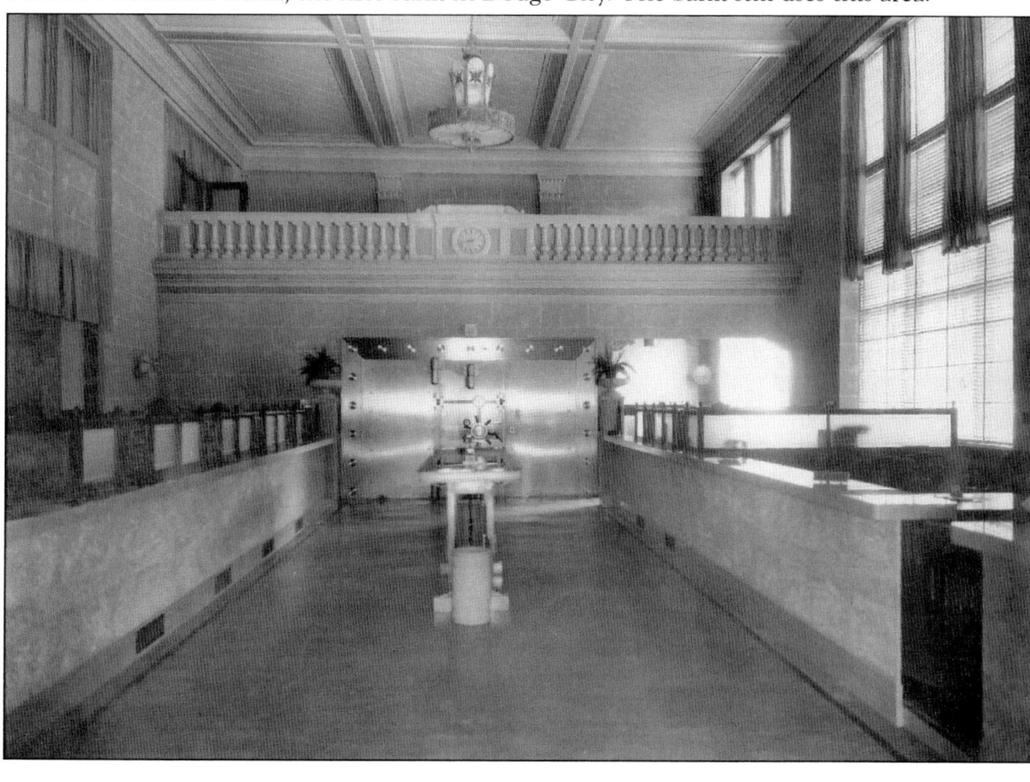

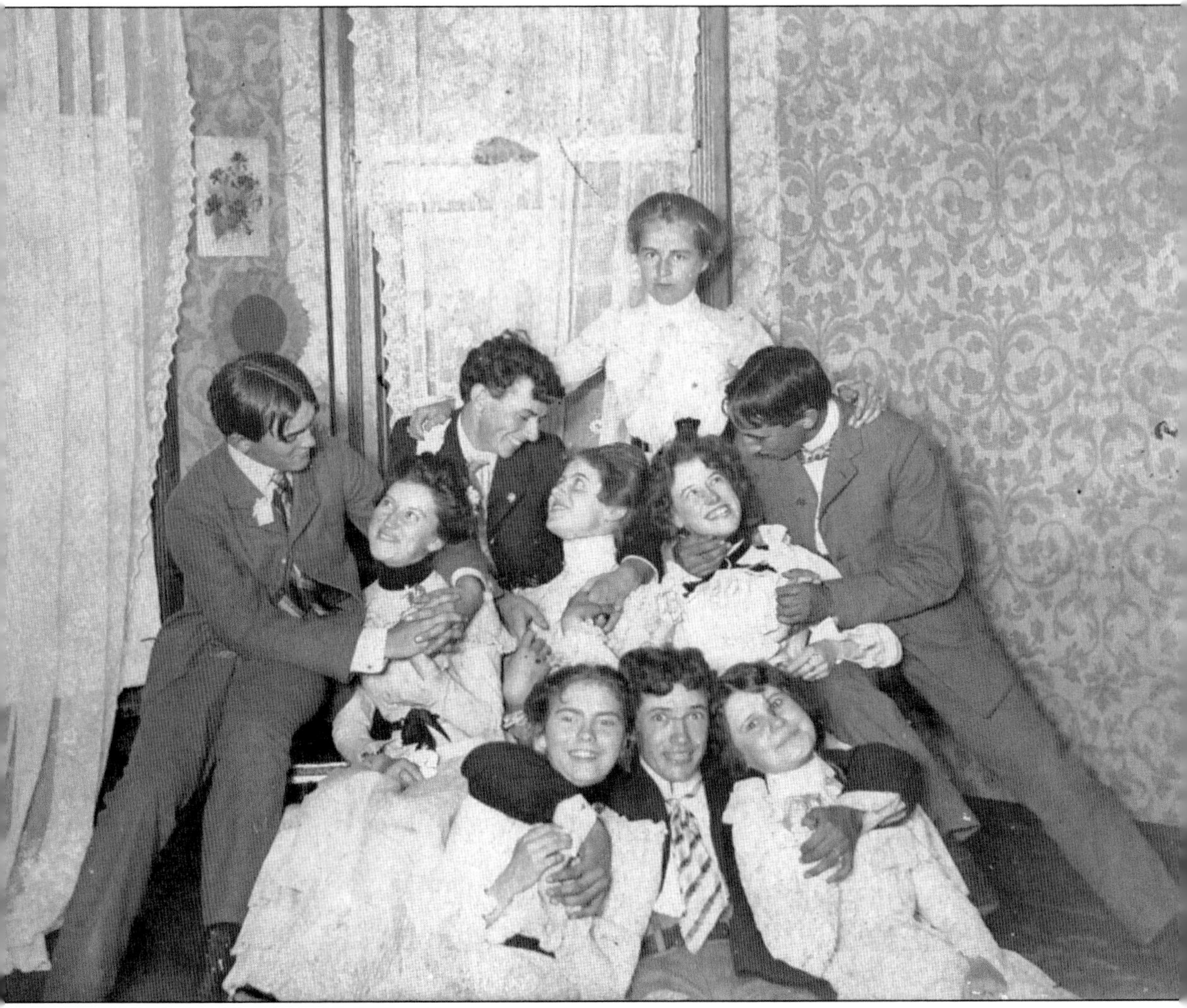

Young couples pose for this 1900 photograph.

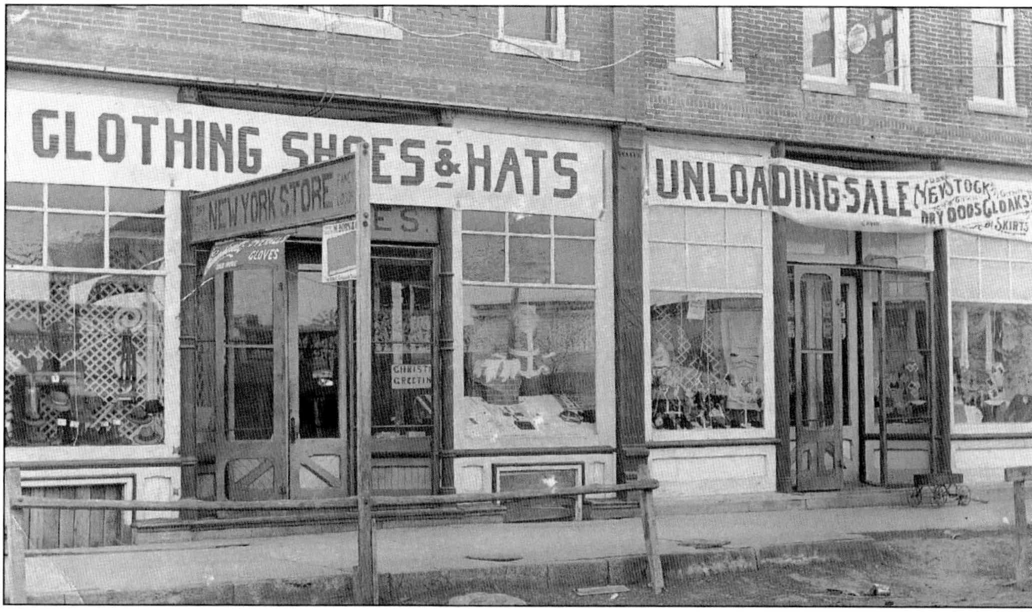

Dodge City's historic, brick, 1885 Front Street blocks were destroyed by urban renewal in the late 1960s. These blocks are now parking lots. Town president Robert M. Wright and first merchant George M. Hoover, among others, developed Front Street into a commercial area of constant business activity and built classic Victorian-era brick buildings to replace the wood-front structures destroyed in two fires during the 1880s. The destruction of the brick Front Street buildings in 1970 (i.e., "urban renewal") is a reminder of promises made and not kept. In 1967, the first announcements were made concerning urban renewal for Dodge City. Although more than 1,300 signatures were obtained in Dodge City to stop the destruction, it rolled on. When the outer panels of the building wall where the Long Branch saloon had been were removed, the Long Branch doors were found still hanging inside. They were given to the Boot Hill Museum. The last of the dirt streets of pioneer Dodge City are visible here before around 1914.

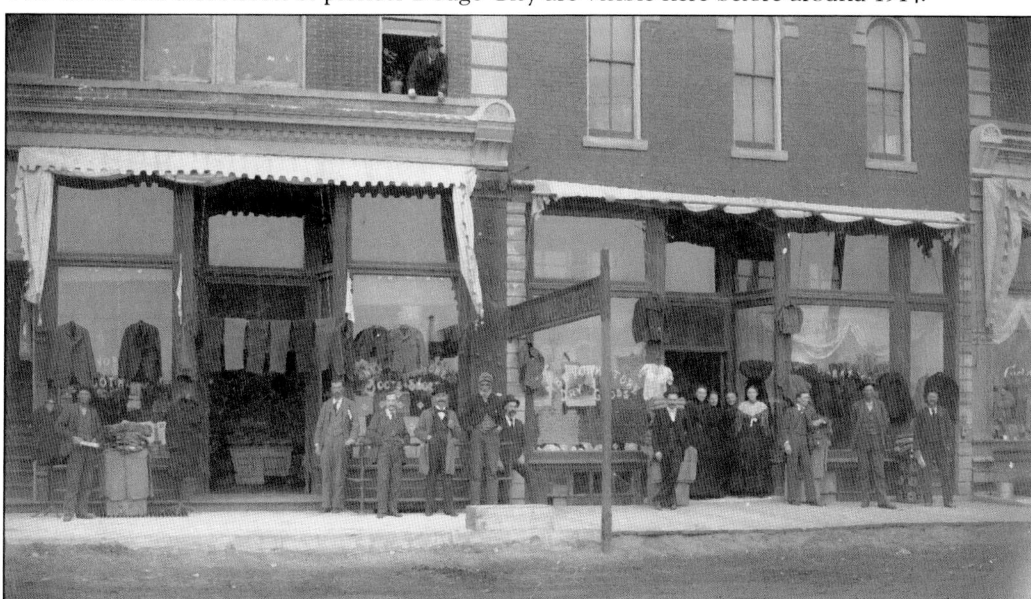

Bibliography

Braddock, Betty and Jeanie Covalt. *Dodge City: Cowboy Capital, Beautiful Bibulous Babylon, Queen of the Cowtowns, Wicked Little City, the Delectable Burg.* Dodge City, KS: Kansas Heritage Center, 1982.

Earp, Josephine Marcus. *Cason* manuscript (original), Glenn Boyer Collection. Dodge City, KS: Ford County Historical Society, c. 1940.

Ford County Historical Society, Lola Adams Crum, editor. *Dodge City and Ford County, Kansas, 1870–1920 Pioneer History.* Spearville, KS: Spearville News, 1996.

Ford County Historical Society Website. www.skyways.org/orgs/fordco/. Topeka, KS: State Library of Kansas.

Haywood, C. Robert. The *Merchant Prince of Dodge City: The Life and Times of Robert* M. *Wright.* Norman, OK: University of Oklahoma Press, 1998.

Isenberg, Andrew. *The Destruction of the Bison: An Environmental History, 1750–1920.* New York, NY: Cambridge University, 2000.

Rath, Ida Ellen. *Early Ford County.* North Newton, KS: Mennonite Press, 1964.

———. *The Rath Trail.* Wichita, KS: McCormick-Armstrong, 1961.

Wright, Robert M. Dodge *City, The Cowboy Capital and the Great Southwest.* Wichita, KS: Eagle Press, 1913.

Young, Fredric R. *Dodge City: Up Through a Century in Story and Pictures.* Dodge City, KS: Boot Hill Museum, 1972.

———. *The Delectable Burg; An Irreverent History of Dodge City—1872 to 1886.* Newton, KS: Mennonite Press, 2009.

ABOUT THE ORGANIZATION

The mission of the Ford County Historical Society is the collection, preservation, and display of the artifacts of the Old West—primarily pioneer Dodge City and Ford County—and the protection of Mueller-Schmidt House (1881), listed in the National Register of Historic Places. The FCHS is an official archive for Ford County, and is a nonprofit organization dedicated to the preservation of the history of the Old West and the New West. A special feature of the museum is the display of pioneer mothers, with over 150 different women represented by photographs, biographical history, and personal artifacts. The centerpiece of the collection is the artifacts and original furniture of the two pioneer families that lived in the house: the John and Karoline Mueller family (1881–1889) and the Adam and Elizabeth Schmidt family (1890–1960). John was Dodge City's first boot maker, and a leading cattleman, Adam was the first blacksmith, Elizabeth was the daughter of the first baker and restaurant owner. Robert M. Wright, Dodge City's town president and founder, is also featured in the Mueller-Schmidt House Museum. Robert's desk, where he wrote *Dodge City, The Cowboy Capital and the Great Southwest*, and his personal portrait, are displayed.